EDWARD BLAKE

THE MAN OF THE OTHER WAY

EDWARD BLAKE

THE MAN OF THE OTHER WAY

(1833-1881)

Joseph Schull

Macmillan of Canada
TORONTO

ISBN 0-7705-1278-X

Printed in Canada for
The Macmillan Company of Canada Limited
70 Bond Street, Toronto M5B 1X3

CONTENTS

LIST OF ILLUSTRATIONS

(between pages 114 and 115)

Sir John A. Macdonald, 1877
(Public Archives of Canada)

The opening of Parliament, 1879
(Metropolitan Toronto Library Board)

Edward Blake, in 1878
(Public Archives of Canada)

The material for the J. W. Bengough cartoons listed below
was supplied by the Public Archives of Ontario.

J. W. Bengough, November 5, 1869 (*p. 92*)
Grip, August 23, 1873 (*p. 106*)
Grip, August 16, 1873 (*p. 109*)
Grip, February 21, 1874 (*p. 118*)
Grip, May 15, 1875 (*p. 136*)
Grip, October 31, 1874 (*p. 138*)
Grip, May 29, 1875 (*p. 148*)
Grip, March 25, 1876 (*p. 154*)
Grip, December 8, 1877 (*p. 182*)
Grip, March 2, 1878 (*p. 184*)
Grip, November 22, 1879 (*p. 198*)
Grip, May 8, 1880 (*p. 210*)

PREFACE

This attempt to produce a study of Blake's life has been supported by a member of the Blake family, by Blake, Cassels & Graydon, the law firm he founded, and by Canada Permanent Trust Company, now merged with Toronto General Trusts Corporation, of which Blake was president for fourteen years. My thanks are due to the University of Toronto for its administrative role in the project and to the Canada Council which provided funds for the research.

As the original inspirer of the work, as the superintendent of all arrangements, and as the man who persuaded several distinguished scholars to take an interest in its production, I have to thank my friend W. R. Wright, a great-grandson of Edward Blake.

Advising the writer was a consultative body consisting of Professors J. M. S. Careless and Robert Craig Brown of the History Department of the University of Toronto; Professor Peter B. Waite of the History Department of Dalhousie University; and Professor Margaret A. Banks, Law Librarian of the University of Western Ontario and author of the book *Edward Blake, Irish Nationalist*, which deals with Blake's work in the British parliament on behalf of Home Rule for Ireland. With Professor Frank H. Underhill, who had also agreed to be consulted, there was time only for an occasional conversation before his death. Through the kindness of Mrs. Underhill a large body of her husband's papers on Blake, accumulated over many years, was made available to the writer.

In the note on sources I have acknowledged the invaluable help of archival experts and of others who assisted in the work of research. I should like to restate my particular gratitude to Mr. Peter Yurkiw of the Dominion Archives and to Mrs. Marion Beyea of the Public Archives of Ontario, whose interest was unflagging and whose judgment and expertise were indispensable. While in no way making them responsible for anything said in the book, I should also like to acknowledge the kindness of Senator H. Carl Goldenberg and Senator Paul Martin, who were generous with their time and advice on certain questions.

To the historians of the consulting board I am indebted for advice, for guidance, for some of their own notes, for the indication of sources, for the correction of many errors, and for continual kindly encouragement. They offered their knowledge and judgment, while specifically refraining from any attempt to shape or direct the work. For the manuscript in its final form they are in no way responsible. The disclaimer, however, while made in justice to a group of distinguished historians, in no way lessens my gratitude for the help given.

As to the work itself, it is an attempt to produce a portrait of a vastly complex and many-sided man who was and still is a force in the development of the nation. In the almost twenty-four years, between July 1, 1867 and June 6, 1891, there were two Canadian Prime Ministers: John A. Macdonald and Alexander Mackenzie. Blake could have been Prime Minister in place of Mackenzie. As the leader of the Liberal party in two general elections, he was the alternative force to Macdonald and might have supplanted Macdonald. He made Laurier as a politician and a leader. Without a knowledge of Blake, it seems to me, there is a whole segment, and a very important segment, missing from the picture of the first quarter-century of the Dominion of Canada. If this book can supply some aspects of that knowledge for the layman, it may be of use and interest.

I have to thank my sister Helen for much work in the typing of notes and manuscripts, and my wife Hélène and the children for enduring a man who, for three years, was "busy with him up there".

JOSEPH SCHULL

EDWARD BLAKE
THE MAN OF THE OTHER WAY

CHAPTER ONE

THE CHANCELLOR'S SON

HE WAS to begin his life in politics, more or less by design, with the beginning of the life of the new Dominion of Canada. In the spring of 1867 Edward Blake was a rising Toronto barrister, thirty-three years old. He was tall and well enough built, but obviously unathletic; the steel-rimmed spectacles hinted of weak eyes. Yet they were eyes of clear blue, penetrating behind the lenses, and the chestnut hair with a wave in it swept back from a massive forehead. In court before a judge, in the silks of a Queen's Counsel which he had acquired at the age of thirty, he was an impressive figure framed in an appropriate setting. On the way from the courts to his office through the workday rush of the metropolis he was something else again. He carried a blackthorn stick and favoured a wide black hat and rumpled tweeds. There was usually a large cloth bag slung over his shoulders, lumpy with books and documents. They were obviously matter of weight; he was obviously in haste to get back to them; and he moved with an air of reserved and deserved distinction. He might have been a country gentleman, a scholarly country gentleman, who disliked the commotion of the vulgar and was not to be long detained.

In either case and on all counts there was much to support the manner. A brilliant graduate of the University of Toronto, he returned to the campus often as an admired lecturer in law.

He had championed student radicals in wresting control of the University Senate from the hands of Egerton Ryerson. A member of the Senate himself, he was a powerful factor in every major decision. He was a leader of the Evangelicals of the Church of England in Toronto, and equally important and dominant in the affairs of the Toronto Yacht Club. He drove in to his business from the family estate of Humewood, four miles north of the city. With his brother Sam beside him he was head of his own law firm, and he was the son of Chancellor Blake.

He was also the son of Catherine Blake, who had come with her husband from Ireland thirty-five years before.[1] The brig *Ann*, when it sailed from Dublin harbour in the summer of 1832, had carried William Hume Blake, twenty-three years old, graduate of Trinity College, former student of anatomy and presently a student of divinity. On a passenger list of twenty there had been a total of nine Blakes, all of them from County Galway and all related to Humes. There had been his mother and three sisters and four departing ministers, one of them his older brother; Catherine Hume, his cousin, was then his bride of a month. The intertwining of names, like the pervading influence of the cloth, was to carry down through the future from knotted and ancient roots.

Anglo-Irish landowners, the invaders of the twelfth century, Blakes had arrived from England and Humes had arrived from Scotland with the cross and sword in their hands. They had used both and been used by both through the seven hundred years that followed. Walled off from the natives, a part of Britain in Ireland, they had grown, branched, and established themselves in a profusion of clans and families. They had risen with the rise, and fallen with the fall, of kings, and they had been divided, torn, and separated by the swirl of religious war. They had interbred in the faith, they had bled and died for the faith, and they had changed faiths and betrayed them with equally involved facility. They had lost lands as Catholics and got them back as Protestants with the advent of

Protestant Ascendancy. They had become steadily more Protestant and more inclined to the cloth as the established church
and the gentry became pillars of the landed class. Yet Ireland
remained Ireland and the pillars had begun to crack. They
were sinking now under the wave of reform in England that
was bringing with it Catholic Emancipation. It threatened the
established Church, it threatened the loss of land, it threatened
the livings and prospects of a beleaguered Protestant clergy.
All this had sailed with the *Ann* as it sailed from Dublin
harbour. It was a shipment of Irish history, of uprooted Irish
gentry, and of Anglo-Irish Protestantism as seed for the new
world.

The seed was soon falling among the Upper Canadian backwoods. For precariously established Anglicanism, with its vast
territory to cover, sowers were in great demand. Arriving in
the town of York, which was on the verge of becoming Toronto,
the four Irish clergymen were quickly despatched to missions.
William Hume Blake, however, was forced to a change of
plan. In the home of the Family Compact and of the future
Bishop Strachan there had been due welcome for a graduate
of Trinity College. There had been something less, however, for
a mere student of divinity. Ministers the Church could use but
it would require time to make one, and William Hume was not
a man for delay. Within six months of his arrival, seated on a
farmer's wagon with his pregnant wife beside him, he was
bound west from Hamilton to take up a grant of land.

It was a day's ride from The Forks where his friend and
fellow-emigrant, the Reverend Benjamin Cronyn, was busy on
a half-built church. The Forks would be London one day, and
Cronyn would be its bishop. Brother Dominick Blake was a
few miles off at Adelaide, engaged in the same work. William
Hume would be near them, but to none of his other hopes. In
the clearing at Bear River, where the log house was to be built,
there was the gloom of the rainy forest, the decaying wreck of
a cabin, and nothing more to greet him than the serried ranks
of the stumps.

He could afford labourers, but they were scarce and un-
dependable. The gentleman farmer worked with his hired
neighbours, too often working alone. There were stumps
cleared through the summer and by autumn the house was
done. It was here, on October 13, 1833, that the first son was
born and was christened Dominick Edward. The winter closed
them in, closing away the world, and when spring came there
was a ribbon of cleared land. William Hume sowed it and
turned to the stumps again, driving himself with the horses.
The crop came up to be withered by a summer of drought and
blight, and he ploughed the stubble under. There would be
more land and another crop but it would be work for the next
year. And the next year and the next, amid forest and flies,
and backaches, while the world went on without him. He came
home one night from his ploughing to be met by Catherine
Blake. She carried the boy in her arms and she held the small
hands out to him in their first gesture of oratory. Was this child,
she asked, to grow up only to this?

It was the first of the family legends that the boy would
remember later, centering about, embellished by, and embel-
lishing, the image of that mother. The world of Catherine
Hume had been the world of the county family, the world of
"the great house", the world of the sober parsonage and the
church that served the elect. She had left it without fear, carrying it all within her. She had come through the woods in the
wagon with her guitar carefully in her lap, cherishing the ways
of gentility and her faith in the gentry's God. He had made
the established order, He had established her in her place, and
in that place she would serve. She had endured the trials of
the wilderness, she had not complained, she had prayed, and
she had been given guidance at last. She had guided William
Hume. Within three months he was back again in Toronto,
embarked on a career in law.

Thirty years later, in some Toronto circles, it was not considered an entirely unmixed blessing. William Hume Blake —
at the bar, in parliament, in the judiciary, and in education —

had strewn some enemies behind him. He was a big man, confident of his own abilities, as confident as Catherine Blake in the abiding care of Providence and in the gentry's claim to care. With his Trinity College accent and his soft Dublin voice went a vinegary view of privilege and of most colonial pretensions. The privileges he did not yet share, and the pretensions he could not endure. He was remembered by old lawyers as the terror of inept judges, and by old Tories as the supporter of Robert Baldwin in the work of liberal reform. Never known in his lifetime to be neglectful of his own interests, he could defend the interests of other men with passionate force and vigour. At one stormy session of the parliament of the two Canadas he had been challenged to a duel by the young Kingston lawyer, John A. Macdonald. He had promptly accepted the challenge, but friends had intervened. In the reform and secularization of Ontario's schools and colleges he had fought Bishop Strachan and he had fought Egerton Ryerson on his way to becoming Chancellor of the University of Toronto. As a powerful Solicitor-General in Robert Baldwin's cabinet, he had pulled down ancient courts, removed decaying judges, and risen to another Chancellorship as head of the equity bench of Upper Canada.

There, however, he had stopped, hardly in midcourse. He was a man worn out, in his family's view, by the burden of public service. Certainly he was a man with headaches, a man with inflamed eyes, unable to sustain the drive of work and worry. Gout came, diabetes followed, and still in his early fifties he was embarked on the quest for health. There were leaves for travel in Europe and they were always generous leaves, arranged by that same Macdonald who was now the Attorney-General. The duel that had not been fought was long since forgotten. The two were almost friends now, though friends in opposing camps, each deploring some of the other's qualities. Blake was a good judge, Macdonald would have liked to keep him, and even Catherine Blake was moved by his efforts. There were more rests and returns, there were offers

5

of lesser appointments, but the end of it all was final resignation. In 1862, with the usual generous arrangements, William Hume retired. By 1867, an aging, burnt-out man, enjoying only his pension and the courtesy title of Chancellor, he had passed the torch to his son.

∽

Edward Blake, whose first name "Dominick" soon slipped to oblivion, was three years old when he accompanied his father to Europe. It was a visit of two months, partly for the child's health and more than that to renew links at home. There were innumerable Blakes in Ireland anxious to see the boy, for they were still close to their kinfolk. They always would be close, and there would be as strong a tie in Canada between the migrants come by *Ann*. There would somehow always be need, and somehow always money, for rest, recuperation, and family visits. Health, travel, and kinship, on either side of the Atlantic, were to be major themes in life.

Education came next. The first home in Toronto was a comfortable house on John Street, and it was immediately a place of teaching. While her husband studied for the bar, and later commenced his practice, Catherine Blake conducted a school for girls. The voices of young ladies, most of them daughters of the best families in the city, were the first classroom sounds. Meanwhile the children came, to be followed soon by tutors. Samuel Blake was born two years after Edward. Anne Margaret and Sophia arrived three and four years later. The Blake fortunes improved and the school for girls was closed. The family moved to a larger house in Yorkville and from there to one still larger at the corner of Wellington and Bay.

The third house, a testament to growing affluence, was a spacious red brick mansion designed and built to the orders of William Hume. Life here was the life of a man of status, with visitors to be entertained, wide grounds to walk in, a pleasant view of the waterfront, and a boat for the boys to sail. They were coming near to their teens by then, and were rather too much alone. The tutors were still with them, Catherine watched and supervised, and the father shaved in the mornings to the sound of Latin declensions. He had few evenings to spare but they were always precious when they came, with much reading aloud, discussion of what was read, the unravelling of knots in lessons, and the bellcord summoning the servants for family prayers at the end. Life was lively and good, throbbing with worthy work, but education went on in the closed circle.

The breaking-out, when it came, was to Upper Canada College and from there to the University of Toronto. It was obvious that parents and tutors had done their work well, more obvious still that Blakes were aware of status. The Chancellor brought his problems home in the evenings, and father was always right. He spoke here of his ambitions, though in terms of public service, with compensation and advancement incidental. Catherine supported him in everything on the highest of moral planes; one worked for the long hereafter but there should be due reward in the here. The friends and relatives came, many in Holy Orders, applauding goals and achievements with the authority of men of the cloth. The Reverend Dominick Blake was one of the frequent visitors, as were the Reverend Charles Brough and the Reverend Richard Flood, each of them married to a sister of William Hume. There was the sustaining force of his mother, Grandmother Anne Margaret, and the Reverend Benjamin Cronyn was often one of the group. They formed another closed circle enclosing the inmost circle and shutting it off from a crude and common world. The long evening discussions were better than lessons for the boys as they came to be permitted to join them. They were cerebral celebrations of the worth of the great Chancellor, and from first youth they had been inspiration and command. The Blake air, always thick with religion and alive with learning, had been equally quick and electric with the excitement of getting on.

"The Blakes," said one of the teachers at Upper Canada, "were the only boys who knew what reading was."[2] If it was true of the assured Sam, already an ebullient dogmatist, it was rather less than the truth with his older brother. The problem with Edward Blake, from the time he was five years old, had been to get him away from reading. His father, mother, and tutors, impressed and then appalled, had tried to check his progress through the family library. They all had failed. Vague, listless, and dreamy, a worshipper of both his parents, he could be held by none of their restrictions against his own compulsion to know. He had been hauled out, book in hand, from forbidden places in the shrubbery. He had been plucked from under tables reading in a half dark, and whatever the conditions of acquiring it he remembered what he had read. He absorbed it, organized, and built on it, and was not to be stopped by teachers. During his first year in college he was a strained and fretful boy, but it was the strain of weak eyes. Taken off by his father for a second trip to Europe, he returned equipped with spectacles and in headlong haste for his books.

His one sport was sailing, and he carried his books to his boats. He was clumsy at school games, diffident and shy with friends, but his upward progress through the classrooms was strewn with scholastic honours. He was head boy at Upper Canada College. He graduated at twenty from the University of Toronto with the degree of Bachelor of Arts and the silver medal in classics. In another two years, though still working for the Master of Arts degree he would acquire in 1858, he also enrolled as a senior student in law. In that capacity he could engage in limited practice and the first shingle, "Edward Blake, Solicitor", went up on June 14, 1856. Six months after that, twenty-three years old and with final examinations safely behind him, he was Edward Blake, Barrister.

Another step remained before he was established to his own taste. During his first thin months as a solicitor he had joined forces with the young Stephen Maule Jarvis, another scion of an important Toronto family, who had already set up practice. Now, with both men barristers, there was a question of precedence and fees. The son of Chancellor Blake was likely to be the business-getter, but the firm was Jarvis and Blake. It was dissolved in July of 1857, after a life of less than a year. Edward Blake, installing himself on his own in an office in Wellington Chambers, had completed his first and last experience as a junior partner.

~

He was twenty-four when the greater change took place. For as long as he was able to remember the young Blakes of Toronto and the young Cronyns of London had been much together. They had stayed at each other's houses, attended the same schools, and had begun recently and significantly to sort themselves into pairs. Sam Blake was attracted to Rebecca Cronyn. Verschoyle Cronyn had eyes for Sophia Blake. Of Edward's feelings for Margaret Cronyn there had never been much doubt, and once securely established he dispelled what doubt there was. On January 6, 1858, he and Margaret were married in St. Paul's Church, London.

As they drove back with the wedding party toward the bishop's wide frame house they were blazing a path for others. Sam and Rebecca Cronyn would follow a year later, and Sophia and Verschoyle Cronyn in 1860. They would soon be back with their children and another twining of names, Cronyns mingling with Humes and both mingling with Blakes. The house and the snowy streets that were still lanes among the pine trees would be a second centre of homecomings and a part of the Irish past.

The bridegroom of that January day, no longer a retiring student, was already a man who felt the pressures of authority. There had been drastic change for him arising from the affairs of his father. Only three years earlier William Hume Blake, secure in esteemed eminence, had been building plans for the future. He had done his time in politics and it had given him what he wanted; he looked down as Chancellor on rivals who had coveted his place. There had been the promise of good investments, the sufficiency of present funds, and, above all, the hopes for the farm at Humewood. It was a property already purchased and bearing the family name, just beyond Bloor Street, on the northern fringe of Toronto. Well-treed, rolling land, it was suitable for a fine estate, requiring only a house fitting the estate. There had been plans for the new house, and for the sale of the house on Bay Street, but they had had to be laid away. The talk of the family evenings had been turned to doctors and symptoms, plagued by the fretful outbursts of a sick and failing man. As Edward became a barrister with his career opening before him, the Chancellor's career had begun to approach its close. There had been the first of the many breakdowns, the first of the long leaves, the first of the periods of deputizing for an invalid recovering in Europe. The son commencing his practice had been head of the family in Canada and the burden had left its mark.

From the parents travelling together the stream of letters had come to him, each with its batch of worries and its assortment of new commissions. William Hume at the health resorts, in spite of "perseverance and cold water", had been sunk in black depression. His devouring of Canadian newspapers had only deepened his gloom. He had been tortured by gout and tortured by thoughts of money, lamenting his thin shoes, the state of his one coat. Imagined indigence had haunted every letter, yet so had the dreams of Humewood and the house still to be built. He had been unable to relinquish anything, unable to deal with anything, and impossible to reassure. He had had thoughts for the crops on the farm, for every head of his livestock, for every parcel of property, and each maturing note, and he had poured out the thoughts to Edward. Catherine had fretted in absence over every family ailment and the state of every soul, and there had been new resources of piety and fresh suggestions on medicine to be transmitted with every letter. All this the family barrister had dealt with while he tried to conduct his business. Driving himself, fretting himself, and sick with overwork, he had laboured over cheery letters into the small hours of the morning. He had renegotiated mortgages, disposed of the crops at Humewood, and arranged for the servicing of Conquest, his father's purebred cow. He was enjoying a respite now for his parents had returned to Canada, and William Hume seemed well. It was remarked by a guest at the wedding that he looked no older than Edward, and it might well have been true. There had never been much of a boyhood for the scion of this father, and the weight of the home-made legend was imposing itself on youth.

The fine, delicate mouth was already a little too firm. There was a sense of strain, of inward-looking withdrawal. A shadowy edge of mutton-chop fringing the strong face was a deliberate aid to the impression of the aloof barrister. It was well to seem what he was, to look a Blake. There were clerks under him in the office and a profitable flow of business. He was head of a firm which now included his brother, for Sam had joined him in December. Where Sam was, Edward's work would be done, Edward's fees collected, and Edward's interests pressed with a righteous zeal. Vigorous, loquacious, sharp-tongued, and abrasive, Sam had the drive that had once belonged to his father. He had his mother's religious certainties with never a relieving doubt. God and the low church, the established order, the law and Edward Blake, frequently in reverse precedence, were to be his lifelong causes. It made him difficult to live with, for all but the senior partner, and it made him indispensable.

"You will have the goodness to recollect," Edward wrote to a client a few months later, "that at present my brother is merely my managing clerk in the Common Law department and that I have the sole responsibility in all matters."[3] It was large, flat, truthful, and as insufferably pompous as he sometimes seemed himself. Yet Sam would have understood, and would have endorsed the statement fully. It was the Blake public image projected for the common eye; it had nothing to do with the family feeling of brothers. That they both knew, that they both shared, but the business of life came first. The large, young man with the spectacles and the fringe of mutton-chop whiskers had his way to make in the world, and the way to make for the Blakes. He had been forced to it; it went by

11

the name of duty. Whatever the Chancellor's appearance, the thrust and grasp were gone; the goals he had fallen short of could be reached only by the son. Edward Blake was the senior hope of the family and was shaping himself to the mould.

"Although she is thought plain", Margaret Cronyn came to him that day "beautifully dressed in a rich white silk made with double skirts, the waist trimmed with lace and a close-fitting lace cape, a tulle veil with a pretty wreath of roses and orange blossoms and veils."[4] Today she looks out from her portraits, a woman of gentle beauty, elderly, serene, resigned. For the man she had known and grown with she was to be the frame and centre of life, warden of his private heart. She was never much of a housekeeper according to family legend. She could neither find maids nor order them about when found; all this had to be done for her. In her daily relations with Edward, wherever they were seen in public, she accepted the second place as second nature. It was noted on one occasion, returning from a trip to Europe, that her single dress for evening wear was strapped outside a bag, while her husband's books and documents filled the interior.

It was around her, however, that the sons and the daughter would grow and the nephews and nieces of the future love to gather, always certain of a welcome. Her piety was quite as deep as Catherine Blake's but it was less oppressive to children, even on rainy days. "Oh darling, you must not complain about the weather. God sends the weather."[5] She was not without quiet humour, sometimes dry, and a glimpse of her in her later years capsules much of her life. Staying at a hotel in England, preparing to leave for Canada, she was subjected through a long evening to the advice of elderly ladies. She listened meekly to prescriptions for seasick remedies and warnings of marine perils, and rose at last to retire. "Perhaps I should tell you, ladies, that this will be my thirty-seventh Atlantic crossing."[6]

CHAPTER TWO

"YOUNG BLAKE OF TORONTO"

THE WEDDING TRIP was brief and the married barrister returned to a heaped-up desk. When he left it late in the evenings it was for a new and crowded home. He had sold the house on Bay Street while his father was still in Europe, according to original plan. It was the first step, and he intended to take the second; in spite of hard times and in spite of his father's worries Humewood was going to be built. It was to be the reward due, and the sign proclaimed, of the achievements of a great life.

Meanwhile, in a rented house on Peter Street, the newlyweds were installed with the Blake parents. There was no room for Sam and he had moved to rented lodgings. Even so there were cramped quarters for the servants, and Margaret was under the thumb of Catherine Blake. The mother-in-law adored the girl but where she was she ruled, and it was not fair to a wife. The husband knew it and was distressed by it, but it was part of the cloud of duties. They had not lightened with his parents' return from Europe; they had settled in permanent shape. Querulous, indecisive, and no longer equal to his work the Chancellor could fret and hope, but it was the son who would have to act.

The goals were clear enough, at least in the short perspective, and with present preoccupations it was as far as he cared to look. He was steering his way through depression in Upper

13

Canada and preserving the Blake investments. He was even adding where he could. It was the first duty, that preservation of property, that building of property on property toward affluent independence. It was only in such condition that a gentleman could face the world, that a gentleman could look onward. To what? A barrister now and perhaps the bench later, a second Chancellor determining and dispensing justice? "Let right be done" — the words rang down the centuries challenging the best in a man, the essence and soul of law. The strong man doing right, seeing that right was done — that would be good. Yet before that and beyond it there came the making of law, the first work, the creative work, the greatest. And at that thought one stopped.

Parliaments made laws, politics made parliaments, and William Hume Blake had been scarred by the wounds of both. His son was drawn to neither. Certainly not to the politics of Upper Canada, locked and blocked in its union with the Lower Canada of the French. He was not drawn by the men he saw around him, wrangling and warring too — this George Brown of the *Globe*, bigoted, Presbyterian, and raw as a highland morning, that charming, dissolute, too-familiar Macdonald, Cartier the little Frenchman with his smell of railway money. He was not drawn by the crowds and sweat of the meeting halls, the rant and roar of the hustings, the drink, the bribes, the flagrant, bald vulgarity. One could only look to that road if he hoped to change it utterly; it was best not look at all. Or certainly not till there was confidence, prominence, and freedom; the power to effect a change. Meanwhile, leading to all roads, there remained the cluttered desk.

He had handled some sixty cases in his first year of practice, and there were five hundred pounds in fees entered on his books. It was a startling sum for those days and much remained to be collected, but whatever came in went out to good purpose. Mortgages were resting easier now and payments were duly met. There were even occasionally a few surplus pounds, always promptly disposed of. In times preoccupied with money,

money could not be idle, and who knew better than a barrister with his long list of foreclosures that there was land going for a song? There were town lots in London, he wrote to Verschoyle Cronyn, that he would buy "if they are *real* bargains".[1] There were other bargains that promised much for the future, but with half-payments down and balances at six months they had an accompanying refrain in the present: "I am in so deep with my bank that I could not just now arrange for anything" . . . "I can do nothing with my bank just now" . . . "I am in such a position with my bank that I cannot ask for accommodation."[2]

He was as deep in work, however, as he was in the bank's books, and there was money at hand when needed. His routine business was pyramiding, and he was already becoming selective. The shrill client could be certain of a sharp answer. "In the face of a letter couched as yours," he wrote to one of the type, "I do not feel bound to continue taking up fresh business of yours . . . you had better communicate with some professional gentleman who will be disposed to put up with your style of correspondence."[3]

With Sam in charge of the office work, the senior partner was now much in the courts. As the son of Chancellor Blake he was certain to be well watched, and there were enemies as well as friends among the watchers. He had known that, and it had added to his doubts of himself. The law moved to its own majestic rhythms, but there was no man of the law immune from politics. Tory and Reformer, High Churchman and Low Churchman, the friends of the University and its dearest enemies would be sitting across the counsel table or looking down from the bench. He stood in his father's shoes, the inheritor of his father's wars, and he had been inclined at first to stand a little aside. His earliest briefs had been argued by senior men, with himself as second counsel.

That changed quickly as he sniffed the air of the arena and found himself on his feet. He was still an emerging novice but he was a born man of the law, with the love of law an essential part of his being. He could not touch a subject without

15

exhausting it, he would not accept a case without exploring its depths. He was always well prepared, often better prepared than his imposing seniors, and he was soon doing without them. He could speak, he could cross-examine, he could hold a jury; and, with that confidence established, a glimmer of limelight came.

It was provided by the "State Trials" which followed the "Double Shuffle", renowned in the chequered history of the parliament of the two Canadas. Politics had been brought to court at the hands of George Brown. The towering Scot from Edinburgh would never be a favourite of the Blakes; he was brash, crude, and narrow, he was authoritarian and tactless, but he had been suffered by William Hume, and he would be long endured by the son. He would have to be, for there was no denying his powers. He had been fourteen years in Toronto, his *Globe* was a national force, and he had replaced Baldwin in parliament as the leading man of Reform. It seemed for a brief moment in the summer of 1858 that he had replaced the Conservative government of John A. Macdonald.

That government, strained and straddling as usual between the interests of its two sections, had rested on a shaky majority of a half-dozen votes. It had gone down on the 28th of July. Macdonald of Upper Canada and George Etienne Cartier, his associate power as leader in Lower Canada, had crossed the aisle in defeat. George Brown, with Antoine-Aimé Dorion as his leader of French Canadians, had succeeded to Macdonald's place. Brown as the new Premier had duly named his cabinet, but he had not yet power to govern. Until he and his ministers were confirmed in by-elections they had no vote in the House; the actual majority was on the other side of the aisle. It was used with prompt skill. By August 6, four days after he had become the head of the government, Brown was out again. Worse still, Macdonald and Cartier were in, and some fine print in the electoral law was being put to excellent use. Designed to deal with routine shifts of duties within a cabinet, it provided for the waiving of by-elections in the case of resigned ministers who were sworn to a new portfolio within a period of one month. It hardly applied to the whole of a fallen government, but the law had forgotten to say so and the ministers had been out a week. By the ninth day they were back, with Cartier taking Macdonald's place, Macdonald taking Cartier's, and each of the other ministers trading chairs. And on the tenth day, with a new series of swearings, except for Macdonald and Cartier they became what they had been.

There was no recourse in parliament; the deed and the government stood. Nor was there much hope elsewhere, but the sting of the outrageous tumble was not to be endured by Brown. On September 20, with the *Globe* thundering support, suit was opened at Toronto in the Court of Common Pleas, charging John A. Macdonald et al. with illegal assumption of office, various other crimes, and claiming £500 in damages for each day the offices had been wrongfully held. It was, according to the *Globe*, "the most interesting suit ever brought before a Canadian court",[4] and the prestigious battery of counsel included Edward Blake.

There were six weeks of imposing legal liturgy which accomplished nothing at all. The suit was dismissed in December. For the young counsel, however, there had been much notice in professional circles and high praise in the *Globe*. Mr. Edward Blake had shown "great oratorical powers, as well as sterling talent. This gentleman promises to take his father's place at the bar."[5] He was now a father himself. Sophia Hume Blake, his first daughter, had entered the world while the trial was still proceeding. It was enough to brighten Christmas and make up for the lost suit, and there was more cheer for the family as the winter ran its course. The promise of spacious Humewood was at last to become a fact.

As snow turned to mud with the coming of spring there was a clutter of excavation round the property. Then, as the roads hardened and the fields flowered, Edward and Margaret could drive out in the evenings to watch the walls rise. William Hume seemed always there, Catherine showered suggestions, and it was clear that the son and daughter-in-law were expected to share the house. On that point the son was a little hesitant. He was not not so sure of Margaret's feelings and he had some doubts of his own. There was plenty of land for another house, not too far away, and he thought of building for himself.

He was still thinking when his father's house was finished. It sat familiarly in the mellow autumn landscape, with its conservatory and covered bowling alley a flanking wing to the west. A cedar hedge that had been planted long before enclosed the front of the property and was now well grown. The fields ran off behind it, the fruit trees and berry bushes had been carefully preserved by the builders, and there were flowers and ripening vegetables in the undisturbed gardens. The house, served by the farm, seemed to be welcomed and accepted by the farm.

From the rank of bay windows facing south one looked down through a fine avenue of pine trees onto the road that led to the city. It was a long road; there would be a four-mile drive to the office, and there would probably be days in winter when one went on foot through snowdrifts. But it would be well worth it for a man with his way to make; this was a house of status. His father and mother wanted the young ones with them. Margaret would love the comfort of the large, commodious rooms. The thought of building his own house could be put aside for a while.

It was in Humewood, on June 28, 1860, that Edward Hume Blake, his first son, was born. There was an heir now, there was standing, and prosperity was becoming a habit. He owned *Rivet*, one of the finest yachts on the lake, though he had little time to sail her. He owned more than that. As the sport he had loved since boyhood was pushed aside by business, business itself was bringing compensations. He could thank those growing fees and he could also thank his father. William Hume Blake, during his far-off days in parliament when the House sat at Quebec, had been led to discover the delights of the lower St. Lawrence. He had taken his children there, they had gone again and again, and custom had become a permanence as the children's children came. Now as Toronto sweltered in the heat of July and August, and even Humewood lost some of its attraction, there was another home to go to. It looked out over pine bluffs from the little Pointe-au-Pic, and summers at Murray Bay were a part of life.

For Edward Blake they would be the best part through another fifty years. A summer missed, and there would be many of them, would be a loss not to be recovered. Year after year — the lucky ones — he would come to the spring worn out, baked by hot stoves, snuffling from airless offices, racked with the eternal headaches from squinting through reams of paper. There would be the wounds of the lost battles and the glooms of the pending battles, but there would be an excited family round him and the thought of relief ahead.

There would be weeks of office bustle to clear up the last of the work, a wilder bustle at the railway station as the train left for Quebec. Then it would be the little steamer and the heave of the great river, the church spires and clustering whitewashed cottages, the towering, pine-clad bulk of Cap Tourmente and the great cleft in the mountains opening on Baie-St-Paul. There would be the high scarp and its villages fringing the north shore, the curve of a bold headland, and at last under its shadow the first glimpse of the quay. It was the place here, called by the French La Malbaie, on which Wolfe's General Murray had somehow imposed his name.

The bay was a broad semi-circle opening in from the St. Lawrence, with a rugged upland valley climbing behind it. At low tide fishing schooners lay high and dry on sand, with huge rocks glistening about them and little pools and rivulets of trapped water. When the tide came in, however, it flooded up to a height of twenty-two feet, sometimes whipped by the wind into great lashing waves. From the high uplands on the landward side the La Malbaie River plunged down rocky gorges, twisted lazily through the long level stretches of *les eaux mortes*, and tumbled in falls and rapids to sea level. The weather here, where the St. Lawrence widened toward the sea, was as changeable as the river itself. It was a place of many moods, fresh with the scent of pine forests, and salt with the sea air. In all moods and at all times it would be a haven for Edward Blake. There was sail, canoe, and calèche, there were the wild, rocky walks, the shouts and games of children, and the murmurous silence of the woods. The barrister here could lay aside the mask; he could almost be young again, or as young as he had ever been. Humewood yelled of success, of position and worth in the world; here sometimes in the solitudes one listened to the inner man.

᧐

"It is too bad to have one's last years spent in calculating the utmost capacity of a pound of cheese or an ounce of butter."[6] By 1862 the Chancellor was abroad again, sick, retired on pension, and writing the familiar letters. Catherine travelled with him and echoed his complaints and fears. Divorced from Humewood, deprived of the dignities of office, William Hume and his wife were once more in the company of the invalids, the superannuated civil servants, and the retired officers on half pay. They were moving with the dismal procession, always in search of another change or cure, through the spas and the seaside boarding houses and the cheaply-genteel lodging places of Switzerland, France, and Italy.

It was all totally unnecessary. In Ireland and England there were rich and high-placed relatives always glad to receive them. But the two were never at ease; they could never prolong a stay. The Chancellor's pension was large but he insisted on saving half of it, for mortgage payments that did not yet have to be met and eventualities that were not likely to occur. The more one tried to reassure him the less he was reassured, and the more his frettings for Humewood poured in on the son. "You know how my heart was set on carrying out our plans."[7] There were calving cattle to be seen to, fruit trees requiring pruning, crops of apples to be sold. The wheat and oats, the currants, vegetables, and gooseberries all had to be disposed of. There were compost heaps to be built, new fields to be ploughed, gaps in hedges to be filled. And every weekday morning, at the end of the four-mile drive, there were clients waiting for the barrister and the growing pile of briefs.

Sam was a full partner now, and the work of the firm was reaching out through the province. There was a web of agencies forming with barristers in other towns. The Blake name was familiar in all courts. There was too much work in Toronto, more than enough on circuit; and rides in dusty trains, nights in country hotels, and hours in jolting livery hacks were becoming a part of life.

More hands were required, and in October of 1862 Robert Maere Wells and James Kirkpatrick Kerr joined the firm. They were both friends of the family, both in their early twenties, and would prove to be valuable men. Yet more partners meant more clerks and overhead, and there were months when work was slow and when fees lagged behind expenses. At the end of one that was rather worse than usual the burdened barrister, answering his father's fretting, snapped a little himself. There was always that throbbing head, always those strained eyes, always those parents and partners and the rest of the family to be thought for. He was sick of Toronto, fed up with his staff and concerned for himself and Margaret. "I wish we were young enough to get out of it. I would be glad to go anywhere. I am sick of hearing complaints of nothing to do."[8]

He had provided a new worry which promptly absorbed his parents. He was working too hard, William Hume warned. "You have an example before you which proves how easy it is to wear out the constitution." He should have change, exercise, and rest; he should have pans of water on top of the stoves in his office to preserve moisture in the air. He should have a high desk at which he could work standing. "That, I am sure, would be better than sitting cramped up as you are obliged to do for your near eyesight."[9]

Catherine's injunctions followed in their own specialized

vein. There should be "good roast beef or boiled mutton, fresh, the best part . . . plenty of rice and vegetables, no fat or pastry, regular hours, cold water within and without." Apparently unsure of Margaret's care of his diet, she was equally concerned for the health of the spiritual man. "Do, I pray you, read your Bible upon your knees and pray that your heart may be open. . . . Be careful not to waste the precious Sundays on any common work."[10]

There was more of the same through the winter and early spring, but there were always new involvements. By March of 1863, when his parents returned from Europe, the barrister was a member of the Senate of the University of Toronto. For two years he had been giving lectures in law, and they had earned him a name on campus that was now being put to use. With Adam Crooks, another brilliant alumnus and newly-elected Senator, he was confronting Egerton Ryerson as his father had done before him.

Ryerson was now sixty and for nineteen years had been Superintendant of Education for Canada West. There were few to deny his achievements, least of all himself. A born journalist and educator as well as a Methodist minister, he had lectured legislatures, overawed their leaders, and helped in the making and unmaking of several provincial governments. The system of public schools, which he had spent his life in building, was a great and permanent gift to Upper Canada. There was less to be said for his ideas when he extended them to the university. He had entered here, dominant, self-educated, garrulous, and egotistical, on the ground of Robert Baldwin, the ground of George Brown, and finally the ground of William Hume Blake. Those liberal secularists were for a university free of religious ties; Ryerson was for a cluster of five religious colleges, each receiving its share of the public funds.

He had been defeated but not converted when the university was established, and he had regained control of the university Senate. He had gone on with the benignant support of a friendly provincial government to obtain a Royal Commission and a report tailored to his taste. His proposal now, fortified by the Commission's report, was to reverse the work completed by William Hume. The university was to be stripped of the greater part of its revenues, and was to share the bulk of its endowment with the five religious colleges.

The report came to the Senate for what was usually routine acceptance. Ryerson, however, accustomed to somnolent compliance at half-attended meetings, found a new body awaiting him. It had been made so by the younger elements who had elected Crooks and Blake. Youth was in the ascendant, with these two men predominating. They would not accept the report, they were in a position to block a vote, and they intended to take the matter out to the public. On March 5, 1863, when the public crowded into St. Lawrence Hall, it consisted mainly of determined undergraduates seated in a solid block. They were in no mood for formalities, they had no ears for their opponents, and their series of resolutions was simply bellowed through.

Student power had emerged, and it had come to listen to its own. Of these, as chairman, the shy Adam Crooks was a skillful orchestrator but the evening went to his friend. "Mr. Edward Blake . . . concluded a very eloquent speech amid loud cheers"[11] and the evening was all but won. Three weeks later, in spite of much manoeuvring to postpone decision, the Senate met again. It averred that it "could in no way sanction . . . any scheme for the partition of the endowment or for the perpetual alienation of any part of it for the benefit of any institution other than the Provincial University and University College."[12] It was the crucial resolution, and it had been proposed by Edward Blake.

An embittered Ryerson showered the press with letters and despatched a lament to John A. Macdonald. It was the wrong Macdonald at the moment since his Reformer namesake, John Sandfield Macdonald, was then heading the government. John A., from the shades of opposition, could only offer sympathy and predict failure for the foe. Nor was he very sure of that. He had been informed by one of his friends, in connection with changes in John Sandfield's ministry, that "there is some talk of getting young Blake of Toronto to accept the Solicitor-Generalship."[13]

Whatever the source of the rumour, nothing came of it. There was more prominence but there was to be no politics yet for the busy barrister of Toronto. If he saw the approach of a turning-point he remained the aloof observer. He could hardly have failed to see it, for it had been coming most of his life. He had been eight years old when the union of the Canadas was made, with the rebellious French locked into it. He had grown through his teens and twenties as they became the "dominant" French. The joint parliament with its equal representation for a Lower Canada of six hundred thousand people and an Upper Canada of four hundred thousand people had been built in defiance of the realities of population, built to control the French. It did not change as the realities changed and they had come to favour the French. Upper Canada, richer and steadily enlarging, had a quarter-million majority in population, yet it was still balanced in parliament — usually blocked in parliament — by the province of the new minority. It was the province of the "stubborn" French now, the wall in the way of progress. Representation by population — that "Rep by Pop" that was bellowed for by Brown and the Toronto *Globe* — would certainly have to come. Yet how? The expedients within the union had all been tried and had failed. There was always that other talk, old almost as the Conquest, of a wider union of all the British colonies. It might stimulate new hopes, it might dilute some enmities and fears. Yet there were the realities of North America, there was the American Civil War, there were the thousands of miles of wilderness and the scattered, diverse peoples. It was not a thought for today, not for the lawyer of Toronto.

The creaking parliament of Canada went on as usual, with its hostile balanced sections, its game of hairline majorities and its strained machinery always nearer to collapse. The ministry of John Sandfield Macdonald and Louis-Victor Sicotte limped to its downfall in March of 1864, the last real government of the dual province. The other Macdonald came in again and in ten weeks was out, with nothing ahead but deadlock or a new, enormous challenge. It was a challenge that was taken up, but by the men already in the arena, the tired, scarred, brawling, and baffled veterans. Blake would watch from the sidelines as Confederation came.

⌇

On June 14, 1864, in the legislative building at Quebec, the ministry that was led by John A. Macdonald for Upper Canada and by Etienne-Paschal Taché for Lower Canada resigned office. It was the fourth government to have fallen in two years, and there was no man or ministry that was now prepared to replace it. In both Canadas politics had been played out; there would have to be a complete divorce or there would have to be that wider union. On June 15, as the sombre House assembled, Macdonald crossed the aisle to his greatest enemy. There was no charge of corruption, hardly a possible insult, that had not been flung at his head by George Brown. He had returned them all with interest. It was Brown and Rep by Pop, those two grim rocks of Upper Canadian intransigence, that had finally wrecked the union. Yet the time had come for a truce, and in the event more than a truce. Out of the mutterings of that afternoon and the manoeuvrings of days later came the coalition government that would join the men from the Maritimes to make the Dominion of Canada.

It was to be a work of a little less than three years, and in the meantime life went on. From the home of Edward Blake his sister Anne Margaret, married to the favourite partner J. K. Kerr, left for her own house. Two children were born to Margaret Blake, a boy who died before the end of his first year, and little Catherine Jane who died in her third. To the end of Margaret's life she would carry the children's min-

iatures in a gold locket, and outlasting her husband's life
would be a round wooden pillbox, small as a child's hand,
with the note scrawled on its cover: "Given to me by my darling
on my birthday not long before she died. E.B. January,
1867."[14]

William Hume Blake, a confirmed semi-invalid but a moderately contented man, was a Judge of the Court of Appeal.
He had again been appointed by Macdonald and it was at
least a tribute to his worth, though he was seldom able to sit.
He pottered about Humewood, played with his children's
children and left affairs to his son. As a sign of his new status
he had deeded his estate to Edward and could not complain of
the result. The debts dwindled, mortgages disappeared, and
investments began to grow with improving times. The firm
flourished as always. The apolitical barrister moved through
his days in Toronto wearing the mask of authority and success.

Inwardly he was a fretful man, measuring other men, measuring the coming change. It bristled with threats and promise.
Upper Canada would be stronger, freer than in the old union.
Yet what would sustain the new? Federalism, that new word,
so obviously disliked by Macdonald. The key to everything and
yet the key to what? Provinces linked together, united in a
central parliament, yet managing their own affairs in their
own legislatures. The lawyer looked at the scheme and shook
his head. The loopholes grinned and the traps swarmed too
thickly. There were still the French, there was still geography,
there were still those cloud-hung visions that were painted as
sure hopes. Railways — railways haunted the scheme — it was
said to be and it seemed to be a scheme of railway builders.
The railway to the Atlantic provinces, perhaps yes; that at least
must be thought of. It would balance the hopes of the east with
the hopes of Upper Canada for expansion to the new west,
the lands of the Red River. Yet those hopes would be enough
for a generation at least. That other phantom, that steel glim-
mering to the Pacific, could be left to the unborn future.

It was to be a union of the two Canadas and two of the

Atlantic provinces, forced at least in the case of Nova Scotia. It was being forced on much of Quebec, in spite of Cartier's assurance. Antoine-Aimé Dorion, the cool, clear-headed lawyer, always the friend of reform and no enemy to the English, was bitterly against the scheme. So was Luther Holton, dark, lanky, and impressive, the business magnate and railway builder who was first of English reformers in the lower province. Both men thoroughly distrusted the new proposal of federalism. They did not believe it would free their province for the management of its own affairs; they did not believe that Macdonald meant to do so. Even in Upper Canada there was John Sandfield Macdonald, ultra-politician but a pawkily honest Scot, who would have no part in the work. It was too big for him, it was too broad, and he distrusted men and motives. He was being ground under like the others by the force of politics and events, yet none of his objections was stilled for Blake nor any of the fears quelled.

Yet there were the other voices too. The barrister had followed, fascinated, as the debate on Confederation rose to its height. He had spent his nights in the study of the Quebec proceedings. He had copied out huge sections from the speeches of many leaders, and he had gone back of them to study earlier words. He was impressed by D'Arcy McGee, the Irish Catholic of Quebec, with his lyric visions of peace between the races and of the nation sea to sea. He was impressed by the new George Brown, the ogre of French Canadians and equally of Roman Catholics, who was changed now and working for conciliation. He gnawed at the problems propounded by lesser men, stubbornly French and Catholic or stubbornly English and Protestant, jealous of long-held rights. He knew little as yet of Alexander Mackenzie, the gaunt Scot from Sarnia, always at Brown's right hand. A dour, self-made man, a Baptist Grit and reformer, another of the established pope-and-bishop-haters. Yet there were certain words of Mackenzie that Blake had copied out: "As to the people of Lower Canada who are of French origin, and who are Roman Catholics, I have always heard it said in their favour that a large degree of liberalism characterizes their conduct toward their Protestant neighbours. Lower Canada, I believe, was the first portion of British territory to give political freedom to the Jew."[15] There was a new man here, groping away from the old positions of Brown, as Brown was himself. There was a man growing, reaching for the scope and breadth of larger work. There were many men growing amid this turmoil of nation building, and it would be good to grow along with them. It would be terrible to be left behind.

For Edward Blake the tide had begun to set, and it was not to be turned back. The quarrels came and the nation-builders parted, but the building was almost done. Brown's truce with Macdonald came to an end. He stamped out, shattering the coalition, calling his friends after him and some of the friends came. His old cry rose; the "corruptionists" had seized control; Macdonald and all his works must be rooted out of the Dominion. But there would be a Dominion now, and there would be a Dominion general election. The old war, when it resumed, would be on new and wider ground.

It would be a fight for the grip on central government and on provincial government as well. There was still the coalition shaping the paper plans, wielding the levers of power, hoping to hold them. There was still and always Macdonald, that cork on the sea of politics, who had somehow bobbed to the top. There was Cartier with him from the new province of Quebec, another of the indestructibles. There were the other old familiars and there were the new men unassessed; Charles Tupper, the bellowing Nova Scotian, and Leonard Tilley, the former druggist from New Brunswick. It seemed likely that there might be another Macdonald, for John Sandfield was wearing the signs of change. Whether convinced or converted — and it was better to think he had been bought — he was somehow moving into his namesake's camp.

Worse still, there were the other men, the renegades of reform. They had entered the coalition at the same time as Brown, but they had not left when he left. There could be no forgiveness for them, least of all for the tallest man among them, the affable, all-too-clever William McDougall who had grown under Brown's wing. He had been a hard bird to subdue and would have been a valuable one to hold, but he had found his nest and Macdonald and was well hated for it now.

All this Brown was preparing to fight. It was not these Tory remnants with their spattered rabble of turncoats who would shape the new Dominion. It was to be a new-built, fresh-built party of liberal Reform. It was to be the party of George Brown, confronting the party of Macdonald. There were to be federal elections and provincial elections and men were in much demand, notably Edward Blake. The hint of an overture from Macdonald, which was brusquely turned aside, had been succeeded by an offer of two places from men in the other camp. The constituency of West Durham was open to Blake in the federal election, and South Bruce in the provincial. He could run for both and he was wanted for both in the cause of Brown and Reform.

It was a nebulous cause as yet, unshaped and vague in its purposes as the coalition itself. The one clear hope of reformers seemed to be to pull Macdonald down. Yet Edward Blake was the son of William Hume; he had been born and bred to reform. He did not like George Brown. But it was Brown more than any man who had steeled and galvanized the hopes of Upper Canada and bent Macdonald to the work of Confederation. There had been Clear Grits before him with their roots going back to William Lyon Mackenzie. They had been parochials and men of the soil, of the western fringes of the province, demanding American ways, totally elective governments, a universal levelling that was not to be had in Canada. Robert Baldwin had fought them and they had ended Baldwin's career. But George Brown had tamed them. He had absorbed those rock-ribbed Calvinists and he had made reform

29

possible. He was a clear Grit himself now, but a Grit in his own image, and for all political purposes it was the image of Edward Blake.

On March 29, 1867, the British North America Act received royal assent. Seventeen days before that Brown was sure of his recruit. "Blake is ready and will be a host," he wrote to Alexander Mackenzie on March 12. "As a lawyer he is admirable, excellent common sense, immense industry and great pluck. Not much of a politician but anxious to learn, and sharp as a needle. He has a great opinion of you and I am persuaded you will be immense helps to each other."[16]

Opinions might change later, but the tide was in flood now. By April, as the party feverishly reorganized, Blake was deep in committee work and preparing for the convention of reformers that had been called by George Brown. It was to fill Toronto with the faithful, elucidate party doctrine, and establish the election mood. William McDougall and his ilk, the reformer renegades still with the coalition, were to be excommunicated with bell, book, and candle. On Thursday, July 27, amid the gas-lit blare and tumult on the stage of the jammed Music Hall, the first of the resolutions was proposed by Edward Blake.

During the same week, at Humewood, there was the familiar commotion of an invalid preparing to leave. William Hume Blake, without much interest in politics and with little hope of health, was again on his way to Europe. One hardly had time for the farewells, less still for brooding on the fact that they might be final. There were too many public meetings, too many urgent voices, too much work of a new, distasteful flavour.

The lawyer was preparing for the Court of a million judges. In his own spectacled eyes he was accepting a new brief, somewhat different from others. It was to establish the Dominion of Canada on a sound and proper footing, and to assure that his own province had its due and legitimate place. It would be a large work and it would be shared with many men, some of them no doubt inferior. But there were law, parliament, and reason, ultimately the masters of all. He intended to serve them honestly, he intended to give his best, and his best had always — or almost always — prevailed.

There were, as he had known there must be, the preliminaries he did not relish. He had been prevailed on to offer himself to the constituency of West Durham and the constituency of South Bruce. The electors now must be prevailed on to accept him. Both territories were new to him, his fate depended on strangers, and he was only beginning to learn how strange they were. He had felt it necessary to establish certain positions. He was a private, prosperous barrister who had heeded the call of duty. He could serve prospective constituents only as time permitted. Nor was he over-anxious to serve; he was quite indifferent, he said, as to the result of either election. He would not buy votes nor permit votes to be bought for him, he told his party organizers, and they agreed and went their way. They liked the look of their man and he had been a hard man to get; they were going to see him in. They had learnt their trade on the hustings of old Canada, and they had heard political fledglings cheep before.

CHAPTER THREE

FRIEND OF THE CONSTITUTION

IN AUGUST of 1867, with the Dominion one month old, the election campaigns began. They would be dual in the case of all Ontario ridings, since all Ontario constituencies were provincial as well as federal. Also in this election, and for a few years yet to come, a man might stand for both a federal and a provincial seat.

The statesman at the head of affairs, with his own title like the Dominion's hardly a month old, was Sir John A. Macdonald. It was his piously expressed hope that the former divisions of party might be forgotten. The coalition that had made the Dominion should be given a chance to govern it. He conceded that as years went on there would be new issues developing and parties dividing round them, but he did not concede that there were any such issues yet. The great work was to consolidate the new nation, and it should be begun with the *tabula rasa* — the clean slate.

It was a happy phrase, hit on by William McDougall, who was rather good at phrase-making and had need of one of the best. Still a member of the government and firmly committed to Macdonald, he had defended himself vigorously against the fire of the reform convention. It had not helped him in the eyes of his onetime friends. He was the first target, next to the greatest target, for the fire of the Toronto *Globe*.

Nothing was less likely or less possible than an election with a clean slate. To George Brown, who had risked his political career in the making of Confederation, Macdonald remained what he had always been, the devious seeker of power. It was Macdonald and his corrupt band, supported by corrupt deserters, who had seized credit for the achievement and were now enjoying the fruits. They were asking for a plenary indulgence which would only confirm them in their ways. They would not get it; there would be nothing forgotten or forgiven. The government must be thrown out, the helm wrenched from its hands, and the Dominion set on its course by true reformers.

It was a view which appealed utterly to Alexander Mackenzie, the bearded Scot from Sarnia. Now forty-five years old, Mackenzie had come to Canada in 1842 with sixteen shillings in his pocket. He had settled first at Kingston and later moved on west, with his stone-mason's kit of tools, his Baptist religious convictions, and his belief that government could be honest, clean, and workmanlike. As a builder he had done well, and could probably have done better, but for almost a quarter-century politics had competed with his business. A Grit of the old Grits, rooted as deeply as they were in Protestant Upper Canadianism, he had widened out to a larger view of the country. He had been one of the first of the reformers to speak for Confederation, but his detestation of Macdonald and his scorn of men like McDougall went even beyond Brown's. For Mackenzie there could be no truce nor even a thought of terms in the war with such enemies.

It was not quite so with the new reformer, Blake, just on the verge of politics. His antecedents were known, his abilities had become obvious, and he was certainly his own man. There had been hopes among coalitionists that he might be detached from Brown, and even as the hopes gave over there was still temperate regret. "It is a melancholy thing," commented the Conservative Toronto *Leader*, "to see a young man of talent, as Mr. Blake undoubtedly is, come to the threshold of public life under the guidance of a faction leader." He was rash, moreover, to be trying for a seat in the Dominion parliament as well as in the provincial house. Under Brown's guidance he would fall between the two stools, "and when he is down, there will be none to pity him."[1]

The tone changed as the campaign got under way, and West Durham and South Bruce had a first look at their candidate. This thirty-three-year-old Toronto barrister, wearing the aura of the law courts with an air of chilly elegance, was something new on the hustings. He was a stranger in both ridings and his enemies made much of that, but nothing promised to make him an object of pity. He had few jokes in his repertoire nor did he listen to jokes very often, but he had a sudden, warm smile. It came rarely, but it brightened meetings when it came. He seemed to appeal to women and women influenced husbands, even though they had no vote. He detested political platitudes, of which there were always too many around, and beyond that he was rich.

He wanted the last fact known; he was totally independent. He had made the resolve, he announced, that he would not enter politics until he had gained a competence of a hundred thousand dollars. Office meant nothing at all to him as a source of personal income; it would be what he felt it should be, a sacrifice and a service. He earned now annually more than the combined salaries that would be paid to a provincial cabinet. All this he hammered home to gaping electors, and the visible proofs of his status were occasionally almost painful. At some of his lakeside towns he arrived under full sail, standing at the helm of *Rivet*. "Mr. Blake," said the *Leader* sourly, "publishes an address to the electors of South Bruce in the morning . . . and on the same day jumps into his yacht and sets out for West Durham. We very much fear that the political wooer in his yacht, the eyeglasses and the high style of convention eloquence will be too much for it."[2]

The hopeful worries all proved to be groundless. In West Durham, as the campaign moved toward its climax and sleep became a rare thing, the crowds at open-air meetings and in the drill sheds, halls, and school houses could not get enough of his eloquence. On a sweltering evening at Newcastle, according to one watcher, the audience listened restlessly to a round of local speakers. Then about ten in the evening "that impressive figure arose with his ringing voice and majestic sentences and imposed silence on all. The effect was magical. With no tedious exordium, no funny stories, he was at once into the exposition of his subject in his clear and dignified manner. Tired backs straightened, the hubbub of voices ceased, and a hush of admiration fell on the audience."[3]

He moved on to Orono to be faced by William McDougall, speaking for the opposing candidate. It was a noisy confrontation with a dangerous and experienced veteran, yet it was McDougall who was shouted down. Blake, it seemed, was a match even for the elements. He was in mid-course of his argument when a sharp midnight thunderstorm threatened to end proceedings, but his hearers refused to leave. They waited the storm out, Blake resumed his speech, and the meeting ended triumphantly with dawn grey on the windows. "We went home to build the fires for breakfast and milk the cows. We took our politics in large doses in those times."[4]

Beautiful little Bowmanville was the centre of West Durham with a fine harbour on the lake, half a dozen sawmills, and rich farms rolling away inland. On September 4 it was the site of nominations. For miles around there were acres of ripened wheat crying out to be harvested, but on that Wednesday most of the workers left them. From early morning carriages and wagons were streaming away toward Bowmanville and rolling up to the drill shed with farmers in their best clothes. By one o'clock there were twenty-two hundred people packed in the hall, crowding the doorways or massed at the open windows. George Brown had come in support of Blake and Sir John A. Macdonald had found it convenient to attend. It was proof enough that this was a crucial meeting and that it centred on a rising man.

Macdonald, as usual, outmanoeuvred Brown. He had been much in evidence before the meeting began, ambling about through the clutter of arriving wagons, laughing and slapping backs, telling his stories. As the first of the principal speakers he had sat smiling on the platform through an hour or so of preliminary local addresses. When his own turn came, however, his chair was empty; he had been called by nature or summoned by great affairs. There was "an awkward pause" as the *Globe* reported next day, "the Prime Minister and his candidates were afraid to speak first."[5] Brown knew no such fears. He leaped up and launched himself on his speech, throwing away the advantage of second place. As he soared on, climbing to heights of angry denunciation, Macdonald sat grinning up at him from among the first row of listeners.

The Prime Minister, when he came to speak at last, was rebutting familiar arguments and was quite in his usual vein. He was the amiable, reasonable man, deploring faction. He chaffed Brown on his long face and on the long finger "that he has so often shaken at us". He was, according to an admirer, wholly winning. "Looking on us with his faintly waggish air, he said those simple, sensible things which generally carry conviction."[6]

This time, however, they carried a little short. The man who had come by *Rivet* was the centre of interest here. He was fresh and tanned from the lake, determined on his own direction, and unimpressed by the antics of the rival leaders. When the cold young lawyer rose Brown seemed a little passé, Macdonald a little soiled. Blake was a new enigma, curiously apart from both, refusing to be quite entangled in the threads of the old quarrels. He was not forgetting the past but the future had to be looked to, and he focussed his eyes on that.

There was the frame of a nation now, and a provisional government asking to be confirmed in power. Power to accomplish what? Macdonald came to the country with no policy — how could he hope to be elected? Let him submit a policy, accept the duty of defending it, and be judged by what he said. The so-called coalition was only a rump of remnants, a mockery of what it had been. It was a clutch of quarrelling office-seekers, bound together by nothing but the ambition to remain in power. Was it faction to oppose these men, to speak for an opposing party?

William McDougall — his scorn of William McDougall was as great as Brown's or Mackenzie's — had had much to say recently about the Intercolonial Railway. He was hinting in appropriate quarters to his new Conservative friends that the fifteen million dollars required to build it would keep the party in office for another ten years. Did the electors want that? Was it not an argument in itself for a watchful opposition? It was a time for clean government by clean men; the old ways would not do. He pointed to Macdonald's cabinet of thirteen members, where seven would have been enough. Those six superfluous offices had been sops to various regions and to the demands of hungry friends. Was that wanted? In his innocence, Blake thought not, though he would learn more later of the strength of friends and regions. For that day, as the seven-hour meeting ended, he was sure enough of his election. He would be a member of the Dominion parliament for the constituency of West Durham.

That confidence was to be confirmed, but at South Bruce across the breadth of the peninsula politics swirled more darkly. John Sandfield Macdonald, converted or perverted by John A. Macdonald, was now Premier of Ontario under the wing of the coalition. He had put together his "Patent Combination", a cabinet of old reformers and onetime Tory enemies whose positions were as confused as his own. It promised trouble as a government but it was an efficient force to fight the provincial elections and John Sandfield, often side by side with the other Macdonald, was leading a strong campaign. In South Bruce, which was an important and chancy riding, his henchmen knew their work.

They went at it in old ways against a candidate with much to learn, and Blake's unwary relatives provided them with ammunition. Bishop Cronyn, writing from London to a friend, had urged support for his son-in-law and the rumour was soon around. Religion was meddling here, defiling the purity of politics. Verschoyle Cronyn appeared, shaking hands with the citizens, and involving his own law firm in a train of sinister suspicions. Cronyn and Cronyn, as the *Leader* watching from Toronto hastened to point out, were solicitors for the Huron & Erie Permanent Building Society, and the Huron & Erie held mortgages on the properties of Bruce electors. "Mr. Cronyn can easily, by hinting at a relaxation or tightening of the legal screw, exercise, he thinks, an influence over their votes."[7]

There was also the question of the Toronto, Grey and Bruce Railway that was seeking a charter in Bruce, and was a favourite project of many of the important citizens. Blake had doubts of the project, admitted as much in public, and flatly refused to support it until he had had time to assess the facts. He held to the tight-lipped promise that he would use his best judgment, and it was hardly enough in the face of hostile meetings. He had a first taste, as he had not had in Durham, of the bitter brew of the underdog whose cause appeared to be lost. Yet something changed in the atmosphere as soon as polling began. Whatever the force of his arguments, and however little he knew of some of his supporters, he had busy henchmen too. Teams came to the polls provided by Blake organizers, tavern keepers grew generous and uncertain voters decisive after contact with Blake's friends. By September 16 the friends seemed to have succeeded. He was in by a narrow margin.

Yet it was too small to be flattering and it was not even quite safe. For another week there was talk of a contestation which would involve a new campaign. The candidate was irked by that, and he had learned a great deal more. On the 24th he wrote to his principal organizer. He would be unable, he said, in any case to stand again for the constituency. He had just been presented with a bill for $2,500, most of it to cover election expenses he had flatly and publicly forbidden. The bulk of the money, moreover, had been spent on behalf of his riding-mate who was contesting the federal seat, "so that in effect I am made to pay for both".

All this he repudiated utterly. "My principles do not admit it . . . and my circumstances do not permit it. I am making, on entering public life at all, an enormous sacrifice independent of this additional loss which I cannot in justice to my family again incur." Also, since he was informed that the expenses were absolutely necessary to win the election, "it is evident that the riding cannot be carried on the principles on which alone I can stand for it.

"I have therefore determined never again to become a candidate for the riding, and the only question on which I am at present in doubt is whether I ought not to resign my seat. What supported me under the great disappointment of the narrow majority was the conviction that we had been fighting our battle on pure principles and without evading the law, and now that I find myself obliged to discard that conviction I will say to you frankly that I wish I had been beaten. At present my feeling is that I ought not, consistently with the views I entertain and have expressed, to retain a seat which I have acquired by such means, but I will further consider this point before coming to a conclusion.

"You will not understand me as expressing any censure on yourself or indeed on anyone . . . I do not wish to blame . . . but rather to part with my friends in a spirit of hearty kindliness. I hoped till today that we might not part at all . . . but these things are managed for us by a wiser Head than ours and we must not repine . . ."[8]

The dismayed battlers of Bruce looked up from the letter dizzy with its contradictions. What did the screed mean? — and what sort of man had written it? Did he object to spending money — or to spending too much money — or merely to spending his own? He doubted his right to the seat — yet he had not decided to resign it. "Pure principles" — the "wiser Head than ours" — he parted with friends in kindliness yet left

39

them all in the lurch, faced with another battle in which he now refused to join. Had he fought through two campaigns, this maker of enormous sacrifices, without learning at least a little of what politics really was? Or was he now beginning to learn, and was that the real trouble? Had he come from his chilly courtrooms and the Olympian quiet of his study to be faced with the sweat and breath of a living nation? Had he looked out from his platforms and sensed the size of the task, the tools he would have to work with?

No one knew in Bruce, and no one would ever be sure. In the event it was not necessary; there was no new election and he did not choose to resign. But he had confronted his shaken organizers, as he would confront many later, with a manifestation of the ways of Edward Blake.

∽

By early October, with the results of the elections final, the political landscape cleared. There were clouds overhanging the scene for both parties. George Brown's reformers, for all the regeneration they had brought about, were not to be the guiding force in the new nation. Brown himself had been defeated in his own constituency, and was never to take a seat in the House of Commons. John Sandfield Macdonald, the coalitionist convert, had carried the provincial elections and would remain Ontario's premier. John A. Macdonald, with Ontario and Quebec won and New Brunswick just safe, was sure of a good majority as Prime Minister.

There were no such certainties, however, for the Confederation itself. Rebellious Nova Scotia under the leadership of Joseph Howe had elected eighteen members, out of a total of nineteen, who had pledged themselves to work for repeal of the union. Charles Tupper would be the only Nova Scotian in the House of Commons who was in favour of Confederation. He was former provincial premier and a burly political wonder-worker who had proved too much for Howe. Tupper had forced the union on Nova Scotia and was determined to make it hold, yet it still seemed all too evident that Howe spoke for the people. For William Hume Blake, writing to his son from England, it was difficult to see how Nova Scotia could be retained against her will. "And if she succeeds in liberating herself the Union is doomed."[9]

For all the achievement of nation-building there was little unity anywhere, on either side of the rickety political fences. The problem of Nova Scotia, dragged in by the heels, was only the worst of many. Quebec was almost as restless. It had voted for Confederation, but only by a narrow margin and only through the supreme efforts of George Etienne Cartier, whose enemies were still active and some of whose friends were weakening. The nation builders themselves were becoming at odds with each other. Macdonald had been made a Knight Commander of the Bath, while Cartier and some of his colleagues had been offered mere Companionships. Cartier had refused the honour and it had been accepted with an ill grace by Alexander Tilloch Galt, who had been one of the first proposers of union and had framed its financial terms. Both men were rumoured with good reason to have their knives out for Macdonald. William McDougall, with the election won and his reform following lost, was becoming a wasting asset and was aware and resentful of the fact. The whole cabinet was a mass of unstable forces whose power seemed very doubtful and whose direction was not resolved.

On the other side there was the certainty that there would be a party in opposition. That point, at least, the reformers fighting the election had made abundantly clear. But what sort of party? — and in opposition to what? Blake complained that Macdonald offered no program, yet the whole work of the leader was to affirm Confederation. Did reformers oppose that? What was their own program, beyond penny-pinching on cabinets and raising the corruption cry? Where, in fact, was their leader and what were his proposals?

All the questions were dangerous, and some presently unanswerable. For every reason Brown was leader by right. But how would he assert the right? He was not now in parliament nor did he seem inclined to return; he seemed to be ascending rather toward the position of grey eminence. But he was not grey, and he had none of the mystic calm, the unimpassioned remoteness that would suit him for that position. He was the red-headed George Brown, the thrusting activist autocrat, wielding the club of the *Globe*.

Yet he was changed and somehow cautious, perhaps because of defeat, perhaps more because of the problems he saw beyond it. He had tamed Grits and he had bent reform to the work of Confederation. There was Rep by Pop now, the promise of better government, deliverance from the entangling French. There was freedom for Upper Canada to expand to the North-West, the west beyond the Lakes. Yet how much of freedom, how much of deliverance? — everything had been gained at a price. There were those separate schools for the French, those assurances given Cartier, those hopes for the St. Lawrence basin competing with the North-West. Competing and yet complementing, the one essential to the other, all and each a part of the developing nation. The reform party, in process of evolution toward a national Liberal party, would have to be made to accept them.

It would have to do more still; it would have to win back the angry *rouges* of Quebec. Those red reforming nationalists had roots going back to Papineau, and they had fought Confederation tooth and nail. They had fought Cartier's *bleus*, those pragmatists and Conservatives who had yielded with him on terms. There was Antoine-Aimé Dorion, indispensable leader and still leader of the *rouges*. There was Luther Holton who supported him with a handful of English liberals. There were few men, with the possible exception of Mackenzie, whom Brown respected more, liked and trusted more than these two, yet they had broken with him in the battle over the union. They were returning now, taking their seats in parliament, prepared to accept the inevitable. Yet they must be for a while defeated and resentful men. There would be distrust in their minds, there would be distrust of them in the minds of Upper Canada and there would be their followers beyond the Ottawa, recalcitrant and unconvinced. There must be a union of minds and hearts preceding a political merging, and it would be a slow and painful growth. "I think," George Brown had written to Mackenzie in mid-August, "it would be better for each party to paddle its own canoe a little longer."[10] He was of the same mind in September, and the implications were clear. Until Quebec *rouges* were tamed and the worst of the scars healed there could be no national party, no national policy and no national leader.

Of all this Blake was thoroughly aware. "Blake concurs" — the expression was becoming common in Brown's letters to Mackenzie. Blake seemed naturally to be included in the discussions of the two men. He was drawing closer to Mackenzie, and the first impression was good. He could work with this man, there was none of the rasp of Brown; there was diffident, labourious honesty with a sense of rock-ribbed purpose. Though he was the senior by ten years and by a quarter-century of experience, the self-educated former stone mason was inclined to defer in most things to the brilliant Toronto lawyer. Mackenzie was a man of the Upper Canadian west, uneasy still with the French, uneasily conscious that they were stiff with him. He did not aspire to lead them, or in fact to lead at all.

With Brown out of parliament he would be standing in Brown's shoes, but there was a general impression that Brown would move the feet. That was natural enough, and Blake shared the impression, yet it imposed no obligation that he himself must accept. If there was an obligation for Blake it was to keep himself free of Brown, to resist his obstinacies and crudities, dilute his old rancours and help in shaping a party for the work of changed times. There was a new excitement in the thought and by October it had begun to seize him, washing away his soreness over the squalors of South Bruce. He was after all and above all the elected of West Durham, and the

Dominion parliament would be opening in another month. At a banquet held in Bowmanville to celebrate the federal victory he was a confident politician, prepared and eager for the fray.

It was a temperance banquet, and he was jovial on the subject of temperance. The beauty of the ladies present was enough to uplift his spirits. He had been much helped by the ladies. He had heard of one of them, he said, who had been tying her husband's scarf as he prepared to go to the polls. She had threatened to pull it tight, strangling her stubborn helpmate, if he did not vote for Blake. For Alexander Mackenzie, who was also present at the banquet, the speaker had kind words with a shading of condescension. His esteemed colleague, he said, was obviously a man who knew the political ropes. Toward the new government shortly to be faced in Ottawa he was as harsh as Brown or Mackenzie. There was to be no *tabula rasa* in Dominion politics; the sins of the coalition could not be blotted out. Macdonald asked for forgetfulness and a fair trial, yet he persisted in his old methods. He had sought Blake as a candidate for his own party and had fought him because he refused, because he would not deny his principles. Could this government of false pretences stand for long? — Blake did not think so. The opposition newspapers had been offering him much advice, coupled with much abuse. One of them had kindly suggested that as a raw political novice he would be best to keep his mouth shut for perhaps the next ten years. He had no such intention; he would speak when he had a mind to. He would hold the government responsible for its every act. There would be no amnesty for the past, and there would be no quarter in the future.[11]

On Thursday, November 7, 1867, the first parliament of the Dominion of Canada convened. The impressive buildings stood on their noble site, dominating the flag-hung lumber town that had become the nation's capital. Lord Monck, the Governor-General, arrived in state, there was the usual display of troops and splendid uniforms, and the Speech from the Throne was read with ancient ceremony. That much was familiar from the parliament of the old Canadas. Yet over it all was a feeling of larger scale, a sense of new beginnings, and in the workday world of government there was less of serene order.

Blake, the new member, had arrived in Ottawa not by comfortable *Rivet* but in a jolting railway car. He had exchanged the amenities of Humewood for Mrs. Brown's boarding house where he was now lodged with Mackenzie and some of his other colleagues. He had been duly sworn, had duly received his travelling trunk and box of official stationery, and had been allotted his seat in Commons. At three o'clock on the 7th, responding with other members to the summons from Black Rod, he had been jostled up to stand at the bar of the Senate. An hour or so later, returned from the upper chamber with the Speech from the Throne behind him, he could at least agree with Mackenzie on the deficiencies of his new home.

The great Gothic building, in the opinion of the tart stone mason who had tendered unsuccessfully on some of the construction, was more suitable for monks than legislators and was "one of the greatest examples of magnitude without convenience on the face of the earth."[12] Its ventilation and drainage worked in an evil combination to assure a continual supply of foul air. Its gas-lighting and pot-bellied wooden stoves consumed enormous quantities of whatever oxygen was left. It was well supplied with bars, ill-supplied with committee rooms, and always too hot or too cold. There were no private offices for private members. For Blake the newcomer, used to the spacious quiet of his Toronto legal chambers, there was now a corner of the common room reserved for Ontario reformers. Or there was his desk in Commons itself, the fourth in the second row to the left of Mr. Speaker.

In the early November twilight the view from the desk was not particularly promising. On the treasury benches to the right of Mr. Speaker, Sir John A. Macdonald and the tall William McDougall were splendid in court uniform. But they were already uneasy colleagues and they were alone in their fine garb. Cartier sat in morning dress at the side of the Prime Minister, still deprived of his title, a study in surly dignity, and in the eyes of anxious enemies a hopeful sign of disrup-tion. Adams G. Archibald, Secretary of State for the Provinces, was not present at all; he had been defeated in Nova Scotia. Even more significant was the vacated place of Alexander Tilloch Galt, the brilliant Minister of Finance. He had just resigned from the government after a final quarrel with Macdonald, and he had left in his empty office the problem of the Commercial Bank. One of the large banks of the country, it had failed some weeks before, and was now shaking the props of several others.

There were men outside the ministry as symptomatic of problems as those within. Thomas D'Arcy McGee, Catholic Montrealer and prophet of Confederation, was sitting as a private member. So was Charles Tupper, the Protestant who had borne the battle in Nova Scotia. Macdonald had wanted both men and had found a place for neither. The multiple pressures of cabinet making had crowded each of them aside, until there was a single seat left. For that seat religious balance had required an Irish Catholic, while regional balance had forbidden a man from Quebec. The result had been a hasty Senatorship for the mild Edward Kenny, who could only claim significance because he was a Catholic Nova Scotian. He was not to be seen here, for he sat in the other place, but he had served to complete this government which was now before the House. Congratulating itself on the achievement of nationality, faced with the building of the Intercolonial Railway, it was in the midst of financial crisis, shaken by Galt's departure, and none too sure of some who remained behind him.

There were as many more uncertainties reflected across the aisle. Incongruous in the place of leader of the opposition sat John Sandfield Macdonald, who was a federal member as well as premier of Ontario. He had come to both places largely through his recent alliance with John A. Macdonald, though he was still a wayward reformer and uneasy in Confederation. Dorion and Holton were beside him with Lucius Seth Huntington, another of the Quebec liberals who had opposed the making of the union. Beside Huntington was Mackenzie, as granite firm for the union as he was against the two Macdonalds, but a seat away from Mackenzie was the glowering Joseph Howe. For all Mackenzie's presence, it was a front bench that reeked of anti-Confederacy, the government's favourite charge. To the man who watched from the fourth seat in the second row of benches it was a reminder of many difficulties, and might well have presented more. Howe had been assigned originally to the seat reserved for the leader of the opposition, but had refused to take the place. At least now, by a hasty exchange with John Sandfield Macdonald, he had reduced his own pre-eminence among the men on the Speaker's left.

Yet it still remained for Howe to reduce himself. Until that threat was lifted from the young Dominion all else was preliminary. He rose on the night of November 8 with thirty years of service to his home province behind him, one of the first men who had talked of a nation spanning the continent, of hearing the whistle of a locomotive in the passes of the Rocky Mountains, of travelling from Halifax to the Pacific in a mere matter of days. Yet he had fought Confederation because it was not made to his shape, and when he sat down at the end the fight was over. Nothing remained ahead of him but the long agony of surrender. He had come before his time, a man who had dreamed too high, and too many of his dreams had been centred on Joseph Howe.

It was the man who had done what Howe had hoped to do who established the final irony. Charles Tupper, for once, had no need here of his own verbose bluster. He rose after Howe to quote in Howe's own words the prophet's great imperatives for the nation sea to sea. "Between Canada and the Pacific ... five or six noble provinces may be formed, larger than any we have ... will you then put your hands unitedly, with order, intelligence and industry to this great work? Refuse, and you are recreant to every principle . . . refuse, and the Deity's handwriting upon land and sea is to you unintelligible language." With the last relentless passage not only was Howe demolished but the vision he had turned away from seemed more impelling than before. "God has planted your country in the front of this boundless region; see that you comprehend its energy and resources — see that you discharge, with energy and elevation of soul, the duties which devolve upon you."[13]

The parliament that would witness many tragic downfalls had seen its first that night. But on Monday, November 11, when Blake stood up in the House for his maiden speech, there were signs of a new rising. The tall, erect figure, with the blue eyes steady behind the glinting spectacles, was already known and watched for. The sheaves of notes before him and the thumb hooked in the lower pocket of the vest were soon to become familiar. There was no barrister's gown here but he did not seem to miss it; he carried the air with him. He asked, as a young member, for the kind indulgence of the House, but however seriously it was requested indulgence was not required. As *rouges* and reformers groped toward a leader of Liberals, the talk was rising in caucuses that here was the potential man.

He dealt gently with Howe, welcoming him to the federal parliament and urging him to share the work before the nation. But how could the work begin without a program? — where was the government's plan? He smiled bleakly on the Honourable William McDougall, who had spent years as a reformer in condemning Macdonald's work. Suddenly, as he reached the ministry, McDougall had found that the devil was not so black; he was a devilish good fellow. He paid his respects to Galt, the departed Minister of Finance, whose one consistent policy seemed to have been to increase the national debt. "At last, like some will-of-the-wisp which had led us into a quagmire, the honourable gentleman left us in the very worst spot of it to flounder out as we could."

John Sandfield Macdonald, still positioned as leader on

Blake's side of the House, was next to come under the guns.
He was one of the oldest of the other Macdonald's enemies
but in recent months had become his attendant shadow, "tall
and thin as a shadow ought to be, which followed his every
footstep, re-echoed his every word, applauded his every sentiment." The long feud of the clan Macdonald had ended, the
barrister informed the House with chill irony, and the sole
purpose of the peace-making had been to sweep the Ontario
elections.

He looked around him at friends sitting by enemies, and
commented on the confusion of the House. Which of these
gentlemen supported the present government and which were
prepared to oppose it? He hoped to learn later from the gentlemen's own lips. Some of the gentlemen squirmed under the
steely glint of the spectacles; they had seen this cross-examiner
at work in the courts.

He returned to an old theme, criticizing the size of the
cabinet; its present vacancies should be allowed to remain
vacant. He warmed from his own experience to the subject of
bribery in elections and the growing cost of campaigns. The
whole electoral system, with its weeks of open polling, was a
basic cause of corruption. All general elections should be held
simultaneously and confined to a single day.

Finally he returned to Howe, who was still looking toward
London for repeal of the act of union. Blake did not think the
repeal movement would succeed. The Imperial Government
had approved of Confederation, and would insist on a fair
trial. Until that trial had been made, the members from Nova
Scotia should accept their situation and make the best of it.
The speaker hoped, for his part, that they would join faithfully
in the working of the constitution. So long as it made for the
good of the whole Dominion he hoped nothing would change.
Stability was to be hoped and prayed for. "There is on the
floor of the House no truer, though no more humble, friend
of the constitution than myself."[14]

It had been a powerful and confident speech from a new

member, and it brought the acclaim of one ambiguous friend. The thirty-two-year-old Richard Cartwright of Kingston was sitting across the aisle, elegant, assured, and wearing the crop of whiskers he seemed to have been born with. He was of Empire Loyalist stock, his family background in Canada was older than that of the Blakes, and he had crossed the Atlantic to become, like William Hume, a graduate of Trinity College, Dublin. He had returned to politics and finance, and had been a Conservative for four years. He was now an independent, though still nominally a Conservative, and a man with much on his mind. He had been president of the Commercial Bank, recently defunct, and he had his problems with that. He resented the fact that Macdonald had refused to save it by means of government help. He was soon to resent the new Minister of Finance, Macdonald's friend, John Rose. He was to break finally with Macdonald in culminating resentment when he failed to secure the appointment as successor to John Rose. In the meantime, as a battered financier and an ambitious politician, he was building tentative bridges. He rose after Blake to extend felicitations on the speech he had just heard. He had always found, he said, that the honourable gentleman who had just sat down was a worthy friend as well as a worthy foe. On that point, in the years that lay ahead of them, each of the honourable gentlemen would have much cause to reflect.

As the session moved along toward the Christmas recess the work of the future shaped in massive outline. The Intercolonial Railway was still to be begun, and the territories of the Hudson's Bay Company were the problem beyond that. To Macdonald, to McDougall, and even to George Brown it was an imperative necessity to acquire that great Northwest. If the Dominion of Canada did not, the United States would, and it would end the hope of a nation sea to sea. Blake saw no such certainties. Who knew the intentions of the United States? In any case what could Canada alone do to forestall them?

How could she defend and administer that vast region when she could not defend herself? Since the territories would depend for years on the strength of British arms, they would be better as a Crown Colony. There was no need for this headlong plunge toward bigness; it was an assumption of liabilities which the country could not support.

The Ontarian and the eastern Canadian was sounding a basic theme; work should begin at home. Yet there was no doubt that the decision was moving against him, and Maritime members were becoming tired of the debate. The west was too remote, and their own affairs were slighted. The party bickering of Upper Canadians bored them, with its threshing of old straw. Talk drifted toward parliamentary housekeeping and matters of organization, with members' expenses and indemnities becoming a moot point. Six hundred dollars a year did not go far in Ottawa, and you could buy a meal in Halifax for a third of the price here. In the other place there was a grumbling of honourable Senators that was soon to become familiar. Macdonald's unformed legislative program was giving them nothing to do. Just before Christmas the session ground to adjournment and the members left for their homes. For a friend of the constitution there had not been much to complain of, and there was still less to applaud. The gears of the new machinery had hardly begun to mesh.

CHAPTER FOUR

"A GIANT AT MY ELBOW"

H UMEWOOD sat calm and inviting amid its white fields and snowy trees and hedges. Yet it was not to be a good Christmas; for the elder Blakes the best of such days were gone. William Hume and Catherine were across the Atlantic, still failing in the cheerless quest for health. The office distracted Sam, politics and the neglected practice weighed on Edward, and there was to be another family parting. "Old Gran", William Hume's mother who had been living with the Broughs in London, was now awaiting the end.

It came on the 26th, and the matriarch of Dublin, dying at ninety-six, remained a Hume and a Blake to the last. As the family surrounded her bed and the Reverend Charles Brough stood murmuring scriptural comfort, her eyes opened and she turned to her youngest daughter. "Ann, dear, get a Bible. Charles is misquoting shockingly."[1]

A day later the Ontario provincial legislature convened for its first session. Amid a confusion of party loyalties that matched conditions in Ottawa, there were also physical signs of improvisation. In the legislative chamber itself a last-minute rush of carpenters, plumbers, and upholsterers had achieved an air of order. Yet elsewhere throughout the building, according to the critical *Globe*, "chaos reigns supreme." In the committee rooms and the offices of various departments, books, records, and furniture were piled high in confusion, everywhere thick with dust. Many of the new administrators would have battered chairs and tables, purchased second-hand. John Sandfield Macdonald, lax enough in many of his political practices, was at least bent on economy.

With the funeral of Gran delaying him, Blake was absent from the ceremonies of opening day. Yet around his vacant seat — again the fourth in the second row to the left — there was more speculative gossip than there had been in the Dominion House. "Who is to lead the opposition?" the Toronto *Leader* had asked. "What of Mr. Blake?" As the protégé of George Brown, he had been pushed forward by the *Globe*, yet even the *Globe* had seemed to have second thoughts. They were well-advised in the *Leader's* opinion; Blake was still unproved. It conceded him much ability, and dwelt more on his faults. He was a highly successful barrister, but the courtroom manner followed him into the House. He was a fine speaker, but inclined to speak too long. His grasp of facts was coupled with a short temper, and he was often brusque and rude with the ill-informed. The sea of politics required experience in a navigator, and Blake had none at all. "We are not without hopes of Mr. Blake's future usefulness, but . . . they do not solve the present question of leadership."[2] In the event he had solved it himself by a flat refusal to serve. It was the rotund Archibald McKellar, a genial veteran of the wars before the union, who would be opposition leader.

For Blake, the thought of his provincial duties was stirring some latent doubts. He had had one half-session in the Dominion parliament, and why was he there at all? Duty was a half-answer, ambition had rightful claims, and there was the all-pervasive thrust of the home he came from. It had made him a successful barrister and had edged him into politics, but it had not defined his purpose. For William Hume Blake and Catherine Hume Blake the Creator's designed order had imposed the urge to rise. It was as much a part of religion as the Sunday walk to church, the ritual of evening prayers. There had never been a moment for the son when that pressure was

relaxed, when it was not expected of Edward that he would
stand above the herd. That much he had achieved; he was sure
of his capabilities. He had achieved a measure of affluence,
the all-important preliminary. Yet now there were the obligations entailed by the Creator's gifts, by money and high abilities, and the sense of the leader's place.

Those obligations had also been driven home; they were a
part of the Sunday walks, a promise with every prayer. One
prayed for the means to serve, for God watched well. Victorian
in stiff gentility and in respect for position and money, Blake
had centuries behind him of place in an established order,
and of striving to improve that place. All this must be, for order
tended to good, and advance within the frame was a right
and duty. He saw the plane he stood on through the eyes of
father and mother and of reverend friends and relatives who
were Irish gentlemen of the cloth. He saw the good man's
purpose through the eyes of Victorian poets. Tennyson's words
filled many pages in his notebooks. The young barrister, home
from his liens and mortgages in the late evenings, had dreamed
in lamplight over the mighty thoughts. He intended like old
Ulysses "to strive, to seek, to find and not to yield". He had
kindled to George Eliot, sharing the golden hope:

> Oh may I join the choir invisible
> Of those immortal dead who live again
> In minds made better by their presence; live
> In deeds of daring rectitude, in scorn
> For miserable aims that end with self,
> In thoughts sublime that pierce the night like stars
> And with their mild persistence urge man's search
> To vaster issues . . .[3]

Vaster issues. Yes, there were vaster issues waiting man;
challenging and tremendous issues in this young country. He
intended to aid the search, to join the choir. But where did a
man begin? In that raucous Dominion parliament, smelling
always of alcohol, presided over by Macdonald? Among the
back-slappers in the corridors, the whisperers in smoky bars,

or out on the roads and hustings from which all this tumult flowed? He had heard no immortal notes in such places, and he expected them less in the dreary provincial house.

He had made it clear to his South Bruce electors that he was a man with limited time. The Dominion parliament came first, the claims of his business second, and provincial business only a poor third. In any case he was still resentful of the campaign. Since only about half the constituency had voted to retain his services, he was disposed to offer only a fractional effort. Yet these were first broodings, impossible to hold for long. Whatever the work he was faced with, Blake could not nibble. He was hardly into his place before he was taking a full bite, and in the two months that followed there was considerable bark too.

He was not remote from his office as he was in Ottawa, and it claimed him every morning. There was never enough time there, and there were often days in court. He came to the House at three in the afternoon, nagged at by loose ends, fretful with his own affairs, to be faced by relentless quibblers and the rasp of provincial problems. He was not patient with quibblers, he was bored by provincial problems, and he had little respect for John Sandfield Macdonald. He was inclined to brush the mild McKellar aside. He was sometimes quite insufferable in the eyes of his dearest critics. Yet there could be no doubt that the party's centre of gravity was shifting in his direction, and somehow work got done.

When the session came to its end, on March 4, 1868, Ontario was under way as a province of the Confederation. John Sandfield Macdonald was at least a good administrator, and for the success of some of his measures he was inclined to credit Blake. There had been storms across the aisle but considerable cooperation behind the scenes, and as an easy-going lawyer he had been glad of Blake's advice. But not overly glad; he was already a man in difficulties who saw more reefs ahead. An unconvinced Confederate, he was still balky and difficult with the Macdonald sitting in Ottawa. He was at sea on many of the dividing lines between federal and provincial powers. Blake was not, and some of their ideas clashed. There was a report of Egerton Ryerson's on provincial education, which John Sandfield approved of and Blake was eyeing coldly. Dual representation, the right of a member to hold a federal and provincial seat, was already a bone of contention. Sandfield liked it; Blake was determined to end it. Above all it was clear, as McKellar diminished daily in relation to his chief supporter, that Blake would be the man to beat at the next election.

$\wp$

In that view McKellar heartily concurred, and so did George Brown. They made their professions on the evening of March 4, at a large banquet celebrating the end of the session. Blake, said Brown, had achieved unprecedented success, from the very start of his career. There was no doubt that he might soon lay claim to the highest offices in the country. McKellar, in his own opinion, had been the wrong man in his place. It obviously belonged to his "excellent and gifted friend . . . who is destined to be our chieftain in a very short time and who ought, in fact, to be so at the present moment." Throughout the session, he said, he had sat "with a giant at my elbow".[4] The giant replied with a modesty he could now well afford, but already his thoughts were straying. So, in fact, were Brown's. It would soon be time for Ottawa, the greater parliament was resuming, and there was high intrigue in the air.

It had begun with a letter from Cartier, directed to George Brown. The two men, enemies so long in the past, had become almost friends during the making of Confederation. They had each risked more than Macdonald for considerably less reward, and they shared a mutual resentment. Now Cartier, still in the coalition but often at odds with his chief, was regretting the absence of Brown. There actually seemed in the letter to be rather more than regret. "It may be," he wrote with a curious significance, "that some difficulty might spring up before long, and your presence in the House might be so useful, and so conducive to solve it."[5] He longed for a private talk, or at least an exchange of letters, and in the meanwhile hoped that the friends of Brown would reflect his views in the House.

What did it all mean? To Blake, Brown, and Mackenzie, deep in plans for the session, it posed some exciting questions. Cartier was making overtures and they ran in the direction of what? — a complete break with Macdonald and a new alliance with Brown? Did Brown wish for it? Would he go back to parliament at all? He thought not, and yet he was certainly tempted. Yet there was the question of his own leaders, the essential men in Quebec. Would Dorion and Holton ever accept Cartier? Would they in fact accept Brown, in alliance with the detested *bleu*? And was any of this credible or in fact even desirable? With Cartier or without him, could the government be brought down?

For a few weeks, as the session opened in Ottawa, Blake was inclined to try. He met with Dorion and Holton and with trusted men from Ontario, all of them eager at least to defeat Macdonald. He shuttled from conferences with Mackenzie to consult Brown in Toronto, and for once was the urgent man. It was Brown who was cautious now, cool and almost indifferent. He had seen more than Blake of the shifts and changes in politics, and Cartier was no longer pressing. His relations with Macdonald seemed to be on the mend. He was still said in Ottawa to be anxious for a talk with Brown, but he had not repeated the request. Should Brown come down to the capital and be near if the request were made? Mackenzie rather doubted it; it would raise a cloud of rumour. Mackenzie distrusted rumour and distrusted Cartier's intentions. He was somewhat inclined at the moment to distrust his novice friend. Blake, he reported to Brown on March 19, seemed rather too strongly influenced by Luther Holton. "There is a little danger of Holton's getting ready the bullets and allowing Blake to fire them."[6] In the end there was no firing, and the glint of power passed. The present state of the parties provided confusion enough. Cartier remained with Macdonald, Brown remained in Toronto, Blake remained with Mackenzie, and Dorion and Holton held their separate way.

When the session ended in May there had been little done. It had been a period of waiting and groping, with the real work still ahead. By the late spring Joseph Howe was in London on his last attempt to gain repeal of the union. Tupper was there to oppose him. The question of the North-West Territories remained unsettled, and the building of the Intercolonial was not yet under way. In the meantime, between Ottawa and the provincial capitals, the problems of jurisdiction began to rise. None of them was serious yet, but there was a trend running through them all, the determination of Macdonald that power should accrue to the centre. Blake was alert and watchful whenever Macdonald moved. He nagged at every question, little or great, where the federal government intruded on provincial powers. He pursued his points interminably, he was legalistic and dogmatic, and he ranged through aeons of history in support of his own views. He was a daily cross to the journalists who had to report his speeches, and a mere obstructive party man to his enemies across the aisle. Yet there were a few, even among these, who saw a good deal more. There was a basic struggle developing here between the centralizer and the federalist, and it would determine much for the nation.

Through the next year and the next, and in the sessions of both Houses, much was revealed of Blake and much foretold of his future. He was a sharp-eyed Grit in Ontario, careful of money, jealous of railway spending, watchful of provincial rights. On educational reform he was savage with Egerton Ryerson, a graceless Blake renewing the family feud. Or he seemed so to Ryerson whose new proposals, supported by Sandfield Macdonald, were to be the crowning work of his life. The system of common schools at the elementary level was now engrained in the province. It was to be expanded and carried forward by the absorption of the old "grammar schools" into a public system of high schools and collegiates that might carry the student to the doors of the university. Education was to be free both on primary and secondary levels, and it was to be made compulsory for all. There were to be increased municipal grants, higher qualifications for all teachers and inspectors, and a widening of the curricula of secondary schools to include teaching in science.

All this, good and necessary as it seemed, Blake opposed head-on. Was compulsory education to include the compulsion of Catholics, who had their own separate schools? Where were these new inspectors and qualified teachers to be found, at the salaries now paid? He was unimpressed by the standards that Ryerson had maintained in the past. Compulsory schools in the cities would be mainly for the sons of working men, anxious to learn a trade. They would therefore have to be trade schools, or the law would be a dead letter. It would be a dead letter in any case in most of the rural regions. Who could imagine a local country school board fining a father for keeping his son on the land? Who could desire that science, the function of a university, should be taught as a smattering of ignorance in second-rate secondary schools? The practical objections were there and undeniable, but the deeper war was beneath. The trained mind of the bar and the university, of the estate and the private tutor, could accept neither the standards nor the work of the self-taught man. Nor would he accept haste and half-measures in democratic advancement; the gentleman could afford to wait.

On the other hand, in the daily work of the legislature, Blake was not much bound by the division of parties. He was an often-rejected counsellor of John Sandfield Macdonald, and occasionally went with his views to a higher court. Between the Prime Minister in Ottawa and the opposition member in the Ontario House, there was a considerable correspondence and a close identity of views, at least in regard to Sandfield. The Cornwall Scot was a slapdash reformer, anxious to get things done, with little regard for the long effect of his actions. "I regret," sighed Blake in one of his letters to John A. Macdonald, "that we do not seem to understand the importance of legislating on general principles here."[7]

General principles. It was in the name of general principles that he straddled the provincial House, always dominating McKellar, sometimes Sandfield Macdonald and often bullying his friends. It was more so in the Dominion House when the greater issues rose. In April of 1869 he watched as Joseph Howe entered the chamber, a member of Macdonald's government. Better terms had been promised, dissident Nova Scotia appeared now to be reconciled, and the young nation set more firmly on its course. It was not so to Blake. The man of principle deplored the secret bargaining and the work of the smoky rooms. The Grit accountant thought of the money involved, the Ontarian of provincial rights. It was the lawyer, however, preaching the virtues of contract, who took him fully over. For long months, ridiculed by all opponents, feebly supported by friends, and savagely hammered in the newspapers he fought those better terms.

How had they come to be granted, and what was the effect of the granting? It was the weight of votes from Quebec, adding weight to the votes of Nova Scotia which had made them possible at all. Two partners in the union had united to bilk Ontario which would carry most of the load. The British North America Act, an act of the Imperial parliament, had set the terms of union. They included the financial terms; those terms were part of the contract. In entering Confederation "Our province agreed to part with a certain portion of its legislative power upon certain conditions, which conditions were to be embodied into an Imperial Act — first, because that was the proper and constitutional mode of making the contract; and secondly and no less importantly, because . . . that was what would give us security — that was what would make it really a charter of our rights . . . Well, sir, here is a partnership . . . we agree that we shall go into partnership and put a certain sum into one common stock to carry out the objects . . . And I may say this, that this compact under which we have surrendered so much of our rights is not alterable except by the power that made it."[8] This was the doctrine of the law, and it horrified men of politics when they thought of its application. The agreement made by the provinces would have to be re-negotiated and once more ratified in London. The work begun at Charlottetown would have to begin again.

There was more than that to the subject and Blake said it all, reviving the tone of the wars before the union. What province was safe if the contract were not adhered to? Subsidies increased today could as easily be reduced tomorrow, though the disastrous trend would probably be in the other direction. It was Nova Scotia who came with her hand out now, and she was supported by Lower Canada. Why? Because the province of the French would be next; it was living beyond its means. Blake was sure of that; he had "taken some little pains to investigate the accounts of Lower Canada."[9]

In himself, as he foresaw for others, that prospect of mutual pocket-picking was reviving the old jealousies. The old names — Upper Canada, Lower Canada — recurred in his arguments now. Common nationality, the achievement of Confederation, became a dwindling and fitful strain. As between the provinces, for Blake, "destiny" became "destinies". "These separate interests," he said, "must be directed by separate governments."[10] As to the interests of Nova Scotia he was not disposed to be niggardly; to satisfy and pacify her "I would cheerfully take the responsibility of going in a constitutional way very far indeed,"[11] but the constitution was all. If there were to be a change in the terms of partnership it should be made in due form, and if the province could not be satisfied it should be allowed to leave the union. Better that than "this pension of two million", this pitiful bribe to remain. "When will the flood-gates now opened be closed again? Never!"[12]

It was all basic legalism, and there would be cause to remember it later. But it was unendurable to practical men of the day. There were lawyers to denounce Blake's law and there was hardly a politician who was prepared to endorse his principles. Joseph Howe leaped up in the name of common sense. Was the constitution to be unchanged, immoveable, dead? He wished for his part that it had been thrown in the fire in London, but the hope for that was gone. A measure of wrong had been remedied and it had brought a measure of peace. Did Nova Scotia care how the money came? As to the whole of Blake's argument, "a piece of political quackery" was the kindest view in most of the daily press. "Everybody says so, and what everybody says must necessarily be true."[13]

Nor could Blake develop enthusiasm for the gaining of other provinces, at least in the short term. Newfoundland talked of entering Confederation, but he considered her price too high. He had the same view of the demands of Prince Edward Island which, as he tactfully noted, could be dropped into Lake Ontario. He opposed the taking over of the North-West Territories, and glumly watched that done. On December 1, 1869 William McDougall, exchanging his cabinet office for the appointment of Lieutenant-Governor, set out for the Red River to proclaim Canadian authority. He was not to be allowed to do it, but that was not known yet; no one thought of the Métis or had heard of Louis Riel. The nation was on the move, it seemed, with Macdonald the skillful pace-maker and Blake already the man who was out of step.

At the same time, for most of the past two years, he had been a man at a private crossroads. Early in 1868 William Henry Draper, Chief Justice of Upper Canada, had decided to retire from the bench. Philip M. Vankoughnet, another of Macdonald's seasoned political friends, was presently Chancellor of Ontario and the obvious man to replace him. The Prime Minister, however, was not quite pleased with the obvious, and discussed an alternative with Blake. There should be a general reorganization of all the courts, with Draper's going providing the opportunity. In the course of the change, moreover, politics would be laid aside. Vankoughnet would have the lesser post of the Court of Common Pleas. The office of Chancellor would be open to Edward Blake.

He was thirty-five years old, and he would be standing in his father's shoes, at the very pinnacle of his profession. But it would mean departure from politics, as it had for William Hume. Was that what Macdonald wanted? Was that what Blake wanted? In the little parliament of Ontario and the greater parliament of Ottawa he had had a taste of the actual work that built a nation. He would give over the work forever, in all likelihood, if he consented to become a judge. "Be on your guard,"[14] his father warned him from England. The offer had been made in confidence and Macdonald might yet withdraw it. He might be forced to withdraw it, if Vankoughnet balked or his political friends rebelled. Yet Macdonald had seemed sincere. The session ended in Ottawa, the summer waxed, and the doubts of the family waned. The attractions of office grew as the son wrestled with himself and his parents plied him with advice. "We have always found J.A.M. kind and considerate," Catherine wrote. His mode of life was regrettable, his political methods deplorable but he had done much for the Blakes. She was inclined to recall that now and to urge the acceptance of more, with her gratitude "infinitely increased by his considerate treatment of our darling boy".[15]

From political friends in counterpoint came anguished cries of dissuasion. The thirty-seven-year-old David Mills, handsome, earnest, studious, and only slightly a bore, was already a man of considerable weight with Blake. He was certainly a devoted admirer with perhaps a shading of envy, for his way was harder in the world. A school teacher risen to school inspector, he had been elected as federal member for the constituency of Bothwell but was still studying for the law. He would be at it for years yet, he would always be studying something, and conveying the fruits of his diligence to a largely ungrateful House. For the ironic Prime Minister, he was to become "the philosopher of Bothwell", but if any compliment was intended it was certainly not returned. Always suspicious of much and invariably suspicious of Macdonald, Mills had nothing for this offer but angry scorn and dismay.

63

The only possible motive, he wrote Blake, was to remove a threatening adversary from the field of politics. When had Macdonald ever made an appointment in his life with a single regard to the public welfare? Blake's going would shock the country and be a shattering blow to the party. More than that, it would be a total renunciation of his own destiny.[16] It might well be so, it was an echo of Blake's own thoughts, yet August came and he could not make up his mind. He did not at the moment have to, and it was almost an irritation; Macdonald had not yet asked for a yes or no.

Murray Bay was as usual in the hot and lovely summer of 1868, but the barrister-politician did not respond to the spell. He was troubled not only by headaches but by a squalid attack of boils. Catherine sighed from England over the state of "the weary judgeship" that was affecting her son's health. She offered much new counsel, all on a high plane and almost all equivocal. William Hume Blake contributed more confusion. He still distrusted the motives of the Prime Minister, yet they were no cause in themselves for the son to refuse the appointment. "There is not, I think, the least foundation for the accusation that you could not with honour accept the seat." Yet, in the father's own case, he had been so bitterly attacked for taking the post of Chancellor that he had often regretted the act. If that should be the case with Edward he would be inclined to advise against it. There was more honour in the world's eyes to be won in the political arena, and more money as a barrister than as a judge on any bench. Yet, on the other hand, he coveted the honour for his son "and indeed still covet it earnestly because it would afford leisure and opportunity for communion with God, which is after all the great business of life."[17]

The son went back to Toronto burdened with many letters, and waited two more months. It was November 5 when the word came from Macdonald. The plans had not worked out. Vankoughnet would not be moved and it would therefore not be possible to offer a place to Blake. The decision was acknowledged affably in a note two days later. "I am personally rejoiced," Blake wrote, "at the conclusion to which you have come, which as you know coincides with my own wishes."[18]

Yet it was not to be the end of the affair. A few months later the ailing Vankoughnet was dead, the office of Chancellor now definitely open. Vice-Chancellor John Godfrey Spragge, the next in line of succession, was determined to have the appointment. Macdonald's closest henchmen supported Spragge for the place, or at least were firm that it should go to a man of the party. It was a large political plum; Macdonald the politician was required to think of that. Nevertheless Mr. Justice Joseph Morrison, long a sound Conservative but a friend of William Hume, appeared in the son's office. He had three questions to ask on behalf of the Prime Minister. Would Blake accept the Chancellorship if offered? Or would he demand a definite offer before returning a definite answer? And in the latter case, if the answer proved to be no, would he be prepared to treat the offer as never having been made?[19]

They were routine political precautions so far as Macdonald was concerned. The party pressures were steadily building under him but he had damped them down before. He would risk an explosion if he could get Blake, but not if he were to be refused. To Liberal oracles, however, with their usual opinion of Macdonald, it seemed to be another trap. Where would Blake stand — this potential Liberal leader — if he reached for the fruit that the tempter could snatch away?

It was new matter for brooding and the potential Chancellor settled himself to that. Meanwhile the parties rumbled and the newspapers caught the scent. There was much favourable comment to increase the force of temptation, and enough of another nature to induce second thought. Why, asked the *Kingston Whig*, was the Dominion government coquetting with Edward Blake?[20] By what right, the Toronto *Telegraph* demanded in a somewhat different tone; should "this mere novice and nincompoop" — "this upstart of a parliamentary prig" — aspire to follow a father who had "sat long enough in the parliament of 1854 to get a measure through it which has provided him with a large pension for life."[21] Through it all Macdonald was silent and there were no further messages; the offer floated in air, a kite of rumour. On December 18, 1869, it was abruptly hauled to the ground.

"I regret," Blake wrote to the Honourable Mr. Justice Morrison, "that a pressure of public business will prevent my calling on you today and so I am obliged to write." The letter was not private, was soon to be made public, and recited in full Macdonald's propositions. It went on to deal with the iniquity of the secret offer and, that being made the most of, to Blake's own conclusion. "I beg you will inform Sir John Macdonald that I would not accept the Chancellorship if offered to me."[22]

Liberals would now be soothed and Conservative aspirants stimulated to new resentment. William Hume might regret it, or perhaps he would understand. In any case it was done. There were to be no years yet of leisurely communion with the Deity. For now at least the road to the bench was closed.

With the die cast for politics, another decision followed. There had been strong rumours since November that McKellar was stepping down as provincial leader and that Blake was to have the post. On February 3, 1870, rumour became fact. In the opinion of the Toronto *Telegraph*, "the noisy Chancery pleader" — "this bellowing young man" — had pushed McKellar aside. Actually, he had been pushed himself, and not without much manoeuvring, by the elders of the federal party.

Affairs on the national scene were as confused as ever. Ontario and Quebec Liberals were still at arm's length, often divergent on policies, and unable to choose a leader. Dorion and Holton were inclined to assert claims, each in support of the other, but Mackenzie was wary of both. His relations with the two were good but he distrusted their present politics. They were too eager, as one-time anti-Confederates, to justify their old positions. It tended to distort their attitudes and it was reflected in the party in Quebec. It was dangerous to the party in Ontario, which had special difficulties of its own. After three years in parliament reformers were still fighting the myth of the *tabula rasa*, still justifying their function as a party in opposition. And they were still themselves leaderless, or over-blessed with leaders, while direction centred in the unelected Brown.

In Brown's eyes Dorion and Holton were possibles, but only as a last resort. He could not really conceive of any man but an Ontarian as occupying the leader's place. His first choice was Mackenzie, but there were obvious difficulties in that. His old friend was of the old wars, as Brown was himself, still uneasily reconciled and with little appeal in Quebec. He was accused with too much reason of being Brown's voice in the House. Always his own man, yet always painfully aware of his own deficiencies, he had no desire for the leadership and the one alternative was Blake. Both men had to be kept, and both men at the same time were members of the provincial House. They were overworked and impatient with their dual responsibilities, and Blake at least was inclined to break the traces. He had no wish, he insisted, to be leader in either House, but he would not go on much longer serving in both. It was at least obvious that he could not remain as second in the provincial legislature, and McKellar wholly agreed. With all this, and with Brown's guidance and approval, the caucus came to its decision. The federal muddle for the most part would be left to the experienced Mackenzie. The forcing-house of Ontario would be used to mature Blake.

At Stratford, on February 10, 1870, he was honoured in his new position by a large banquet. Brother Sam, now an enthusiastic organizer, had been in charge of the careful arrangements. Opposition newspapers gave much credit to "Mr. Samuel Pecksniff Blake" for the fact that five hundred guests were present at fifty cents per head. On Edward Blake they were more than usually vehement, with the not ill-founded fear that "the Stratford half-dollar festival" might be the first gun of an approaching election campaign. They made much of the image he had begun to present in parliament. He was a difficult man who followed the party program until "some latent consciousness of principle and consistency will occasionally assert itself, and then with one elephantine kick he upsets the Grit applecart." They were diligent in seeing dissension in the party's councils, and in sowing what more they could. McKellar had been kicked out and a boy placed in his stead, an obnoxious scion of the law courts "who turns up when his shystering operations are completed to harangue the House as is the manner of the bully of the sophomore class." It was Brown's egg that had hatched "this one solitary chicken of the hyena species", and the strange bird or beast was threatening Brown himself.[23] "But will Brown consent to be quietly snuffed out by this politician of two years? 'Tis a happy family, truly!"[24]

Brown himself seemed oblivious to such a danger, or at least prepared to accept it. He had written six days earlier to William Buckingham, later to be Mackenzie's secretary, with frankness if not with tact: "I have known all the public men of Canada intimately for twenty-eight years past, and I believe Edward Blake to be the ablest of them all."[25] To friendlier newspapers who had watched Blake in action the savagery of the abuse aimed at him was proof of his growing stature. He was the rising man in Canada; he threatened not only John Sandfield Macdonald but the greater Macdonald as well. The tall, stooping, muscular young man "of the nervo-sanguine temperament . . . peering through his goggles out and in among the opposition benches" loomed up "like some behemoth among pigmies".[26] He would at once be selected as "the spirit master of the House . . . his faculty for exhaustively comprehending almost at a glance the most difficult subject is little short of marvellous. It is intuition — genius."[27] At the banquet itself he spoke for three hours, during all of which time, according to an admiring listener, "the orator had the breathless attention of his audience, his beautifully modulated tones being as clear at the last sentence as they were at the first."[28] True or not, when the long three hours ended there was great applause. The friends of reform in Ontario seemed pleased with their new head.

↶

He was now to learn about leadership and the ambivalent claims of party. On the Red River McDougall came to his fiasco and returned a discredited man. The Métis, Louis Riel, established his provisional government. On March 26, 1870, word arrived in Toronto of the death of Thomas Scott. He was hardly the stuff of martyrs; he appeared rather to have been a quarrelsome, thick-skulled oaf. But he had opposed rebellion, he had defied Riel and he had been tried in Riel's court. He had been coldly, boldly sentenced and the sentence had been carried out. A young man of Ontario, a young Orangeman of Ontario, had been brutally done to death.

No Ontario reformer could regret McDougall's downfall, still less the fact that he had dangerously hurt Macdonald. One could hardly regret Riel, for he justified so many warnings. There had been blundering, haste, and stupidity in the taking-over of the territory, and there had been no care for the natives. The outburst had been invited, and there was political capital in that for an opposition party. The indignation of the French, when one thought of federal affairs, could be used to break Macdonald's hold on Quebec.

Yet not now, not by an Ontario leader, not with this Scott dead. What Scott meant to Toronto was to be seen on April 6, when Charles Mair and John Schultz, those super-loyal Ontarians, arrived from the Red River with the report on what had been done. The streets were filled for a welcoming by ten thousand people; the two were guests of the city, and the city's mind was clear. There would be the same mind in the Orange lodges of the countryside, and not in Orangemen alone. It was Ontario, Protestantism, and nationhood that had all been outraged here, and the Catholic, half-French rebel should pay for blood with his blood.

Why not? To the Toronto lawyer it was the clear demand of the law. Rebellion, whatever the pretext, was a thing not to be accepted. The killing shocked and violated the instincts of a man of order. He was quite aware of the dangers lurking in the cry. He would inevitably be aligned with Orangemen against Catholic French in Quebec. There were Catholic Irish in Ontario who were no friends of Orangeism and valued friends of reform. Many of them would be lost. One could not speak of Riel without the risk of a parting of peoples. Yet who could remain silent? Brown certainly would not and Mackenzie certainly would not; their Scots blood was up. Blake as certainly could not; he was head of an angry party and his feelings ran with theirs. So did his political interests; policy fitted principle. Or so it seemed to the political leader in Ontario, with Quebec a distant cloud. John A. Macdonald had raised this storm in the territories and John Sandfield Macdonald, who happened to be a Scotch Catholic, would be prisoner of his patron's work. There was a stick to lay on both of them, and it was the stick of right and justice. It should be taken in hand and used.

The effect through a hot summer was rather more than Blake desired or expected. By October of 1870 he was carefully defining aims. He could not blame the Métis of those distant territories for resenting many wrongs. He could not blame their priests, as many were inclined to do. He hoped there would be no division among French and English, still less among the citizens of his own province. "A great outcry has been raised with respect to the religious aspect of the question, and it has been said that it was a scheme for Romish aggression. I cannot, for my part, conceive that this is so." The question should not be treated as one of religion. Nothing and no religion justified murder. "I am convinced that the Roman Catholics of the country will agree with me that their own security, their own sense of the justice of that divine law which says that there must be blood for blood in these cases, demand that such steps shall be taken as shall result, if possible, in the trial and conviction of these miscreants."[29] The tone was already becoming a little abstract. The principal miscreant now, with Macdonald's eager connivance, was safely out of the country. Macdonald himself was still vulnerable, however, and the bland assumption remained. Quietly, peacefully, unitedly — and sanctioned by divine law — Quebec would go out with the Orangemen for the blood of Louis Riel.

There was nothing to sustain that view in the lower province. Blake was fully aware of it, and aware of much that he risked. But he was supported by cold law, he was being driven by hot anger, and he was a political leader of Ontarians whose business was gaining power. One was not required at the moment to think beyond that.

૭

The Ontario House opened on December 7, 1870, with John Sandfield Macdonald prepared for the fight of his life. There was not much of it left, for he was to die within two years and he was already in poor health. The same was true of his Patent Combination, for it was more a clutch of expediencies than either of the federal parties. Yet they were for the most part honest enough expediencies. Sandfield went for his objectives but he had his own rules for the game.

He had been the odd duck in the pond of Canadian politics for something like thirty years. Birth, character, and circumstance all fitted him for the role. He had been born a Scot of Glengarry County, Ontario, where fearsome Catholic highlanders were the neighbours of Lower Canada. He was a considerably lapsed Catholic but the political tinge remained, and it was part of his colouration. So were Frenchness and romance, for he had had a surprising share of both. He had been a young officer serving as a Queen's Messenger during the Upper Canada rebellion, and had been sent on a trip to Washington, carrying government despatches. One of the stops on the route had been at Saratoga, New York, and he had met there a visitor from Louisiana. She was a lovely, lively Creole and the daughter of a rich planter, to whom Sandfield was unacceptable as a suitor for his daughter's hand. This became all too obvious during a visit to Louisiana which Sandfield made at the end of his tour of duty. The result was a prompt elopement, a swift departure for Canada, and a home where French was as freely spoken as English. Sandfield prospered as a barrister, his Ivy Hall at Cornwall became a social centre of the region, and he was launched on national affairs.

Yet he was of Cornwall and the St. Lawrence valley, and a Catholic with a French wife. He had been, as he said, a sort of political Ishmael[30] in the wars of the two Canadas, and he remained that at the union. Subdued by the other Macdonald and reduced to the provincial field, he was the more anxious to defend it against the new intruder, Blake. Aware of the greatest danger, which he saw no way to avoid, he could only hope that Ottawa would be left to deal with Riel. On his own ground he had a fair record of achievement, some forehanded proposals and a few political weapons of a high order. He had abolished the old election system with its days and weeks of polling; voting was still not secret but it was to be done on a single day. He still held firm on dual representation but he had cleaned up some of the features of election practice. He had not satisfied Blake and never expected to do so, but that could be accepted in politics as one of the enduring facts.

There was powerful support for Ryerson and his educational reforms, and there was now a bill that was tailored to Sandfield's taste. He intended to force it through. Better still, there was a railway bill of wide and ample proportions. The government would appropriate a million and a half dollars to be used for building at discretion. The right-voting constituencies would be likely to get their railway grants; the others would be left to grind their own axes. It was potent election medicine and the Speech from the Throne reflected pious confidence. "The state of the province is hopeful in the extreme

. . . let us hope that this flattering prospect may not be marred by injurious dissensions among ourselves."

Under the hand of its new leader, the opposition was quick to dispel the hope. The bill on education and the bill for the railway fund came under savage attack. Both passed, but it was a shaken government that passed them, and there had not been time for recovery when the thud of the next blow came. On February 2, 1871, Blake moved the resolution that would be quoted across the country, in terms that invited the quote:

RESOLVED: That the cold-blooded murder for his outspoken loyalty to the Queen of Thomas Scott, lately a resident of this province and an emigrant thence to the North-West, has impressed this House with a deep feeling of sorrow and indignation, and in the opinion of this House every effort should be made to bring to trial the perpetrators of this great crime, who as yet go unwhipt of justice.[31]

There could be no acceptance of those words by a government committed to John A. Macdonald. They could have no effect on the absent one who was far from the whips of justice. But they spoke not only for Orangemen but for most of aroused Ontario, and they were not to be stilled by a weak government amendment. It brought the House to declare, by a vote of 47 to 28, that it was unwise and inexpedient for a provincial government to pronounce on federal matters. There remained, however, the voice of the court beyond. On February 25, 1871, Sandfield Macdonald dissolved the provincial legislature and went out to face the hustings.

On March 21 the election came, with Riel a principal theme. Yet another theme was the railway bill, and it helped to avert disaster. Blake emerged from his own campaign reconciled to South Bruce; this time it had overwhelmingly endorsed him. Provincial results generally were in a state of uneasy balance, and actually leaning a little in the direction of Sandfield. But not enough; the momentum had passed to Blake. With Mackenzie still beside him he was head of a revived party, set and eager for the kill. There was a wait of nine months, while contested elections wound their way through the courts and the

Premier struggled to shore up crumbling strength. It was a long time but the delays of the law were longer. When the new parliament convened on December 7, eight of the contestations remained to be decided and Sandfield for all his efforts was still in a bad way.

He had a nominal majority of three or four in the House, but several of his votes were doubtful. They were particularly so in two crucial cases. R. W. Scott, a prominent Ottawa lawyer and leader of Irish Catholics, was restless now in the Patent Combination. He disliked the Ryerson reforms as a danger to separate schools. He had had a professional disappointment, as the representative of important lumbering interests, in failing to secure from Sandfield a grant of provincial lands. Another dubious quantity was Edmund Burke Wood, a one-armed lawyer from Brant County who was "Big Thunder" in the House. The huge voice seemed lowered now, though he was still a member of the cabinet, and he was obviously nursing grievances or alert to changing winds. In such case the Premier did what he could. He elevated Scott to the Speakership and left him voteless there. With Wood he hoped for the best. Beyond that he sought to advance a theory. There were eight seats vacant in the House because of elections still in the courts. He hoped for perhaps six of them when the verdicts finally came, and it would be a slender working majority. Parliament, he therefore claimed, until it was supplied with its full complement, should refrain from a vote on any major question.

There was short shrift for his plea. Blake rose, with Mackenzie in grim support of him, to sweep delay aside. The House stood as it stood, competent to decide all issues. On the second day of the session, and on the first paragraph of a glowing Speech from the Throne, the twelve-day battle was joined.

"During no period in the history of Her Majesty's North American possessions," announced William Pearce Howland, Lieutenant-Governor of Ontario, "can there be found recorded of any one of them a condition of prosperity which can approach that now almost everywhere exhibited in this Province, and it therefore affords me great pleasure to congratulate you on so favourable an aspect of our country's stride in the path of material advancement."[32]

After that sonorous example of John Sandfield's prose there was a two-day break for the weekend. The swirl of political in-fighting began outside the House. The parties faced each other, as Blake and Mackenzie calculated, in almost exact balance. There was Wood and there were other waverers who might be detached from Sandfield, but the Premier was well aware of it. He was fighting not only for them but for possible waverers from Blake, and as the man in office he still had potent means. Through a long Saturday and Sabbath, as the empty chamber of the legislature reposed in solemn silence, there was a rumble of threats and bargaining and a stink of cigars and whiskey in the haunts of provincial statesmen. Reports came to Blake, who was not to be oppressed with details, from hoarse emis-saries with headaches that served to increase his own. He was still unsure of the position when he rose on December 11, but he moved his formal reply.

The House, he said, should accept with gratification the sentiments expressed by His Excellency in the first paragraph of the Speech. There was a need, however, of certain major additions. Regret should be expressed at the establishment of the Railway Aid Fund, the one salvation of Sandfield at the last provincial election. It should also be coupled with an in-junction that the fund "be submitted to the approval or rejec-tion of the Legislative Assembly, so as not to leave so large a sum as $1,500,000. at the disposal of the Executive."[33]

To that amendment came a government sub-amendment, establishing Sandfield's theme. There should be no discussion of the question until vacant seats were filled. Debate ran on till midnight, resumed on the 13th, and in the course of that day's session the sub-amendment was lost. Blake had gained the edge, but it was not a decisive edge. There was still fight in Sandfield, there were still attractions in the cabinet, and a

75

second sub-amendment was actually proposed by Wood. It was fought to another midnight and lost on the 14th. With no more road-blocks possible, Blake's amendment was put, and was carried by seven votes. It was a third defeat for the government and should have been quite enough. It was not, however. Sandfield still sat on, grimly mastering his cabinet and holding the shaken Wood. A massive thrust was required from the opposition, and it called for a move by the leader.

For a day and a half the pleadings centred on Blake; he must negotiate with Wood himself. He would not do it; he admitted the man was crucial but principles were even more so. There must be no thought of promises, there must be no unworthy inducement. Yet even principle itself required discussion. He admitted that too, but it was still work for the emissaries, and they went forth to leave him brooding in Humewood. He was still there when his hunters came up the drive, carrying the scalp. Wood had announced his resignation from the cabinet.

Sandfield's fate was decided, but he was not prepared to accept it. As the time neared for the crucial last division he had somehow threatened wanderers back to the fold. The vote now was to be on a sub-amendment of Mackenzie, which flatly declared no confidence in the existing ministry. As the peak of debate neared the House actually seemed to be swaying toward its old balance; the government could yet be saved. But there had been silence in one place, where the man sat who had just resigned as a minister. At his own desk Blake reached for a sheet of paper and snapped his fingers for a page. The immortal note went across to E. B. Wood: "You had better speak now." The "Thunderer" rose obediently in support of Mackenzie's motion and it was carried by a single vote, never to be forgotten or forgiven. A year later in the Commons Blake would be faced with the torn up scraps of his message, rescued from a House spitoon and patched together. The Honourable E. B. Wood was to culminate a long career as Chief Justice of

Manitoba, but he would be haunted and taunted to the end of it by the echoes of "Speak Now".[34]

The reply to the Speech from the Throne, duly amended, and with only six on the government side now voting against it, was approved by a weary House. The diligent toil of the legislators had achieved a strange production. Gratified by His Excellency's words regarding the happy state of the province, it repeated them all in full, went on from there to remind him of the regrettable Railway Aid Fund, and informed him "that we have no confidence in a Ministry which is attempting to carry out, in reference to the control of the said Fund of $1,500,000., an usurpation fraught with danger to public liberty and constitutional government."[35]

There were no props left to support the battered Sandfield, but he hung for three days longer, a premier in mid-air. It was Monday the 18th when Blake brought him down. A long resolution, passed in the early evening by a House that was tired of midnights, informed the Lieutenant-Governor of the present state of the legislature, recalled that supplies must be voted within the next thirteen days, and humbly prayed that His Excellency would take the needful steps. On Tuesday the 19th Sandfield Macdonald resigned, and Blake was Premier of Ontario.

He met the House next day as the Honourable Edward Blake, already a captive victor. If he had ridden out Sandfield Macdonald on the strength of the railway aid fund, he had ridden in himself on the back of Riel. Nor was that the worst of the thoughts. Over the high altars of principle the dust and grime of the practices had descended in their rank cloud. He had been part of that counting of heads, that trading and gaining of men, and he had no taste for the rewards. "I have not slept" — the letter had gone to Mackenzie while the battle was still proceeding, and it had been almost incoherent — "I am unable to bring myself to the conclusion that I ought to approach Wood as proposed. It would be a subterfuge for

me to allow others to approach him and reap the triumph myself . . . take the leadership, I beg of you . . . for the work outside of the House I have long known myself to be utterly unfit,
and I know now that I shall never be more fit for it."[36]

~

It was part of another change that he had lived with now
for a year. At the beginning of 1870 William Hume and
Catherine had returned to Humewood, with the search for
cures abandoned. It had been hard for the son to see the frail
old man, pottering about the garden, taking walks with the
children, occasionally summoning strength for a family visit.
Yet there had been that deep companionship, the deepest he
would ever know, and the accepted certainties joining father
and son. Religion, politics, duty, ambition, interest — they had
talked of them all endlessly yet talked in a kind of code, in stiff,
stereotyped sentiments, in contradictions and fatuities that
merely encrusted fact. The fact itself was the rock that sus-
tained both. They were good men in their own eyes — men who
meant to be good — and the shared strength of the conviction
was the greatest strength they had. Now the sharing was ended.

For a few days in November of 1870, with his old infirmities
steadily gaining ground, William Hume lay dying. Catherine
sat beside him with a pen and notebook, faithful and industrious as always, and as often a little incongruous in her
methods and means of comfort. In the near shadow of mortal-
ity she was recording memories of her childhood to be read by
children of the future, but the scratching pen was torture to
the feverish man in the bed. She changed to pencil instantly at
his first fretful protest, and her work had whispered on for a
few more pages. Then the writing ceased. On the 15th of
November William Hume was dead.

It seemed that something in the fabric of the son went with
him, or perhaps it had been long going. He had hard words
for some of the clergymen at the funeral, and he was impatient
during the rites. He complained to his mother of his deadness

and greyness of spirit and of the spectre of religious doubt. She replied as usual with texts and prayers and protest, but there was no warmth in the reply.

> So thou art gone! and round me too the night
> In ever nearing circles weaves her shade . . .[37]

It was the cold Matthew Arnold that he quoted now, the Victorian of the lost friends and the lost faith, for whom the God of righteousness had been reduced to "a stream of tendency not ourselves".[38]

CHAPTER FIVE

"I WAS A STRANGER TO MY CHILD"

HE ANNOUNCED to the House on his first day as Premier that he would serve without holding a portfolio and without accepting a salary. It was quite in character as a gesture of independence and it left a place in the cabinet for another salaried minister. Even by his own party, however, it was received with mixed feelings. The wealthy Toronto barrister who could afford to scorn his emolument seemed to be rather rubbing it in. On the other hand, to John Sandfield Macdonald, glowering from across the aisle, it was a disguised increase of the ministry by the addition of an unpaid head. He proposed a motion against it and was promptly voted down, but with the disposal of that difficulty Blake had merely begun.

He was now inexorably involved, not only in the necessities of government but in the expediencies of cabinet-making. As the old ministry dissolved amid a murk of recriminations, the friends and regions and interests that had hammered at the two Macdonalds were abruptly hammering at Blake. The confident candidate of Bowmanville, the independent spirit of the House of Commons, had now to study the seamed face of his province. He had to consider the balance of east and west, the balance of Protestant and Catholic, the representation of the cities and the rural regions. He had to consider the deserts of "Big Thunder"; it was another of the joys of power. If he took Wood now as a minister the crucial vote would seem to have been a flagrant purchase. It would not do; there would have to be something later. There would have to be something later for all too many of the loyal; they competed with newer men. There was D. A. Macdonald, brother of Sandfield, who had opposed his brother's politics and was a power in eastern Ontario. His letter arrived with jubilant congratulations; the "millstone about my neck"[1] had now been removed and he was eager to serve Blake. Blake replied instantly with the offer of a cabinet post, and wired next day to withdraw it. He had been too "pushed"[2] — there would perhaps be a vacancy later — D.A. would have his reward.

For two days and nights, amid an endless succession of meetings, bombarded with letters and telegrams, and assailed by urgent callers, Blake sought for the men he needed and evaded those he did not. His first and hardest task was to hold Mackenzie, who had federal politics to think of and was sick of the provincial House. When Mackenzie agreed reluctantly to serve as provincial treasurer the harried leader had gained a strong right arm. Yet he was then faced with the host of the unreluctant and with one most delicate choice. In making Riel an issue he had risked a break with Ontario's Catholic constituency, and the danger was still there. To restore and secure amity there would have to be a strong gesture embodied in a prominent name. By December 22, when the House adjourned for the by-elections to confirm cabinet appointments, the right name had been found. Richard W. Scott, federal Conservative supporter of John A. Macdonald, late provincial supporter of John Sandfield Macdonald and late Speaker of the House, was to be Commissioner of Crown Lands.

He was a prominent Irish Catholic and an able lawyer whom Blake liked and respected. At outs with the late government even before it fell, he had some colour of reason for giving support to the new. The change, nevertheless, even in the present upheaval, was a considerable gymnastic feat. Scott had "turned turtle" in Sandfield Macdonald's phrase, and Blake had now to prepare for what must come. Writing on Christmas

Eve, hardly in Christmas mood, he sought to prepare Scott. The theme the Premier seized on was the rejected Tory argument of the *tabula rasa* days. It had been claimed then, Blake wrote, that there were no issues to divide reformers from Conservatives but that these would rise in time. The time had now come. "You are free, nay bound, to say that issues have been developed on which your opinions are in accord with mine and opposed to those of Sandfield Macdonald and his government. And, this being so, you have taken sides against the government and with me." He seemed to forget that he was the government now, and he was obsessed with other worries. Scott, as a man with wealthy lumbering clients, would be open to attack as Commissioner of Crown lands. He was still federally a Conservative in the greater Macdonald's camp. For all reasons he would have to be specially discreet. "I need not repeat to you how essential it is that you should be circumspect in every utterance, *and do or say nothing to weaken me with my friends.* To do so, besides destroying my political usefulness, would inflict on me *the most painful wound I can conceive.*" He believed, he said, that he was safe in Scott's hands, "but you will know how to excuse an overstrained and nervous man in my present circumstances."[3]

He had not underestimated the risks taken to retain Catholic support. Scott was an uneasy colleague, there were rumbles within the party, and there was an instant cry of outrage from the opposition press. Scott, said the *Daily News*, had been accused for years of seeking huge land grants from his friends in a Conservative government. Would he get them now from Blake?[4] Reformers who had attacked Sandfield for his "patent combination" were now themselves a coalition of parties. When Blake set his "prentice hand to the manufacture of a cabinet the joy of our Grit friends at dropping into office is adulterated with the sad reflection that their leaders have taken the first opportunity of doing what for four years they had condemned in others. The New Combination is a bitter pill even for the most hardshell Grit to bolt."[5]

John A. Macdonald, actuated as he said "by my usual desire to make the best of a bad state of things", took a somewhat wider view. "As it is now," he wrote to Matthew Cameron who had replaced the embittered Sandfield as leader of the opposition, "the government is a coalition one to all intents and purposes." The name "Blake-Scott Administration" should be carefully fastened onto it. "You should avoid driving Scott into Grittism . . . By not making him too much of a black sheep you will keep him there, a disintegrating element in the Government. I believe that his being there has sown the seeds of dissolution in Blake's ministry . . . give them a little rope and they will hang themselves."[6]

The prophecy was not borne out. Blake returned to the House on January 18, 1872, with all his ministers secure in their own constituencies. He had promised to abolish dual representation and that was quickly done; from the time of the dissolution of the present parliament of Canada no member sitting in the Ontario legislature could hold a federal riding. Money was not scarce, and Blake and Mackenzie were both prepared to spend. In the "National Development Budget" which Mackenzie brought down in February there was new emphasis on the care of the sick, the handicapped, the indigent, and the insane. Sandfield Macdonald's railway fund, for all its political potency, had hardly yet been touched. It was to be used now, controlled and watched by the House, and largely in the province's newer northern region. There would be roads built for the advancement of colonization, leading toward Lake Superior and on to the North-West. There would be inducements offered in Ontario and large advertising in the mother country to promote and encourage British immigration.

The standing and pay of teachers were to be much improved, a first essential in Blake's eyes toward the advancement of education. Whatever he thought of Ryerson's reforms, he left them largely untouched. They seemed to be acceptable to the province and he was first servant of the province. He was even changed, or changing a little toward the old man himself. He was still to deliver snubs that would call forth injured letters and there would be diatribes in the newspapers and a glacial period yet. "I dined last evening with Mr. Mowat," Ryerson wrote to his daughter on December 15, 1872, reporting on an assemblage of prominent Toronto gentlemen. "Mr. Brown and I *bowed* to each other, as we have always done, but there was no recognition on either side between Mr. Blake and myself."[7]

Three years later, however, with the long embroglio in decline, there was to be a happier scene on a chilly railway journey. Ryerson had been sitting in the coach, he reported on January 29, 1875, when "Mr. Blake came on board, apparently on his way to Guelph or some place west. He did not see me and we both continued reading, etc. until near Georgetown I prepared to leave the train for the stage. I thought it my duty as the older man to make the first advance. After putting on my coat, etc. and going near where he was sitting to get my little portmanteau, I spoke to him though his back was toward me. He looked up with surprise, not knowing that I was on board . . . smiled . . . expressed very great pleasure in meeting me . . . and insisted upon carrying my parcel, which he did to the platform, *bearheaded* [*sic*], when I told him he ought not to expose himself to the cold wind without his hat. We parted as cordially as we met."[8]

If none of this was foreshadowed when the session ended on March 2, 1872, there had been evolution elsewhere. Dual representation, in Blake's eyes, meant the constant danger of entanglement between federal and provincial interests. He had removed that, but there was a larger frame of reference which he also intended to change. Sandfield Macdonald's ministry, he told the House, "was formed upon the principle and the understanding that it and the Government of the Dominion should work together — play into one another's hands." That arrangement was ended. Federal and provincial governments would henceforth stand as neutrals, each independent of the other in the management of its own affairs. There would be no hostility, but equally there would be no alliance. "As

citizens of the Province of Ontario we are called upon to frame
our own policy . . . we deprecate, nay more, we protest most
strongly against any interference on the part of any government with our perfect freedom of action."[9] It was in the light
of that freedom that Blake intended federalism to develop,
and it was another of his early warnings to the federal Prime
Minister.

Yet he had raised and revived another troubling question,
and he had done little to resolve it. Where did provincial rights
begin and end? — what had Ontario to do with Louis Riel?
For all the pains he had taken to acquire Richard Scott, Blake
refused oblivion to the shade of Thomas Scott. He had moved
early in the session "That this House feels bound to express its
regret that no effectual steps have been taken to bring to justice
the murderers of Thomas Scott, and its opinion that something
should be done to that end."[10] Toward the same end, when the
budget came down in February it carried a notable item. The
Province of Ontario was setting aside the sum of $5,000 which
would be offered by Order in Council as a reward for the
capture of Riel.

It was good provincial politics and an intrusion on the federal field, the more justified in Blake's eyes because the field
was now changing. Riel had forced Macdonald to the creation
of Manitoba, that province the size of a postage stamp on the
map of the North-West. It was too small to be viable, it was
a mere reward to rebellion, and worse than that it was creating
problems for Ontario. The western boundary question had
already risen. There were paramount interests of Blake's province beginning to be involved here, and they were not to be
threatened by boundary makers or rebellious Métis or Macdonald. It was Ontario's young men who would be filling up
that country, and they were entitled to expect a full measure
of protection. "It is entirely competent for this Chamber, in a
matter in which the honour of Ontario is concerned, and in a
matter affecting the life of a citizen of Ontario, to take notice
of the murder of one of its people."[11]

It was seen differently in the west. The postage-stamp province had a House of its own now, and a corps of sharp-tongued legislators prepared to assert their rights. They moved to inform Ontario that they did not require her meddling and would see to their own justice. Blake, in the opinion of some of them, had used Riel as a hobby-horse to carry him into power, and one of the results of his work was "the arrival in the Northwest of people from Ontario burning with desire to wade knee-deep in the blood of a harmless people, hated for imaginary reasons."[12] There was another report from a more official source, significantly directed toward Quebec. Upon the announcement of Ontario's reward of $5,000, Lieutenant-Govnor Archibald informed Cartier, there had been stormy Métis gatherings in the parishes on the Red River. If there were an attempt to capture Riel, who was once again in the country, he would be protected by armed force.[13] The voice that spoke from Toronto had been answered by a warning chord.

There were other warnings and there were symptoms of greater change. On the surface of things, however, relations between Blake in Toronto and the Prime Minister in Ottawa continued to be amicably correct. The Premier forwarded copies of all provincial Acts, and the Prime Minister perused them. Macdonald's comments were cautious and usually in favourable terms. "I quite concur," wrote Blake, "in your observation as to the desirability that the legislation of both the general and local parliaments should be conducted in accordance with the Constitution."[14] There were differences on minor points which Macdonald gently dealt with, and Blake as gently replied. "I should be very glad," he wrote on March 4, "to accept your suggestion of talking this over when we meet."[15]

There would be much more to talk of, but it would be across the breadth of the aisle. The federal parliament was convening in mid-April, and it would open out on a wide and stormy scene.

∽

Blake viewed the scene, when it opened up before him, with all the sick forebodings of a tired-out man. He had been rubbed raw by politics, he was scarred by embittered enemies and he was tired of some old friends. Above all he was weary of George Brown. That greatest of official friends stood well apart, high on his own pedestal, the enduring genius of reform. Yet he was always on hand too, driving, thrusting, advising; colouring the party mood, setting the party tone. It was the worse that he was indispensable, that he was Mackenzie's alter ego, that there was no voice of liberalism as powerful as the Toronto *Globe*. The rasp of that personality still remained, somehow diminishing Blake. It was something more to be lived with, something more to be endured, when there was all too much now. It seemed to be piled onto, and perhaps much of it grew out of, the worries of neglected business, the sleepless nights and the headaches, the coming home to the family a moody and brooding stranger. The second trade of the barrister was beginning to exact its price.

In a period of five months he had fought his party to power, experienced the use of power and confirmed himself in his place. He did not relish the place, but he could claim a measure of success. He was the undisputed leader, and he had done much. With dual representation now abolished, he could see an end to the work. When the time came for a decision between the federal and provincial Houses there was no doubt of his choice. But the time was not yet. He was not only Premier of Ontario, he was also a federal Liberal, and one of the men the party looked to most. He "served in the ranks", in one of his favourite phrases, but there was no escape in that. There was no freedom from Brown, nor from the necessities Brown imposed. Blake was consulted on federal matters as one of the constant advisers. He was still burdened, quite as much as Mackenzie — rather more than Mackenzie — with the ambiguous task of leadership where there was no official head.

Across the country the great issues were rising and would somehow have to be dealt with. British Columbia was a province now at the price of a new railway and the greatest problem of all. At the last federal session, preoccupied with Ontario's election and the demands of provincial politics, Blake had listened while Cartier announced the deal. And deal it surely was in the eyes of the Ontario Liberal, the culmination of many and the threat of many more. Blake had harped from the beginning and always would harp against Macdonald's political methods, the flagrant misuse of patronage, the bribery and jobbery at elections, and the squandering of public money. It was not diminishing, it was growing, and it seemed to feed on itself. In Blake's view it was becoming of the essence of politics, distorting the the will of the voter, and the reckless gamblers who built on it were themselves distorting the nation.

To Blake the original union had perhaps been made too soon, before either the need or will had quite developed. Yet both were there as a sure promise for the future, to be fostered by careful planning. The Intercolonial Railway, that expensive link with the east, would be risk enough for its time, promise enough to secure the Atlantic provinces. Beyond that there should be a generation of growth, centring on the two Canadas, consolidating and strengthening both, and resolving the old differences that divided English and French. Blake had envisioned western expansion from a strong central base, answering in its own time to the outward thrust of settlement. Instead, what had there been? There had been the blunderings in the North-West and the purchase of peace by the creation of Manitoba, a miniscule and mockery of a province, far ahead of its time. There had been the purchase of Nova Scotia with "Better Terms", and the extension of the evil precedent in the wooing of Prince Edward Island. And far beyond that was the purchase of British Columbia with the promise of the Pacific Railway, in Blake's eyes the most fatal act of all. Macdonald had not built, Macdonald had simply bought; and the end of the long process must be bankruptcy, corruption, and ruin.

There was more than that to depress him, though it depressed Macdonald too. On May 8, 1871, the Treaty of Washington had been signed between Great Britain and the United States. Its great purpose, where the senior partners were concerned, was to restore amicable relations after the strains of the Civil War. Its effect on Canada, however, was to exact major concessions in response to American demands. Through months of negotiation Macdonald had served unhappily as one of a British commission resolved to have peace at almost any price. Surrounded by imperial statesmen, dominated by imperial interests, he had seen his own claims ignored and most of the American claims readily accepted. He had had to come back to Canada and confess to an angry country that the navigation of the St. Lawrence and the freedom of the Atlantic fisheries had been bartered away on terms. The terms were wretched enough, there had been no balancing concessions, and the only sop for colonials was the promise of a British loan.

On May 8, 1872, a year after the signing of the treaty and in the midst of the storm it had roused, Blake got up in the Commons to debate its ratification. For a while he was the politician, scathing on Macdonald's "cowardice" and making what hay he could, yet his real concern was the future. Canada, by conceding the rights on the St. Lawrence and the rights in the Atlantic fisheries, had given up the best levers she had for extracting reciprocity from Yankee traders. Macdonald argued that the fisheries agreement was only for twelve years — did anyone believe it would end with that term? There would be "the same hectoring, the same blustering and bragging" from the Americans, and the rights would be ceded again. Canada's injuries from the Fenian raids, mounted on American territory and supported by many Americans, had not even been mentioned. For all that loss and suffering what was Canada to get? Nothing at all from the Americans, but the promise of a British loan — a squalid tip from the mother country for not pressing her claims. The status of the new Dominion, still evolving so dangerously within her own unsettled borders, had been irretrievably reduced in North America.[16]

For all Blake's lashing of Macdonald he saw the major fault in the relations of colony and mother country. He did not believe, he was to say a few months later, that Canada would be long prepared to have her interests disposed of without having a voice in the disposal. It might come, perhaps, in a general parliament of the empire, in some huge reorganization "which would open to us a wider and higher destiny."[17] The old dream of an imperial federation was flickering on his horizon and it would for many others. But it was still a hope of the future and it would not last long with him.

The question of schools in New Brunswick rose that session, small, irritating, unanswerable, the symptom of a deeper fissure. New Brunswick Catholics, a great many of them French, had no legal right to the maintenance of separate schools. Before Confederation they had enjoyed the privilege, and they had assumed its continuance afterwards. With the privilege now removed by a provincial legislature, not only New Brunswick Catholics were up in arms. Quebec was aroused with them, raising the federal question. The Dominion might intervene to protect a Catholic minority, yet provincial rights were supreme in education. They had been made so, on Quebec's own insistence, yet now they threatened one of her dearest causes. They threatened to arouse Ontario, where Blake had made a cause of provincial rights. He could not forsake the cause and he could not justify New Brunswick; he could only beg the question. There was the same dilemma for Macdonald, watched by Ontario's Protestants and needing Quebec's support. On neither side of the aisle, nor in the assembled wisdom of parliament, was there any real answer. Mackenzie moved at last to refer the legalities of the problem to the Privy Council, and Macdonald quickly agreed. The crack was papered over, to go on widening in the future, as Blake could hardly doubt. He had not helped much in the debate. He had "considered from time to time the very difficult question", he quoted the conflicting Acts, he could see no remedy but a reference to the law officers of the Crown.[18] His speech in support of

Mackenzie, according to the Toronto *Mail*, was "tame and dull as the hair-splitting of a college professor and . . . actually bored the House".[19]

Throughout the session, commuting between Toronto and Ottawa, he was harried by provincial problems and the thought of his desk at the law firm. He was driving himself with the last dregs of his strength, oppressed and dominated by the worst foreboding of all. The price for British Columbia was to be greater than she had dreamed of asking. The westerners had demanded a link with the Pacific coast, in the form of a railway crossing the prairies to the Rockies and a wagon-road over the mountains beyond that. Cartier, negotiating for the government, had waved the proposal aside. "No," he was said to have said, "that will not do; ask for a railway the whole way and you will get it."[20] They had promptly asked and they had got it; the Canadian government, still staggering under the burden of the Intercolonial, was to build another railway four times longer across wild and half-known country in a period of ten years.

When the bargain was announced in the House the year before, Blake had greeted it with shock and incredulity. It was claimed that the railway would be paid for by the sale of public lands, that there would be no increase in taxes. Both claims, to Blake, were merely ludicrous shams. He was unimpressed, as in the case of the North-West Territories, with the need for haste to prevent American aggression. There had been too much haste already in the making of the present union. There was too much fear of the ambitions of the United States, and in any case the defence against them still resided in England. The fate of the Pacific region was said to be hanging in the balance. If it was, said Blake, the westerners could not affect it. "While England is true to herself the result does not lie with British Columbia."[21]

He suspected Cartier's sincerity in making the bargain. At best it was an election cry, raised by a threatened government that was soon to face the polls. At worst it was a national

FROM HALIFAX TO VANCOUVER.

MISS CANADA.—"THIS IS WHAT WE WANT, COUSIN JONATHAN. IT WILL GIVE US REAL INDEPENDENCE, AND STOP THE FOOLISH TALK ABOUT ANNEXATION."

JONATHAN.—"WAL, MISS, I GUESS YOU'RE ABOUT RIGHT THAR; BUT I'LL BELIEVE IT WHEN I SEE IT."

swindle, linked as it was by Cartier with the airy assurance to parliament that no man could be compelled to fulfill an obligation if he were prevented by unforeseen circumstances. There was even in it for Blake a motive much like treachery. "I cannot but think that the preposterous proposition of the government with reference to the Pacific Railway is specially framed to defeat a union with British Columbia." Joseph Howe, so long an enemy of union, was concerned with the negotiations as

92

Secretary of State. "Who can wonder that he was a party to bringing down a measure so iniquitous that the House cannot help rejecting it?"[22]

Yet the measure had not been rejected. Now, in 1872, in this last session of the first parliament of Canada, it stood not only confirmed but in process of implementation. British Columbia was a province and her price had grown again. For the company building the railway there was to be a cash subsidy of thirty million dollars, instead of the twenty-five as first proposed. There were to be fifty million acres of the Dominion's best land, a swath forty miles wide allotted in alternate sections along the line of route determined. There was no route yet, for there were no adequate surveys; even the completion of that work would require at least two years. Yet the national faith and credit stood pledged: to complete the line in ten.

The government was engaged in choosing instruments for the work, and they were certain to be political friends. Of two rival syndicates the choice seemed now to be inclining toward Sir Hugh Allan, the wealthy steamship magnate of Montreal. Why? Allan had American connections. Was there a link with Jay Cooke of the Northern Pacific Railroad? Did it involve others of his tribe? Was this greatest of Canadian projects, trumpeted abroad in the name of nationality, to be guided by foreign hands? Was it to be milked and wrecked, like other railways before it, by American buccaneers? The capital of the proposed syndicate was to be set at ten millions, with only a tenth paid-up. For an investment of one million it would acquire the government subsidy and the enormous grant of land. There was no assurance in the proposed board of directors; most of them were names with no money behind them. The money would come from Allan, or from the shadows behind Allan, and once installed as President he would have complete control. Under this man, and on such terms, was Canada to risk that mighty westward plunge?

It seemed she was. The government, forced by the Liberals,

had agreed that the building of the railway must not increase taxation. But, except for that paper assurance, it had held to the original plan. On June 14 the session closed, and dissolution was imminent. The summer and fall would bring a general election, dragged on as usual through weeks of open polling. In this, as in much else, Macdonald had refused reform. To Blake's perennial proposal of simultaneous elections he had given a short answer; it was contrary to the custom of the country and "un-British". It was certainly inexpedient, for he was facing a bitter fight. Yet he might survive — Macdonald had survived so much — and there would be no hope then that Blake could see for redemption from the great disaster.

On June 15, in Toronto, he had a visit from Gordon Brown, younger brother of George. Gordon Brown, for Blake, had all the faults of the older man, few redeeming qualities, and no ability to persuade. Certainly not that morning, one day after the session had closed in Ottawa, and certainly not in Blake's present condition. "My strength is so far impaired," he had written ten days earlier from his desk in the House of Commons, "that I am ordered to abstain from exertion and to look for rest and a change of air and scene at the peril of permanent ill-health."[23] For Gordon Brown's proposal he had a short and definite answer, confirmed to him after he left. "With reference to our talk of this morning," Blake wrote, "I want that you should distinctly understand that my mind is absolutely and irrevocably made up against taking (if I were offered) a lead in the House of Commons."[24]

He had said the same thing to George Brown only three months earlier, and he had opened his mind to Mackenzie during the late weeks of the session. Not only would he not be considered for the federal leadership; he would be unable even to take part in the coming election. The headaches would not let up, he said, he could neither sleep nor eat, and the pasty

face and the strained eyes and the shaking hand confirmed it.
By June 25 he was a man who looked no better, but the mood
and scene had changed. He stood on a platform at Riverdale,
the honoured guest and nominated federal candidate, address-
ing his Bruce electors. To provide silence for his words even
the nearby sawmill of Messrs. Miller and Mason had been
closed down for the day.

South Bruce had redeemed itself; a difficult provincial constituency had been converted wholly to Blake. It had invited
him now to stand as its federal member, and he was touched
and flattered by the move. He could make no promises, he said,
since he still sat in the Dominion House for his constituents of
West Durham and was "theirs as long as they pleased."[25] Yet
it was permissible by law to stand for a second riding; South
Bruce had nominated him and was willing to share with Durham. It was too much to be resisted and he was here to share in
return; he would stand for Bruce as a candidate and her voters
should have his thoughts.

His health, he said, would not permit him to canvas the riding nor to make a long speech here. But "my mind is oppressed
with a multitude of questions upon which I and my friends
have differed from those in power." For an hour and a half
he ranged over the questions, a bleak and indignant man. What
had become of the hopes of Confederation? Had Ontario attained her goals? As the greatest province she had demanded
a proportionate voice in the affairs of the nation. Could she be
said to have it now? She paid more than a half, as the Dominion's greatest tax-payer, of the cost of those "Better Terms"
to Nova Scotia. Yet it was not by her own will but by the votes
of the other provinces. And the terms were still wrong, a viola-
tion of principle that endangered the constitution. There was
the province of Manitoba now, with four representatives in
parliament for twelve thousand people. South Bruce, a constituency of thirty thousand, had only a single member. There
was worse disparity in the case of British Columbia, where

six men spoke in parliament for a population of barely eleven thousand. "Eighteen men in South Bruce count for one man up in British Columbia."

Was this a small matter? Those ten men in the two western provinces, speaking in all for 23,000 people, might decide the result of the coming general election. They might shape the destiny of the nation for at least the next five years. They had been made by the men in power and they would be used by the men in power, first to win the election and then for the government's ends.

In the case of British Columbia there was the promise of the Pacific Railway. He had a word to say about that. Its length was now estimated at 2,700 miles and its cost between a hundred and a hundred and twenty million. On the financial side of the project there was the experience of the United States, in the building of railways less than half as long. Companies with far more capital than the proposed Canadian syndicate were wholly or half bankrupt. Was there any promise in that for the success of the present venture, even if it were well planned?

But it was not well planned; it was hardly planned at all. With surveys uncompleted all estimates were meaningless and no one could even conjecture what the road would really cost. It would run through some of the most difficult country in the world, and it was being projected blindfolded. There were the huge gullies and river basins to be bridged in the Northwest, there was "the sea of mountains" to be crossed in British Columbia. To all this, on the strength of its flimsy guesses, on the promise extracted by the Liberals that it would not increase taxation, the government had committed Canada.

These fears had been voiced in parliament, by himself and many others. He had little to add but forebodings of new evil. If costs outran the estimates, as they almost certainly would, it was not Allan's syndicate but the people of Canada who would pay. There would be new subsidies, still more crushing burdens, and they would be fastened onto the taxpayers by compliant government tools. It was with that prospect and for that purpose that Conservative members of parliament would be installed as directors and shareholders on the proposed company's board. Even that outrage Blake and his friends in parliament had not been able to prevent. He could see but one remedy and it was the defeat of Macdonald's government at the coming general elections. Yet he was bleak about that too, since he would not be present for the fight.

He went on for a while to speak as Premier of Ontario, obsessed with old criticisms of his father as well as himself, defending quite unnecessarily his own personal honour. The pounds and shillings of his sacrifices came to the fore again. He was charged with self-interest, yet in the pursuit of his public duties he had half-withdrawn from his law firm, and had reduced his legal income until it was a third of what it had been. As he went on to other charges there were concerned glances from those on the platform with him; he was making a visible effort. He was in mid-course of a tangled defence of his policy in building provincial railways when he stopped rather abruptly. "I feel that my strength is failing me." He sat down to endure the vote of thanks and the raising of three cheers, struggled to his feet again to answer a question and at last was free to go.[26]

On July 6 he left Toronto with Margaret, bound for England. From the forewarned Mackenzie there was consideration and sympathy, but most of the party members were shocked and openly resentful. There was a cool note, even in letters from friends. "I was sorry to learn from your brother that you were suffering from illness to such an extent as to require a voyage across the Atlantic . . . your absence during the elections will no doubt have an injurious effect."[27]

To the hostile Toronto *Mail* it was merely a strategic retreat; Blake had withdrawn to the sidelines in the face of a critical battle. The game of politics was beyond him. "Mr. Blake's recent exertions in Bruce may be taken as proof that there is nothing very serious the matter with him."[28]

He arrived in England and proceeded like his father before

him to one of the watering places. The headaches were still blinding, and the inward fears and convictions more insistent and he could not yet find sleep. Margaret, worried and lonely and torn away from the children, was anxious for word from Humewood. When it came it was of little Margaret, the youngest daughter, born ten months earlier. She had died suddenly while her father and mother were at sea.

On August 8 he replied to a letter from Mackenzie: "I thank you, my dear friend . . . my wife joins me in my thanks for your kindly words about our dear babe." He was still Premier of Ontario, writing to his provincial treasurer, and he could not escape a discussion of provincial affairs. He had left Mackenzie alone to fight the elections and he had to assume at least a part of the load, offer what advice he could. He did so, letting his pen run on, fascinated and trapped as usual by the swarm of problems. But it would all be to little purpose, and it was not to continue long. "My recent misfortune has added to the reasons in my mind for the accomplishment of my comparative retirement. I was a stranger to my child, and my other children are growing up strangers to me . . . I have a great yearning for a little time to be with them."[29]

CHAPTER SIX

"WE ARE A HUMILIATED PEOPLE"

A GREAT YEARNING . . . "the accomplishment of my comparative retirement" . . . the words left for Mackenzie,
but the man remained himself. On September 12, by then
writing from London, he forwarded his resignation as provincial premier. The letter went to Mackenzie to be used at Mackenzie's discretion, and Blake offered his apologies for the
tone of the accompanying note. It was abrupt and brief, he
said, "owing to the Canadian mail which always gives me a fit
of nervousness."[1] Yet he was "devoured by curiosity" as to
the result of the maritime elections, and eager for more
statistics on the party's showing in Ontario. In that province
at least there had been a massive shift to the Liberals. It was
not as much as had been hoped for, yet it pointed the way to
victory. Politics held new promise in the wider field of the
nation, and the moth was circling the flame.

It was October when he returned to Canada, and his first
act was to shift the provincial burden. On the 21st of the
month, in company with George Brown, he called at the house
on Simcoe Street where Oliver Mowat lived, the Vice-Chancellor of Ontario. The chubby little judge with the spectacles,
steel-rimmed like Blake's, was now fifty-two. He could look
back thirty years to his days at the law in Kingston, when he
was an articled student to John A. Macdonald. Since then he
had had seventeen years in the politics of old Canada, usually

99

at Brown's side and as a thorn in the side of Macdonald. As firm as Brown in the work for Confederation, he had pursued it as far as the Quebec Conference and ended his role there. He was high and safe on the bench, and he was a man who liked to be safe, but his visitors were warm and pressing. This shrewd, cautious Liberal was a born manager of men, certain to be well received by the provincial party. He was also a politician whose hand still itched for the work. By the time Mackenzie arrived to add his pleadings Oliver Mowat had been gained. He would be the new premier of Ontario.

For Mowat an early result was a dry letter from Macdonald. "My feelings . . . are of a composite character . . . with all your political sins you will impart a respectability to the local govt. which it much wanted . . . we must try to work the new machine, with the construction of which we had so much to do, with as little friction as possible."[2]

It was a hope unlikely to be realized, and there was a corollary for Blake. Toward the end of the year, with the office of Vice-Chancellor now open, the beneficent Prime Minister had another appointment for the family. This time it was Sam, the very prop and stay of his elder brother, who was to leave the desk in his office and replace Mowat on the bench.

For the head of the firm it meant the problems of reorganizing, the acquiring of new partners, and more than enough distraction for the private man. Yet he was not private; both South Bruce and West Durham had elected him in spite of his absence, and he made no move to resign. He could not resist, and he would not be allowed to resist, the welter of hopeful prospects provided by the public scene. Macdonald was still in office; he had salvaged that from the election. Yet the results of a savage battle and the growing maze of his difficulties had brought him close to disaster. He had lost Cartier, he had almost lost Quebec, and he had been badly beaten in Ontario. Only the maritime provinces and the votes of his loyal westerners would enable him to face the Commons with a bare working majority. He was weaker even than he seemed, because there were uncertain votes in the maritimes and a hint of incipient trouble in British Columbia. Nor was that all. Over the whole election, and surrounding the crucial issue of the Pacific Railway, there was a hint of impending scandal.

Mackenzie had resigned with Blake from his provincial office. He was now totally immersed in federal affairs. He was insistent on Blake's help, and it was quite impossible to refuse him. He had been left alone to fight the general elections, and Blake felt guilt for that. He felt resentment in the party, and duty's call was clear, the more clear because the prospect was irresistible. Now after long years, and under wise and skillful guidance, the Liberals might hope to bring Macdonald down.

Of that needful guidance Blake seemed hardly prepared to offer much. He would come down, he told Mackenzie, to attend the opening of parliament and "do what I can in the first struggle."[3] The first struggle, however, was in the party caucus on March 4, 1873, and still with the abiding problem of a headless party. The opening of the new session was a day away, and it was necessary now if ever that it be faced by Liberals under a common leader. Throughout the 4th and on to the morning of the 5th, as Ontario and Quebec members debated in their separate rooms, Mackenzie declined to serve, Holton "talked shy",[4] and to Dorion the practical necessities demanded a leader from Ontario. In each of the separate rooms, and finally in a joint meeting, the choice began and ended by hovering over Blake. He thrust it firmly away. He had played no part in the elections, and he knew that it was well remembered. His health he insisted, was still not restored; his business was more demanding, he desired time with his family. At length, quietly and inexorably, the chance and the burden passed. Mackenzie finally yielded, agreed to shoulder the leadership and Quebec accepted him politely. The party embarked on the session with Blake still in the ranks.

He remained a private as the greater struggle began. On April 2, Huntington, the Quebec Liberal, rose in his place in parliament. The first gun of the Pacific Scandal sounded. He had evidence, Huntington said, to prove that Sir Hugh Allan was merely a Canadian figurehead as president of the new railway. It was to be built by American capital and controlled by American capitalists, who would also control Allan. In effect they would control the government, for they had helped it win the elections. He could prove that huge sums, advanced by the Americans and passed on through Allan, had come into the hands of Macdonald and several of his leading ministers. He moved that parliament establish a committee of inquiry.

The tall, cultivated Huntington, always impressive in appearance, was sometimes less so in action. He had made the enormous charges, according to an unfriendly critic, "with a joint air of exultation and timidity."[5] Macdonald had sat quite silent, tapping his pencil on his desk, his face a study in blankness. He did not move when the man across from him finished; no one rose to answer. The Speaker put the motion and it was voted down. It seemed the matter was closed.

No one was deceived in parliament, and least of all Macdonald. He had been much lied to himself and the lying had been done by Allan but he knew the truth now, or at least much of the truth. The Montreal magnate had claimed to be wholly free of his American connections, and Macdonald had chosen to believe him. He had had to; he needed Allan's money to fight the elections. He had taken the money and spent it, but Allan had not been free. He had been totally involved with the Americans, bound hand and foot, and worse than that he had pledged himself on paper. He had pledged the Canadian government, and the pledge might well be enforced, for American money had kept the government in power.

For three months Macdonald had been able to assess most of the facts. He had learned them from George McMullen, the American entrepreneur, the connecting link with the syndicate that was to build the Pacific Railway. Allan, lying to Macdonald, had also lied to the Americans and proposed to escape his bargain. He would not be allowed to escape, McMullen said, and neither would the Canadian government. The syndicate would have the contract and go on as the Americans planned, or Allan's letters would go out to the Canadian public.

There would be more than that go out if everything were known. Even Macdonald hardly knew how much. Cartier had fought the election in Montreal — with Allan's help — pledging himself to Allan. What had Cartier got? What had he given in return? What had he said on paper? One could not know, some of the papers had vanished. Cartier was now in England, already a dying man. Macdonald himself could hardly recall the election; there had been too many frantic meetings, too many calls for money, always too much drink. But there was that one fatal telegram written by his own hand, etched on his own memory, and not in his hands now: "Must have another ten thousand. Will be the last time of calling. Do not fail me."[6]

He was trapped, and Blake knew it. Almost everything Macdonald knew was known to the opposing leaders. The rumours had come in December and by February they had grown firm. On the 21st Mackenzie had written Cartwright who was not yet quite a Liberal but inclining the Liberal way: "I heard an extraordinary story two days ago concerning the Pacific Railway Company . . . It seems Sir John made an agreement with Sir Hugh Allan and Jay Cooke and their Yankee associates that they were to have the contract, they engaging to furnish 3% on their capital, or $300,000., to carry the elections."[7] Much had cleared up since then, in the best tradition of melodrama and the worst tradition of politics. In Montreal there had been money found for the purchase of McMullen's papers, by persons who remain unnamed in pen or print. Other papers had been rifled from the files of Allan's solicitor, J. J. C. Abbott. The means were wholly questionable but the facts were not, and they meant Macdonald's downfall. There only remained the manoeuvring before the end.

⚓

It began within a day of Huntington's defeated motion, and continued for seven months. By April 3 not only the public reaction but the attitude of his own party had convinced Macdonald that he would have to hold an inquiry. He moved that day for the establishment of a select committee, and on the 8th the members were named. There would be three from the government side, constituting a majority, but they would be faced by Dorion and Blake.

Macdonald had hoped that both would refuse to serve, on the ground that their eminence as leaders might tend to bias their judgment. It was a thin argument and a slender hope, but he was already clutching at straws. As this one snapped in his hands he knew that the work of the committee, for all its Conservative majority, would be dominated by the formidable lawyers from Toronto and Montreal. With Dorion close to the source of all the evidence, and Blake already looming as the great inquisitor, it was more than ever necessary that their hands be somehow tied.

The opportunity presented itself as Huntington's witnesses began to arrive in Ottawa. Mackenzie moved that all their testimony be sworn to, and the question of the "Oaths Bill" rose, gratefully nourished by Macdonald. It would require an Act of parliament to enable the select committee to impose an oath on witnesses, and there was doubt that parliament had power to pass the Act. There was still doubt after three weeks of debate but on May 3, under Blake's threat that he would move for the Committee to sit without sworn testimony, the Oaths Bill passed the House. It left Canada for London to receive imperial sanction, and on May 4 the committee opened its sessions. Its first business, however, was to consider a motion of Macdonald, asking for more delay. Three important witnesses who would certainly have to be heard were now absent in England. They were Sir George Etienne Cartier, Sir Hugh Allan, and his lawyer J. J. C. Abbott. It was expected, Macdonald said, that they would have returned by July 2, and he moved postponement till then.

His Conservative majority supported him, and the next meeting of the committee was set for July 2. In the meantime, by May 23, parliament had finished its other business and a new question rose. It involved considerable discussion with a new Governor-General. The tall, handsome, bewilderingly eloquent Lord Dufferin was an Irish peer of peers, regal in all his views. He had opened the current session with much splendour. With large ambitions for himself as an imperial viceroy, and already accused by Liberals of being too close to Macdonald, he was approaching the first of his hurdles in a long and intricate course. He could not prorogue parliament because prorogation ended the life of its committees. The select committee on the affairs of the Pacific Railway would certainly have to live, and have time to complete its work. His Excellency, therefore, acting on the advice of his ministers, merely adjourned the House until August 13. On that day the members would be recalled to receive the report of the committee and prorogation would follow.

Blake was aware of what overhung the plans. Macdonald had been too compliant in the matter of the Oaths Bill, and in too much haste to despatch the text to London. He was said to have despatched his emissaries with it to argue for disallowance. Blake himself had doubts of the bill's reception, but it hardly mattered now. Whatever happened in London, the evidence was safe in Canada; the lawyer could bide his time. Cartier had died in England on May 20, Macdonald was drinking as he had never drunk before; the old order was passing. There would be a few moves yet but Liberals were prepared for all of them. Dorion was prepared, steely, graceful, courteous, always beautifully articulate in either language, and now utterly implacable. On the evening of July 1, as the solemnities of another Dominion Day were concluding in Montreal, Blake arrived to confer with him. On the next morning they walked together to the Court House, expecting what lay ahead.

They joined their Conservative colleagues in the chamber of the Court of Appeals to be officially informed of what they already knew. Lord Kimberley, the Colonial Secretary, had disallowed the Oaths Bill. The Committee was deprived of its

105

power to demand that witnesses be sworn. It was therefore incompetent to proceed, in the opinion of its Conservative majority, and would be required to suspend sittings. The argument went on through the day and concluded on July 3, with the result quite as foreseen. Blake's and Dorion's protests had gone down by three to two.

On the same day Macdonald proposed the alternative of a royal commission, as he had often done before. It had ob-

THE BEAUTIES OF A ROYAL COMMISSION.
"WHEN SHALL WE THREE MEET AGAIN?"

viously been his set goal. Parliamentary committees, even with Conservative majorities, were emanations of parliament and occasionally unpredictable. It was not so with an appointed royal commission. Even if it contained Liberals it was the sole creation of government and could be guided by the maker's hand. From the Prime Minister to Blake came the formal offer of a place, and the freezing reply went back. "I believe that it would be of evil consequence to create the precedent of a government issuing a commission of enquiry into matters of charge against itself, the commissioners being, as they are, subject to the direction and control of the accused."[8]

The manoeuvring in courts was stalemated, but the evidence lay to hand. Dorion, a week before, had been clear as to the next step. "Then let the whole papers . . . be published and commented upon by the press and at public meetings."[9] It happened, at least in part, on July 4. On that day, in the Montreal *Herald* and the Toronto *Globe*, a great mass of the story behind the railway was given to the Canadian public. On the 18th there was more, appearing in Quebec's *L'Evenement* as well as the *Globe* and *Herald*, and standing out from the worst of it was Macdonald's own telegram: "I must have another ten thousand . . ."

Everything was in the open now, so far as Blake was concerned. Macdonald's fate would be decided where it should be, in the great forum of the nation, August 13, the day set for the reconvening of parliament, assumed a new importance. There could be no delivery of a committee report, for there was no report to receive; the committee had been suspended. Still less, however, could there be what Macdonald planned — a mere formal meeting, a report of no report, and immediate prorogation all in a single day. The massed proofs must be presented, there must be the majesty of full debate, and after weeks or months a decision by the whole House.

Nothing like that eventuated when August 13 came. It was hot and stifling in mosquito-ridden Ottawa. There had been wild rumours of Macdonald's death by suicide, and there had been the actual naming of Macdonald's royal commission. He would be quite safe in the hands of three judges, all of them Conservative friends. He had been drunk much of the time but he was certainly not dead, and he was still the Governor-General's principal adviser. If he escaped from the Commons to the Senate chamber to be granted prorogation parliament would be stilled before it found its voice. For all the roar in the newspapers there would be nothing heard in the House. There would only be the royal commission and the inevitable whitewash brush.

For Blake, for Mackenzie, and equally now for Cartwright who had entered the Liberal camp, everything centred on Dufferin. He must be somehow brought to stop Macdonald's escape route, to refuse that prorogation. In the steaming Liberal caucus room on the morning of the 13th every member of the party to the last back-bench novice subscribed to a long petition to the Governor-General. Cartwright left to deliver it and was back in half an hour. Dufferin had been polite but firm and the answer was definitely "No". The procedures of parliament would have to go on as usual. His Excellency had been advised by his Prime Minister, and would be bound by that advice, with a single stipulation. He had demanded, as a testimony of his own concern with the ways of the government, that another session of parliament be called within ten weeks. For this session, however, if Macdonald made it to the Senate chamber he would get his prorogation.

There was a last chance, and a slim one, that depended on the House itself. It would be silenced by Black Rod, summoning the loyal Commons to attend His Excellency in the Senate. But it could not be interrupted in the course of its deliberations if they were once formally begun. Formalities were all-important, and so was timing. The Speaker must be in his place, the doors of the chamber closed, and above all it must be a Liberal who was first man to be heard. That voice, if it could establish itself, might release the eloquent flood.

Under the eyes of packed galleries, and with guards and detectives standing at every door, the chosen servants of the people took their seats. The Speaker entered with the mace following behind him and settled nervously in his chair. Mackenzie leaped to his feet but the chamber doors were open, and he was forced to sit till they closed. They swung shut and he was up again, but they reverberated instantaneously to the three traditional knocks. Once more they opened smoothly

WHITHER ARE WE DRIFTING?

under the hands of well-coached functionaries, and Black Rod was in the doorway for his passage down the aisle. Jostled by protesting legislators in the midst of a wild uproar, he made his way to within hailing distance of the throne of Mr. Speaker, curtailed his three bows, bawled his summons to the Senate and hastily backed toward safety. There was a rush of relieved Conservatives as Macdonald and friends followed him, and the great tribunal closed.

For Liberals, for that day, it was all over. Most of them retired to the caucus room, refusing to go to the Senate, and jammed there in a temperature of ninety degrees, they released their livid fury. Mackenzie spoke, Blake spoke, and there was a train of other speakers until ten-thirty in the evening. At the moment it changed nothing. To the derisive press of the enemy it was only sweat and words.

∽

"We are a humiliated people."[10] Blake was speaking at London on the 28th of August. He had really begun at Bowmanville two days earlier, for his thoughts outran the limits of a single speech. For once, stirred to his depths, he had become the political animal and a leader of politicians wholly resolved on the kill. An icy lawyer, speaking for the prosecution, he had disposed of Macdonald's plea. "It is utterly impossible to urge that those hands are clean, utterly impossible to escape from the conviction that the enormous powers entrusted to the government . . . were used for the purpose of procuring influence and cash from the contractors to whom they agreed to give the contract." It was the same with Macdonald's claim, and the claim of some of his ministers, that they had not sought money for themselves. They were not charged with that. They had used it to buy votes, to commit a greater crime. "Not one but thousands of crimes have been committed . . . the free voice of the people has been overborne and these men rule, not because the free voice of the people has so decided, but in spite of the utterance of that voice."

110

He was finished with the details of scandal when he reached London; he was probing eloquently and deeply now for the effects of political corruption, of the game as played by Macdonald. "What position do we occupy today in relation to the people of the United States? We have been accustomed to pride ourselves on the comparative elevation of Canadian morals ... we can do so no longer." He dealt with all the expedients of the past months — the Oaths Bill, hurried across the Atlantic with a hint for its disallowance; the choking-off of committees; and finally the last and greatest crime, the choking-off of parliament. For what? For this appointed royal commission, chosen by the accused themselves, to be the safe and pliant tool of corrupt men.

He painted a picture brilliant with his own brilliance, moving with his own emotion, of the fight for liberty in England. He felt himself to be fighting the same fight here, and no man could doubt it as he rose toward his peroration. "The appointment of this Commission is a high contempt of parliament, and you are not to listen to those who tell you that the privileges and rights of Parliament are not important to you. The privileges of Parliament are the privileges of the people, and the rights of parliament are the rights of the people. It is for those rights and in those interests alone that we strive today. We are not separate from you; from you we spring, to you we return; in your interests and in your name alone we speak and act, and it is for your rights that we are now contending."[11]

He left London to carry the contention further. "We must bide our time until Parliament meets."[12] He was the man most watched by Macdonald now, and the man most watched by the country. A copy of the London speech went to the Prime Minister, with a glum note from one of the party faithful: "at least 30,000 of these have been printed." There was a month of party mobilizing while the royal commission sat, ignored by all Liberals, leading its supple witnesses toward its own bland conclusions. "The comedy drags," said the *Globe*, "the audience has begun to yawn."[13] The commission would decide nothing and it could buy no more delay. Macdonald's promise stood, exacted from him by Dufferin at the time of the prorogation. There must be another session of parliament within a maximum of ten weeks.

The session opened on Thursday, October 23, adjourned to the following Monday, and the attack began that day. Mackenzie led and the lesser leaders followed, hammering down Macdonald's last defences, cutting his support away. The report of the royal commission was almost brushed aside; it was the whole body of the evidence, so long shrieked from the newspapers, that was heard in parliament now. For six days, while his ministers rose around him, defending the indefensible, the Prime Minister sat silent. The government majority dwindled and the desperate faithful came to Macdonald pleading; it was time for him to speak himself. He would not do it; there must still be some last and damning scrap of evidence; Blake had not yet spoken. It was the game that had been played at Bowmanville and often before and since; Macdonald was outwaiting Blake.

Yet when Blake rose at two o'clock on the morning of November 4, it was with the last echoes of Macdonald's speech dying away in the House. That game he had won; everything was won now. He had half an hour in the small hours of the morning, and he spoke for four more through the afternoon and evening. He had no new evidence and he might have omitted the old, for all the merciless power of its presentation. The tale of scandal had been told now and it remained to decide and judge. Implicit through all the speech, and for all the memories that might have brushed Blake's mind, was a long farewell to Macdonald. "I have no feelings of joy and congratulation at the result," but the man must go and the ways of the man go with him. If that were not to be, "then we may as well at once give up what will have become the farce of representative government."

He did not believe that that alternative would come. He looked about him as he approached the end of his speech.

"This House is to a certain extent, aye to a large extent, a purchased and a tainted House . . . but . . . I believe that this night
or tomorrow night will see the end of twenty years of corruption." He stared challengingly into the faces across the aisle.
"I have never claimed for myself or my friends that we are
the embodiment of absolute purity . . . nor have I asserted that
all the gentlemen who sit opposite are corrupt . . . but to them
I repeat my solemn warning, that they will be strictly judged,
and that loyalty to a party or to a man will not be held to justify
treason to their country . . . we are here to set up once again
the standard of public virtue."[14]

∽

At three o'clock the following afternoon Macdonald announced
the resignation of his government. In the hushed House Mackenzie and Blake were both absent from their places. The
rumour ran about each of them that he had been summoned by
the Governor-General. Yet Blake was still in the ranks and it
was Mackenzie as Prime Minister who wrote to Brown that
evening.

It was a worried, flustered note. He had been called by Dufferin early in the afternoon and invited to form a ministry.
He had accepted the invitation and was immersed in its problems now. "My chief difficulty is to get Blake to accept. I want
you to send him a strong telegram as soon as you can after
getting this. I don't see how I can get along without him."[15]

It had been a long, hard day, and Mackenzie had still a
number of men to see. He was pressed for time and the letter
was not quite clear. What was Blake to accept? Mackenzie had
told Dufferin that Blake should be Prime Minister. Or so he
had told Blake when he returned from Government House.
The two had gone for a long walk together, discussed the whole
of the interview and Mackenzie did not lie. "I don't see how I
can get along without him." He did not, nor was he anxious for
the first place. Mackenzie had said a hundred times that he was
prepared to serve under Blake. But he was not saying that to

113

Brown in this letter. He had after all been the leader of the opposition, he had carried the thousand burdens, and the reward was here at last. He had demurred duly in the presence of the Governor-General, but he had taken the thorny crown.

Or so it seemed to Blake. For every reason Mackenzie had acted rightly, except for the one reason that he was not the superior man. Three days before as the great debate went on, pivoting on Blake's silence, an opposition newspaper had departed from its usual vein. It had pleaded with Blake to speak, to rise to his true height, as the one possible successor when Macdonald should leave the scene. He would soon be arrayed, it thought, against the commonplace Grits around him. "The men he stands beside are mere accidents of the moment . . . it is impossible that a man of his pride of intellect and character . . . can condescend to brook the outrage by which he is made a subordinate to Mr. Mackenzie."[16] Outrage it was not; he had been subordinate by his own choice; yet now Mackenzie's preferment, and his acceptance of that preferment, had confirmed subordination. The fact, or the view of the fact, was to grow and rankle, unreasonable and inescapable in the face of every reason.

For the moment it was hardly felt. The great work had been done, the reaction was setting in. There was only the wish to be free of turmoil now, escape the clatter of cabinet-making, be back with the neglected business and the yearned-for family. He would "help", Blake said as usual, but he would not take office in the ministry. Mackenzie's pleadings were met with the old reasons; he could not imperil his health, he could not neglect his children, he would face the ruin of the law firm without the help of Sam. Telegrams and letters descended on him to be met with the same answers, or with no answer at all. The whole Liberal caucus petitioned him to join the cabinet, seemingly with small effect. Some of the words sank in at last, or the old imperatives prevailed. On November 7, when Mackenzie's government was formed, it included Blake as Minister Without Portfolio. Yet he had declined responsibility,

Edward Blake, about 1867

Catherine Blake and
Chancellor William
Hume Blake, Edward's
parents

Edward Blake and Margaret Cronyn Blake, shortly after their marriage in 1858

Edward's brother and legal partner, Samuel Hume Blake

Downtown Toronto was a familiar sight to the Blake family —
(*upper left*) King Street West in 1866 and (*below*) in 1878.
(*Above*) Completed in 1859, Humewood was, for many years, the Toronto
home of William and Catherine Blake and of Edward Blake and his family.

Edward Blake and his wife, Margaret, about 1874

The opening of the first parliament
of the Dominion of Canada on
November 7, 1867, from a sketch by
Alfred Jones in *Harper's Weekly*.

The Parliament Buildings, Ottawa, 1879

(*Upper left*) With the Parliament Buildings on the right and the Russell Hotel on the left, the Ottawa Post Office was a familiar sight to political leaders of the 1870s — George Brown (*lower left*), Alexander Mackenzie (*upper right*), and Sir John A. Macdonald (*lower right*).

The opening of Parliament in 1879 by the Marquess of Lorne.

from a sketch in *Canadian Illustrated News*

Edward Blake, in 1878

he had taken the lowest place and he would serve there, he stipulated, only for a limited time.

He had known through it all that with one word to Mackenzie their places could have been reversed. Mackenzie would have served Blake as the new master of Canada, loyally and with relief. The half-made nation, with its infinite mass of problems and its infinite opportunities, would have lain ready to his shaping, cleansed and in new light. "We are here to set up the standard of public virtue." It had been near as his closing hand, he had deliberately let it slip, and never in Blake's lifetime would the opportunity recur.

CHAPTER SEVEN

"THE HOPE OF THE HOUR"

O N NOVEMBER 7, 1873, the same day that his new government was announced, Mackenzie asked for the prorogation of parliament. He did not intend to be caught in a Double Shuffle, and his haste both irritated and amused the Governor-General. "I told him," Dufferin reported to Lord Kimberley, the Colonial Secretary, "that there was hardly time to send for my uniform, etc., and that he might very well have the House adjourned until Monday when the ceremony could be performed in the proper manner. Upon this he observed . . . that if a motion for adjournment was made Macdonald might move some disastrous amendment. The situation and the language . . . was such an exact reproduction or rather parody on the conversation which had taken place between Macdonald and myself . . . that I could not help saying to him, 'Why you seem as little inclined to trust these people now as they were to trust you then' — to which he responded by a grim laugh."[1]

There was reason enough to be grim, as the Governor-General knew. He was well aware of the strains of cabinet-making, and sceptical of his new ministers. As a group they were "frightfully deficient" in official experience. "Mackenzie, whom I personally like very much, is cautious but small and narrow. Blake is no statesman and does not mean to become one." Of their announced attitude, however, Dufferin could only approve. "They profess — and I believe both in the case

116

of Mackenzie and Blake with real sincerity — an intention to conduct the government upon far purer and loftier principles than has hitherto been the case, and their first step when Parliament meets after Christmas will be to bring in a good anti-bribery law. After this they will dissolve."[2]

In the event dissolution came first. As by-elections were called through November and early December, every member of the cabinet except Cartwright, the Minister of Finance, was returned by acclamation. Now an outright Liberal with the post he had long aspired to, Cartwright faced an onslaught that was led by Macdonald himself. Yet his solid victory in the face of it was a proof that times had changed, and it was only one of many. A Liberal tide was rising across the country, and Mackenzie shipped with the flood. "We mean to have an election immediately,"[3] he wrote on December 27. With or without the anti-bribery reforms, it was the moment to confirm his government's hold on power.

The dissolution of parliament and the calling of a general election were announced in Ottawa on January 2, 1874. A day later Blake wrote to Mackenzie. "Having come to a decision, it is my duty to let you know at the earliest moment that it will be impossible for me to stay in [the cabinet] after the election. During the election I am 'yours to command', for it might be inconvenient that there should be any announcement pending the contest, but that over and your majority secured, I must go."[4]

This cloud overhanging the future Mackenzie refused to see. "Your retirement we must not discuss now."[5] The thought unfitted him for work, he said, and Blake's help was essential. It came as promised in full and generous measure. Blake was out on the stump before Mackenzie, speaking in sheds and drill-halls, dominating party councils and strengthening doubtful candidates with the mere fact of his presence. It went on till the close of the campaign, and ended with election eve. That night, with his final speech delivered, Blake slept in a hotel at Walkerton and got up early in the morning to pencil

THE NEW DEPARTURE.

Spouse B——e.—"FAREWELL FOR THE PRESENT, DEAR; YOU AND THE GIRLS MUST MANAGE THE HOUSE IN MY ABSENCE!"

a note to Mackenzie dated 7:00 a.m. January 29: "By the time this reaches you the election will be practically over, and I have to request that you will in accordance with my former intimations forthwith acquaint His Excellency of my resignation, which I now formally tender."[6]

It became effective, in spite of all remonstrances, on February 13. Blake was in by a landslide for the constituency of South Bruce, but he would be sitting as a private member.

West Durham, for the moment, had been bequeathed to E. B. Wood as part of his delayed reward. Blake's duties, in Blake's eyes, had been discharged to the last tittle. He had done his share for the party, he had spoken his mind to the people, and he had given support to his friends. He had not spared his strength in the middle of a freezing winter, and he had been lavish with priceless time. When one thought, as he often did, in the terms of a barrister thinking of counsel fees, one could rate in thousands of dollars, perhaps in tens of thousands, the value of all that work and study and advice. He had helped the Liberal party to a tremendous victory. Macdonald's party, in a House of two hundred and six members, would be a rump of sixty-three. Macdonald himself, who had scraped through at Kingston, stood charged with corrupt practices and was likely to be unseated. The old order was gone, the standard of public virtue was flying high, and the legal Cincinnatus who had passed it on to Mackenzie could consider his work done.

It did not seem so to Mackenzie. The Prime Minister, always painfully conscious that he was rated as a lesser man, had been helped by Blake to this imprisoning eminence. He was to be left there now, just as the work began, newly diminished and isolated even among his own friends. The general run of his cabinet were available mediocrities, and over Mackenzie as always there was the shadow of George Brown. He had grown in that shade and the two men worked as one, composing differences when they came to them with absolute mutual trust. But Brown was not in the Commons and could not be persuaded to return, or even think of returning. Instead, half-amused, he had accepted an appointment to the Senate as the gift of the new government. He would sit with "the old ladies" as he fondly described them himself, and he would certainly be as free as ever with advice, encouragement, and help. But if it soured Blake with the government or kept him out of the cabinet it would be help at a high price.

There was Dorion the irreplaceable, who was now Minister

119

of Justice. A man of fifty-six, he was tired and a little deaf, hardly elated by victory or his new position. He was reconciled with the party, he had accepted Confederation, but he retained his old suspicions of the Upper Canadian west. Brown was the very symbol of all the hopes of that west, only partly relinquished. So was Mackenzie himself and so was Cartwright, the strong, ambitious newcomer. Blake had stood for Dorion as a centre of other forces, an antidote to those of Brown, and at least a promise of major redirections. Without Blake, in Dorion's eyes, the party would still be Brown's and he now intended to retire.

Holton, without Blake, refused to enter the ministry. He was friendly and loyal to Mackenzie but he had grief and sickness at home, a dying daughter. That would pass in time — even Holton admitted it — but the deeper reason was much the same as Dorion's. He was also a Lower Canadian scarred by the old wars, and he wanted a government of new directing forces. He was not as tired as Dorion, he was considerably more ambitious, but he would only work with Mackenzie if Mackenzie worked with Blake. He would follow Blake even as a private member, and at every hint of a crisis would be followed by many others. There was already talk of "Blake men" and of Blake cliques and cabals. The party's wandering lode-star, for all its brilliant promise, seemed only to offer the threat of new disruption.

The Toronto *Mail*, recently established as the principal Conservative organ and making mischief where it could, gave its own view of the map of the political heavens. It professed to see in Blake the obvious successor to Macdonald. Conservatives, it said, had seen him so and been prepared to accept him; it was a principal cause of the desertions that had brought Macdonald down. "That Blake did not at once become first minister was a disappointment to many members of the old House of Commons as well as to a great number of people throughout the country. Disappointed in this respect, they at all events hoped that he would be *de facto* the guiding spirit of the

Administration." Instead he had chosen to be neither. The man whom thoughtful Canadians had seen as "the hope of the hour" had turned away from his destiny.[7]

Or had he? The *Mail* had another thought. There was nothing to be hoped from the present government of Mackenzie but a series of bunglings and mistakes. Blake might have sniffed disaster and done well to step aside. But it was likely to be a short step. "Whether or not it be Mr. Blake's ambition to head a new and fresher party, it is evident that if his health permits he cannot long withhold his services from the state."[3]

✌

There were more potent forces than the *Mail* at work around him, and they tended to the same conclusion. The "new and fresher party", though it was no creation of Blake's, had taken visible form. As the Canadian National Association, which had been organized a month earlier, it was a political emanation of the dreams of Canada First.

Canada First was a slogan grown from a sentiment and translated into a movement by youthful intellectuals. Many of them were friends of Blake, most had similar backgrounds and their roots were deep in Protestant Upper Canada. Toronto was their natural home, Ontario provided their base and set their viewpoint. The typical Canada Firster had a disgust for party politics as practised in the new Dominion, an urge toward recognition by a neglectful British mother, and a lust for fostering patriotic unity. As a conscious member of the colonial upper classes, he resented the ignorance and indifference of the British upper classes. He resented colonialism itself, with its restricting ties and lack of real identity. "The normal old-world idea respecting us and our country," wrote W. A. Foster, one of the prophets of the movement, "resolves itself into confused pictures in which frost and snow, falling timber, snowshoes, furs and wild Indians are the most prominent if not the only objects of vision . . . The citizen of the United States has a flag of his own and a nationality of his own

— the Canadian has ever to look abroad for his."[9]

The various achievements of the movement, with respect to national unity, had had an ambiguous turn. Its greatest success had been to rouse Ontario Protestantism to the tumult over Riel, thereby alienating much of French Quebec. Though it remained British to the core in its image of a Canadian nation, Canada First was querulous over aspects of British rule. It deplored, like Blake, the effects of the Washington Treaty, and much as it revered the empire it was somewhat restive in the bonds. Even more than Blake, or at least more loudly and freely, it deplored political corruption and despised the existing parties. "The smaller the pit, the more fiercely do the rats fight."[10] It saw in George Brown no more than the grimy counterpart of John A. Macdonald, and in Mackenzie merely the mouthpiece of the great dictator of the *Globe*.

In 1871 it had acquired its leading spokesman in the person of Goldwin Smith. An Oxford don and a history professor of considerable private means, Smith had arrived in Toronto at the age of forty-eight. He had married well there, quickly establish preeminence in all the leading circles, and was to enlighten, uplift, and frequently aggravate the Dominion for the next forty years. He did not yet see Frenchness as the nonconducting element which must permanently divide the nation; that would be a later view. Other of his views, however, had been formed before he came. "Of the few people in England who thought about colonial subjects in my day, the general opinion was that the destiny of the colonies was independence. I brought that opinion with me to Canada."[11] Nor had he been in Canada for much more than a year when he pronounced on the state of politics. "In this country . . . what is there for Conservatives to conserve or for Reformers to reform? What is there to preserve our parties from gradually becoming mere factions, and our country from becoming the unhappy scene of a perpetual struggle of factions for place?"[12]

His answer to that was Blake. Blake was interested in the new magazine of the province, *The Canadian Monthly and*

National Review and the Oxford intellectual was a highly
valued contributor. As a friend of Canada Firsters, most of
them Blake admirers, Smith moved inevitably to the centre of a
charmed circle. It was from that position later that his overtures began to come. He watched the Pacific Scandal, the
bringing-down of Macdonald, and the final triumphant raising
of the standard of public virtue. He wrote to Blake on November 6, 1873, the day following the speech in the House of
Commons. "If this note seems impertinent, you must remember
that I am under the immediate influence of your peroration."
He deplored the unwillingness of Blake to accept office, and
urged him to reconsider. "To minds capable of great affairs
. . . labour must be lightened by the dignity of the object
which, in the present instance, is no less than that of putting a
young nation in the right path."[13]

He was leaving for England in a few days, he said, "where
I shall hold my head higher for this national victory over
corruption."[14] When he returned a few months later, though
Blake was not in the government, he was almost better than
that. He was newly restive over Brown's influence on Mackenzie, and as usual displeased with the *Globe*. He was becoming
involved with literature, or at least literate journalism, as an
aid to the public servant. With Blake's help the *Nation* had
now been launched, and it promptly welcomed Smith as a
chief contributor. The *Nation* was a weekly, the *National Review* was a monthly; one might look ahead to a daily as the
ultimate weapon. It might serve to counter the *Globe*, to release
the grasp of Brown on the party and the public mind. The
thought was discussed at Humewood, where the two gentlemen
of means were now much together, but it remained for the time
a thought. Blake was a Liberal still, bound to discretion.

Goldwin Smith, as the free spirit and the journalist, was
hampered by no such ties. He began the shaping of *The Nation*
as the organ of Canada First, and had prompt success with
that. The next and obvious step was to give the political movement the cohesion of a political party. That came in January,

1874, with the establishment of the Canadian National Association. Within two months more, as evidence of purpose translated into action, there were plans for the building of a National Club to serve as a party home.

Blake remained apparently aloof from the movement, still a member of parliament and officially a supporter of Mackenzie. Yet the developments seemed to point to obvious conclusions. Lord Dufferin, watching from Ottawa, transmitted his views to his good friend, Lord Carnarvon, the new Colonial Secretary. Blake was unhappy with Mackenzie and with many of the government's plans. He was displeased with the Governor-General and with the Colonial Office and the empire in the handling of Canadian affairs. To his old high strictures on the effects of the Washington Treaty he added new resentments over the disallowance of the Oaths Bill and the grant of the prorogation that had briefly reprieved Macdonald. He was inclined, in Dufferin's opinion, "to put himself at the head of a new party which has lately been organized under the auspices of Goldwin Smith." Dufferin feared that, with "Canada First" as its motto, the goal of the party would be Canadian independence. "One never knows," he reflected with unwonted gloom, "into what dimensions a political germ of this kind may develop."[15]

Meanwhile, on March 26, 1874, the first session of the third parliament of Canada had been convened, with Alexander Mackenzie as Prime Minister. The ceremonies of opening day had been rather more lavish than usual, partly as a sign of optimism in the face of depressed times, and partly to convince the sceptical that a government which was not Conservative might still have a sense of form. The effect had been somewhat marred, however, by a visit from Louis Riel.

An elected member for Provencher, a Manitoba constituency, Riel was still a proscribed rebel in Ontario. He had simply entered the parliament buildings, signed the roll and vanished. Yet the mere whisper of his presence was enough to divide the parties and the question of what to do with him brought on a fierce debate. The tangle of the man's status was now quite inextricable. Macdonald was said to have bribed him, Cartier was said to have promised him full amnesty, and Blake had put a price on his head. Cartier was now dead, and there was no eliciting the whole of the truth even if Macdonald knew it. For Blake there could be no retreat from the legalities of his old position and Mackenzie had to support him in the face of the indignant French. When the vote finally came, much against Macdonald's wishes, it provided for Riel's expulsion from the House of Commons. But it had set Mackenzie and Blake against Dorion and their Quebec supporters, and it had not expunged Riel as a major problem.

The other problems were already gathering weight, and Mackenzie was bending under them. As an antidote to hard times he had turned to an old hope, a reciprocity treaty with the United States. Senator George Brown had evolved most of the proposals, and he had taken them to Washington in February with the cool concurrence of Blake. Beyond that was the pressure for the Pacific Railway, which in spite of the Pacific Scandal would someday have to be built. The question that loomed was how, and on what possible terms, for Macdonald had worsened even the original bargain.

The agreement made with the province had provided only for a terminus on the Pacific mainland. In June of 1873, as the east rumbled with scandal, Macdonald had moved to strengthen himself in the west. He had passed an Order-in-Council stipulating that the completed line of the railway should cross from the mainland to a terminus at Esquimalt harbour on Vancouver Island. Since Victoria, the provincial capital, would grow round Esquimalt harbour, he had made fast and fervent Conservatives of every local landholder. He had also added millions to the prospective cost of the railway which was to be built in ten years. In seven years now, if the country were held to the bargain, for three of the years had gone. Obviously there would have to be adjustments and surely there were reasonable men, even on Vancouver Island. While

Brown was negotiating in Washington James D. Edgar was negotiating in British Columbia, not, in Blake's eyes, with much hope of success.

The lively, literate, always personable Edgar was another Toronto lawyer, and a man of thirty-three. Much interested in railways and even more in politics, he was a prominent Canada Firster and an admiring friend of Blake. He was also an industrious Liberal and an inveterate loser of elections who had failed in his last attempt. Deprived of a seat in parliament but anxious to be of service, he had been sent with Mackenzie's blessing to discuss concessions in the west. To George A. Walkem, the Premier of British Columbia, he was to propose the dropping of the time limit for the construction of the Pacific Railway. The federal government, in return, might not only confirm the extension of the terminus to Esquimalt when the railway came to be finished; it might also consider some grants for local building. The concessions, in Blake's view, had stretched the limits of the possible and gone a little beyond. To Premier Walkem, however, in the superheated atmosphere of the provincial capital, they had not been worth discussion. Edgar could only come home, snubbed and reporting failure, while at the same time in Washington the hopes of Brown for his proposals were withering in the American Senate.

There was to be no reciprocity as a restorative for dwindling trade, and when Cartwright produced his budget it was a herald of new gloom. Revenues were falling and the national debt was rising. There would have to be an increase in customs duties and new government borrowing, even to meet the current needs of the country. As to the project of the Pacific Railway there was only one thing sure; nothing that was done could be allowed to increase taxation.

Blake said nothing on the budget, and whatever he said on the railway question was said to Mackenzie in private. His views came when they were asked for, and they were ominous for British Columbia. They were ominous for Mackenzie him-

self, who somehow had to strike a bargain with the province.
He could not appease the westerners without the fear of losing
Blake, and quite apart from the railway he was aware of his
own position. Blake was outside the cabinet yet he was still
the power within it, consulted by the leading ministers and
by advisers who were not ministers though they were still
Mackenzie's friends. They were loyal to the Prime Minister
but they preferred Blake in his place; in all friendship and
with thinly-veiled urgency they wished for an exchange of
leaders.

Yet what did Blake wish? As close as ever to Mackenzie, or
only a little changed, he was considerate, helpful, friendly,
invaluable, and quite impenetrable. The great enigma of the
House, he sat with his own thoughts while the speculations of
the newspapers and the mutterings of politicians played
around him. To Laurent-Olivier David, friend of Wilfrid
Laurier, the new member from Quebec, he was a fascinating
and dominant figure with "the calm and reflective physiog-
nomy of a profound thinker . . . his attitude careless, his manners modest and affable, his dress that of a substantial American farmer from the state of Vermont. It is curious to see him
in the House, his head resting on his desk, covered with a
black felt hat with a very broad brim. One would say he slept,
but when he rises to speak it is evident that his mind was on
the watch."[16]

There was too much to watch, and it stimulated new resentments. Blake, as it seemed to Blake, had given Mackenzie a
post, or yielded a post to him, that was proving beyond his
capacity. He should be free of detail and he was not; against
all Blake's advice he had taken a cabinet portfolio. The Prime
Minister, who should be viewing the affairs of the nation from
a clear and commanding height, was slaving like one of his
bookkeepers in the Ministry of Public Works. He was determined on honest government, but he saw it through a clerk's

eyes. On every problem that touched the shaping of policy, ministers came to Blake. Yet the ultimate decision was Mackenzie's and it was often a wrong decision, made by a distracted man. For much of it there was no help, much of it could be endured, but there was one critical exception. The problem of British Columbia had need of a guiding hand.

The conviction grew more insistent as Mackenzie revealed his plans for the Pacific Railway. They involved essentially the terms proposed through Edgar, but they had been bettered beyond Edgar's approval and certainly beyond Blake's. There was still the request for release from the impossible pledge; the railway could not be completed within a period of ten years. There could be no agreement to a time limit and nothing done could involve increased taxation, but with those conditions agreed to there would be other pledges in return. Survey work would go forward with all possible despatch. A telegraph line and wagon-road would commence building immediately from British Columbia eastward. There would be rail lines built and large improvements in waterways to connect the central provinces with Manitoba. Though the prairie section would have to await settlement and there could be no building in the mountains until surveys had been completed, the Columbians were offered sizeable compensation. It would involve not only a grant of $700,000 for the province's local projects, but the immediate commencement by government of a railway on Vancouver Island. This last was the great plum, first dangled by Macdonald. It was based now on the assumption that the main line of the Pacific Railway, when built, would come down by Bute Inlet to a point opposite Nanaimo and that Seymour Narrows would be bridged to reach the island. An island section, then, linking Nanaimo with Esquimalt, the sea-gate of Victoria, would transform the sleepy capital into a great ocean terminus.

The proposals fell coldly on a worried and fretful House. There was no hope that Blake could be brought to accept them, and Mackenzie's difficulties in cabinet were approaching a state of crisis. He was losing Dorion to the bench, he was plagued with useless ministers, and in spite of their crucial difference he was urgent for Blake's support. "I don't see how you can get along without him" — it was a tired refrain in letters from men that Mackenzie trusted and from many others he did not. Without Dorion he had greater need of Holton, the second pillar of Quebec, but Holton remained determinedly Blake's man. Overworked, exhausted, and destined seemingly forever to a ministry of second-raters, the Prime Minister went on in trapped gloom. He was quite prepared, it seemed, by the 29th of May, for the one visible solution that was everlastingly talked of. "I see the *Gazette* says you are to take my place," he wrote to Blake that day, "I wish to heaven it were true."[17]

It was not true, not yet. For the Toronto lawyer, deep again in his law business, there was always too much work. There was no Sam to help, yet income had to be maintained; one's first duty was to provide for a growing family. Holton wrote in June after long hours with Mackenzie, confirming Mackenzie's mood. The Prime Minister, it seemed, was prepared for almost anything if it would bring Blake to the cabinet. He would retire himself to the office of Public Works, with either Blake or Holton taking his place. In Holton's eyes Blake was of course the man, and with him as head of the government there would be a complete reorganization. "So you must see, my dear Blake, the whole concern rests on your atlantean shoulders."[18] The answer was still no, the offer was premature, there was always a new difficulty. Blake would advise and help, but he was unable to take office. The work of government went on with a patched-up cabinet, bowing Mackenzie's shoulders.

In June the problem of the railway took on a new dimension. Premier Walkem arrived from British Columbia, coolly averse to the government's latest plan. He had petitioned England against it, and was on his way to London. In Mackenzie's opinion he was a shifty country lawyer with whom no arrangement could be made, but by then he hardly mattered. The imperial hand had moved. Lord Carnarvon, the Colonial Secretary, whether or not inspired by the Governor-General, had offered himself as arbiter in the affair of the Pacific Railway.

There could be no question of the reply to such an offer; in this, it seemed, Mackenzie did not need Blake. Both men were at one, and emphatic in their first reaction. Carnarvon's impossible proposal was merely a new affront. Once more colonial officialdom, bland, ignorant, and remote, was attempting to usurp the powers of a Canadian government. Whatever the bargain made with British Columbia, it would be made by parliament alone. There was, said the Prime Minister in his stiff response to Carnarvon, no question to arbitrate.

Yet he could not hold without Blake through the pressures of a hot July. With his adviser in Murray Bay, and the Governor-General urgent, Mackenzie was driven reluctantly to act on second thoughts. He informed Carnarvon through Dufferin that he was prepared to accept suggestions, and in August the results came. The Colonial Secretary had found for Premier Walkem; there was to be a further upward revision of Mackenzie's revised terms. The proposed grant of $700,000 was to be increased to $2,000,000, and worse than that there was to be a terminal date once more. The Canadian government was to pledge itself to the completion of the Pacific Railway by December 31, 1890.

Blake came back to long discussions with Mackenzie. The Prime Minister was indignant and had replied hotly to Carnarvon, but he had not been able to steel himself to a flat rejection of the terms. Yet for Blake there could be nothing less; the crisis was now full-blown. It was the high moment and the summons. There must be an end to the Pacific Railway as a threat to national solvency. There must be an end to imperial meddling in solely Canadian concerns. And beyond that, the very surveyors in the mountains had exploded one of the bases of Carnarvon's proposed settlement. Bute Inlet was now seen to be impracticable as a route to the Pacific coast. The Narrows would not be bridged, Nanaimo's function would vanish, and the Nanaimo–Esquimalt railway would be a purely local line. If it were built with federal funds it would be a mere political job, a bribe to speculating legislators who had bought land in Victoria. On all grounds Carnarvon had to be resisted and the task was beyond Mackenzie. He was a sick man, fretful and tired out, caught between imperial pressures and the relentlessly demanding province, and half-master of a ministry that preferred another leader.

Blake visited him on Saturday, September 5. There was some of the old affection and much of the old respect, but the imperatives loomed between them. That day they could not be talked of; Mackenzie was unfit for talk, though Blake had come prepared for it. He returned by train to Toronto and his letter went off next day, after a long, reflective Sunday.

"I hope," Blake wrote, "that you are quite recovered from your attack of Saturday. Had you been well that afternoon I should certainly have spoken to you about the subject of this note." It was a portentous subject, surrounded by many hedgings, but the essence was baldly simple. Blake would relieve Mackenzie in the office of Prime Minister, with Mackenzie retaining the portfolio of Public Works. The words of May were recalled when Mackenzie had wished to heaven that this might happen. It had been an impossible prospect then, and it was repugnant even now. Blake could only think of it if he were convinced that it actually accorded with Mackenzie's real feelings. He must first be assured of this, but if it were still true that Mackenzie desired to be replaced "I will address myself to the effort of so arranging my professional and private affairs as to enable me, by devoting my whole time for the future to public business, to meet your ideas."[19]

୶

The die had been cast, the great duty accepted, but there was no welcoming response. From the office of the Prime Minister there was nothing but extended silence. After eleven

131

days of waiting it was more than enough for Blake. He could only infer, he wrote on the 17th, that Mackenzie's feelings were averse to the suggested change. "This conclusion ends the matter for me. I leave town for Peterboro circuit in an hour, once more thank goodness free."[20]

At Peterboro, during the intervals allowed by the law courts, he had a week to absorb the rebuff. It reinforced and released some sentiments already grown. In ten months of brooding he had come to reverse the decision of last November. He had added lights and shadows even to the manner of its making. It had been, after all, Dufferin's and Mackenzie's decision; the Governor-General had called Mackenzie to power. There had been Mackenzie's weak disclaimers but the central fact remained; the Scot had been called first. Since he had been the only man so called, and had promptly accepted the offer, what had been left for Blake but acquiescence?

Now, however, in the divided cabinet, the crisis of the Pacific Railway, the new intrusion of imperialism and all the other problems, the results of the choice were clear. Mackenzie, out of his depth, was returning to the man who made him. He was drifting helplessly in the grip of George Brown, while the real voices of liberalism were crying for new directions. They were crying for Edward Blake; the echoes came to him from everywhere across the country. They were heard from men in the Maritimes with whom he had discussed his views, but they were loudest of all in Toronto through the voice of Canada First. Its young men were insistent, *The Nation* was urgent and eloquent, and the National Club was approaching inauguration.

There was a speech to be made on that inaugural day, and Blake was the man to make it. Goldwin Smith hoped for it and everyone seemed agreed on it, except Blake himself. There must certainly be some pronouncement, some revelation of his attitude, and it would have to be made soon. Blake's thoughts were formed or forming, but the consequences would be portentous, for Liberals, for Mackenzie and the country. What was to be said must be said, but perhaps not yet at the home of Canada First. It would stamp Blake inevitably as the leader of a new party, and he was not prepared for that. It would be better to redeem liberalism at the head of renewed Liberals.

The key Liberal, however, was confirming a first impression that he was disinclined to redemption. When Blake returned from Peterboro Mackenzie's letter had come. It was worse even than the delay, as aggravatingly patient and reproachful as the tired man himself. It recalled the day of decision when Mackenzie had taken office. "I told Lord Dufferin that I would undertake the task but would prefer that you should do it if you would consent, and he had no objection. He made no objection, but you declined." Twice since, Mackenzie reminded Blake, he had offered to step down and Blake had twice refused him. He had been forced now to other cabinet arrangements that he could not easily change. If he did change, it would involve humiliation that he was quite prepared to accept, but he had to consider the party and give some thought to his friends. It seemed odd to Mackenzie that Blake's exact proposals, "the programme laid down for me", were appearing in some of the newspapers and stirring up talk of a cabal. He was overworked and anxious and unable to see his way.[21]

The inevitable reply went off from Blake, again withdrawing his offer. It had been intended only to be helpful and was not to be thought of further. There was another thought, however, that had been roused from a restless sleep. "I learn for the first time, with the feeling of gratification natural under the circumstances, that when invited to form an administration you told Lord Dufferin that you . . . would prefer that I should do it if I would consent, and he had no objection; and that he made no objection. As to my declining, the only reference to me in connexion with the duty arrived after you had intimated to two or three of us that you had undertaken the task."[22] Mackenzie, it now seemed, had suppressed a message from Dufferin, and imposed the decision himself.

Meanwhile September passed. On October 1 the National

Club was inaugurated, with Goldwin Smith delivering the keynote speech. "A principle, if it is sound, a sentiment, if it is genuine and strong, will in due time find an organization and if necessary a leader."[23] They were confident words for the devout of Canada First, already pregnant with the hope of the expected coming. It was only two days off, the preparations were made, and even the place appointed seemed to promise a new dawn. At the little town of Aurora, some thirty miles from Toronto, the message of revived liberalism was to be heard from Edward Blake.

When it came it was delivered from the freshly-carpeted platform and amplified by the special sounding-board of Aurora's new drill shed. Nearly three thousand people had come to hear it, assembled from the surrounding countryside by wagon, carriage and horseback and brought by the Toronto train. None of them would be disappointed. Of all Blake's speeches — and whatever its effect or purpose — it would probably be the best remembered. In less than an hour and a half, eloquently, bitingly, even with shafts of humour, he arraigned Canadian politics and the shortcomings of reform. Much of it was well-ploughed ground — the many defects of the Senate, the gaping faults of the franchise, the apathy and corruption still unchecked at elections. Yet beyond this he opened up wider vistas and imposed loftier demands. The citizen's right to vote should be a duty enforced by law. There should be a new measurement of the actual results of voting, a clearer voice for minorities, through proportional representation in the House of Commons. Speaking as "one who preferred to be a private in the advanced guard of the army of freedom", he gave his hearers a glimpse of the road ahead. "We shall have to settle before long the question of the parliamentary system of the future."

Yet there was more than that to be settled, and the main thrust of the speech was directed elsewhere. It was probably a disturbing speech, he told his hearers, but "not much good can be done without disturbing something or somebody." He offered no solutions for the squalid practical difficulties that beset Mackenzie; he hardly deigned to notice them. He was quite unchanged on the question of the Pacific Railway, unmoved and coldly hostile to the terms suggested by Carnarvon. Standing on his old ground, firm in his old principles, he sought for "the cultivation of a national spirit". How was the work to be done? "How are we to effect a real union between these provinces? Can we do it by giving a sop now to one, now to another ... by giving British Columbia the extravagant terms which have been referred to ... do you hope to create or to preserve harmony and good feeling upon such a false and sordid and mercenary basis as that? Not so!"

The Northwest, he agreed, must be joined by rail and water to the central provinces. "I go heart and soul for the construction of these lines as rapidly as the resources of the country will permit." The demands of British Columbia, however, were quite another matter. The old statistics came forth, newly projected; "the insanity of the bargain thrust upon you," "that inhospitable country," "that sea of mountains" were once more excoriated. He had reluctantly agreed to the terms proposed through Edgar, though "those terms, in my opinion went to the extreme verge." They had been rejected; they were not enough. Those greedy ten thousand beside the Pacific, "representing, perhaps, not so many householders as the audience I see before me", were still insistent on more. They should be told plainly that there was now no more to be had. "If these two thousand men" — he seemed to be reducing the Columbians as he went along — "understand that the people of Canada are prepared, in preference to the compliance with their ruinous demands to let them go ... we shall hear no more talk about secession." The cheers of Ontario taxpayers rose about him. "They won't secede," he concluded to applause and laughter, "they know better."

There remained the other question, simmering in his mind since the days of the Washington Treaty, and not diminished by thoughts of Dufferin and Carnarvon. It was to be deter-

A GUESS AT THE GREAT SLEEPER'S VISION.

mined "not now, not this year, not perhaps during the Parliamentary term, but yet at no distant day". The time might be at hand when the people of Canada would be called on to consider their relations to the empire, and their responsibilities in an imperial federation. It would involve new burdens but there must be a bold willingness to assume them as the price of larger rights. "Matters cannot drift much longer as they have drifted hitherto." There could be no more bargaining away of colonial interests, no more making of treaties in which Canadians had "no more voice than the people of Japan." The cares and privileges of maturity could not be left forever with the parent state. "The time will come when that national spirit which has been spoken of will be truly felt among us, when we shall realize that we are four millions of Britons who are not free, when we shall be ready to take up that freedom."[24]

As he sat down he had bequeathed a galaxy of phrases to later history, and the political waters of the present were already beginning to seethe. From the sounding-board at Aurora the speech went forth to fill the columns of the newspapers, to alarm the Governor-General, infuriate British Columbia and trouble Mackenzie's sleep. Canada Firsters seized on it as the tables of the new law. For a few halcyon months, as Goldwin Smith was to remember in his old age, "the guiding star, the hero of the party was Mr. Edward Blake."[25] Yet he was not to be so for long; he moved in his own orbit. As to the real drift of the words, and the real purpose of the speaker, there were as many interpretations as there were commentators, but one fact seemed to be established. "Blake," said the bemused editor of the *Bobcaygeon Independent*, echoing greater colleagues, "must ere long assume the responsibility of guiding the energies and directing the destiny of the Dominion."[26]

༄

George Brown, the practical politician, took a cruder view of affairs. "Blake," he wrote Mackenzie on the Monday following the speech, "is out on the rampage. Look out for squalls!" He dismissed the Aurora program with brief contempt. "A federal Empire — an elective Senate — a fancy franchise . . . compulsory voting — a more stringent election law . . . pleasant little additions to the burden of work which the Reform Govt. already bears!"[27]

The public reaction had to be less emphatic, and the *Globe* for once was careful. Usually the first with a scoop, it waited

SIGNOR BLAKE IN HIS POPULAR ACT OF KEEPING THE *GLOBE* IN
SUSPENSE.

for three days before mentioning the speech at all, and then
dealt with it mildly. Blake after all, it was somehow gratified
to observe, agreed generally with the government in its policy
on the Pacific Railway. The majority in British Columbia, the
Globe was sure, would accept most of his conclusions "though
they may fail to appreciate the frankness." Imperial federation it dismissed as a familiar idea "which appeals to a certain
class of minds" but was not practical. There had been hard

138

words about the Senate and the organ of Senator Brown was duly reproachful, but its general tone in conclusion was that of the admonishing uncle. "Discussions of fancy franchises have doubtless their uses, but in many cases they must be classed rather with the recreation of leisure hours than with the graver efforts and more earnest work of high and practical statesmanship."[28]

With all this the *Mail* was vastly amused. It was reminded of an angry gentleman with a balky horse; he would like to beat it but was afraid of being kicked. It was tempted to even more and livelier pictures. "We can imagine the effort by which the claw is kept sheathed and velvety and the purr is continued when there is fierce impulse to flesh the talons, suck the blood and growl tiger-like over the quivering victim." The time might come, it thought, when the teeth and claws would be used, for in the Aurora speech there was "the foreshadowed exodus of a great body of intelligent men from the Grit organization, led by one of the boldest and bitterest of spirits among them."[29]

There were other auguries of the same by late November. The *Liberal* was being projected as the new Toronto daily that would invade the field of the *Globe*. It was to be largely a Blake enterprise supported by Blake's money, but Goldwin Smith was also to supply a share. Smith obviously would be editor, rumour was sure of that, and the spectre of a third party seemed actually taking flesh. Yet somehow it did not; something was lacking. The ideals of the gentleman journalist might accord with the politician's yet expression must be controlled, timed and guided by circumstance. In January of 1875, when the *Liberal* finally appeared, it was John Cameron, late of the London *Advertiser*, who brought out the first edition. He was an older friend of Blake, more malleable and alive to circumstance. The *Liberal* in its short life, as viewed by its friend the *Mail*, would be "Mr. Blake's special journalistic mouthpiece and trumpeter."[30] But it would not be the great proponent of the views of Canada First.

It was out of tune with the *Globe* but it was not to be heard for long, and the *Globe* chose to ignore it. Within a short three months it could well afford to do so. During that period, while newspaper comment rumbled across the country, a dialogue of politicians had been shaping actual trends. They were still involved and confused, disturbed by the disturbing speech, but there was no discernible tidal wave in the direction of Edward Blake.

Mackenzie had taken nine days to absorb the impact of Aurora and compose a letter to the speaker. When he did write he skirted the speech with perfunctory congratulations and turned to earlier affairs. He went back to the November day when he had taken office, and he was rankled by Blake's hint. It was not at rest, that matter, for either of the two men. "I did not say that I mentioned to you my conversation with Lord Dufferin . . . I meant to recall my conversation with you on our walk." It was at that time, when the two were quite alone, that Mackenzie had offered to step aside for Blake. He had just come from Dufferin, was aware of Dufferin's feelings and "it would have been idle for me to say such a thing unless I had made the way clear for it first, though perhaps I should have said so explicitly." In any case he had certainly suggested Blake to the Governor-General, and would ask Dufferin to confirm the fact if Blake wished him to do so.[31]

Blake did not. Nor, obviously, did he quite believe Mackenzie. He differed blandly and maddeningly over the "unimportant details". But he had not been informed of the conversation with Dufferin; there had been no offer transmitted. Had there been, "it would have been my duty to give such an inquiry from His Excellency, delivered at your instance and supported by your request, grave consideration, to consult some of my leading friends upon it, and to communicate to His Excellency the decision to which I might arrive. It would, I think, be right that he should even now be made aware of the facts."[32]

What facts? What was he really driving at, this man who

was still being trumpeted as the man to replace Mackenzie? Did he want Dufferin to believe that he had been ready the year before, or was it another of the veiled suggestions that he might be ready now? The reply went off on October 15 in Mackenzie's firm script. "I seem to have conveyed the impression that I carried a message from His Excellency and that you were deprived of the opportunity of consulting friends and conveying to him your decision. I was not the bearer of any message or I should assuredly have said so at once." As to the gist of his talk with Dufferin, he conveyed it in flat words. "He briefly discussed our relative positions and suitability for the post and expressed the hope that you would be one of the ministers."[33]

"One of the ministers" — and obviously not the first. It drew an answer in the too-familiar vein. The matter was of no consequence. Blake imputed nothing that could be unfavourable to Mackenzie. "All I wish is that Lord Dufferin should not be under the impression that I was aware that anything had transpired between you relative to me. You can judge whether it is likely that he is under that impression. If so, you can remove it by a word. If not, the word is needless."[34]

Mackenzie threw up his hands and turned to Brown. He had spoken enough with Dufferin on the subject of Blake, especially since Aurora. For the time being he had spoken enough with Blake. "I gather in a general way that he means isolation if not hostility . . . and if he chooses to go into a cave, why I cannot help it."[35]

The Governor-General, never an admirer of Blake, was now actively hostile. Holton had changed, soured by Aurora too. To his mind the attack on British Columbia was worse than useless; Blake knew, as everyone knew, that there would have to be a settlement soon. Imperial federation was a hopeless dream, not worth serious discussion. If voters were to be compelled to vote, Holton suggested acidly in one discussion with Mackenzie, so should lawyer-members who were so often absent from the Commons "even if Courts of Chancery stood in the way."[36] Holton was enlarging a little as Blake diminished in his eyes, and Mackenzie had hopes that he would at last enter the cabinet. The cabinet itself, faced with British Columbia and the nagging problem of Riel, seemed less inclined to a change of Prime Ministers. Blake, rather than Mackenzie, was being edged toward isolation.

Through November and December government went on without him, always nervously aware of him and often leaning on his help. He offered advice when asked for, but events seldom conformed. It was Dufferin and Mackenzie, rather than Blake and Mackenzie, who evolved a plan of amnesty for the rebels of the Northwest. It would not include Riel, but it would remove Riel from politics by consigning him to five years banishment and perhaps ultimate oblivion. Mackenzie turned from Blake, again with Dufferin's urgings, to accept Carnarvon's views on British Columbia. A Nanaimo–Esquimalt railway bill was to be presented when the House met and an edgy but loyal ministry was determined to force its passage. By the end of the year, in Dufferin's view, that issue was settled. He was also in better heart, he wrote Carnarvon, as to Blake's speech at Aurora. "The greater portion of what he said has fallen extremely flat."[37]

∽

The second session of the third parliament convened on February 4, 1875. Eleven days later it had settled one of its problems. Blake joined with Mackenzie, and was duly opposed by Macdonald, in supporting the Northwest amnesty and the banishment of Louis Riel. The former Premier of Ontario was as much concerned as anyone in justifying his own position, and he had not much more success. All speeches were long, all old arguments revived, and all knew what the result would have to be. There was only glum relief when the measure passed. Riel seemed to be disposed of.

The next great item of business was the establishment of a Supreme Court. It had been a favourite project of Macdonald and it had always been supported by Blake, but there were old difficulties still standing in the way. There was Quebec's civil law, differing from the English law, which would be subordinate in jurisdiction to the decision of a Supreme Court. There were Quebec's fears that the proportion of English judges and their habits of legal thinking might tend to over-balance the French minority. In addition to these there was a new difficulty arising as the bill went on. What should be the Court's relation to imperial judicial authority? Should the Supreme Court be supreme, the last resort in law, or should there still be the old recourse to the Privy Council?

In the late stages of the debate Aemilius Irving rose, a barrister and a back-bench Liberal sitting for Hamilton. He had a lawyer's taste for talk, some familiar legal humour, and the idea of the court displeased him. What, after all, would it do? How many cases would it hear? He could not imagine "a more dismal spectacle than would be offered by six melancholy men living in this city endeavouring to catch an appeal case, which, but for this Act, would have gone to England. They would become rusty and relapse perhaps into a state of barbarism."[38] In any case, to Irving's mind, it had been a very dreary session, particularly for the back-benchers, and he proposed to liven things by moving an amendment. His first attempt was lost but there was a second a day later, fiercely opposed by Macdonald as a severing of imperial ties. The Court's judgments should be final by the terms of Irving's amendment, "saving any right which Her Majesty may be graciously pleased to exercise as her royal prerogative."[39]

Lurking in those words was the almost unanswerable question of the bounds of the royal prerogative. Actually they were empty words, for the Privy Council spoke with the sovereign's voice, in exercise of the prerogative. Yet the Hamilton lawyer's amendment, accepted by the Canadian parliament, took its due place as part of Clause 47 and the Supreme Court Bill was passed. As a constitutional instrument it rivalled in importance the position of parliament itself, and in that one amendment there was the seed of an imperial quarrel. It had been partly sown by the sentiments voiced at Aurora. Yet through all the long debate, and even through Irving's antics, there had been no complaint from Blake. The man who was now recognized as the greatest lawyer in Canada, and who would be of all men the most suitable as Chief Justice of the Court, had sat without saying a word.

The Ides of March came in, and the House quickened with expectancy. Mackenzie was now girding himself in the face of a potential Brutus. On March 19 he brought down the bill for the Nanaimo–Esquimalt railway, with Blake still adamantly opposed. Through another ten days, as it lay on the order paper, the linked problems of Blake and British Columbia became a party obsession. Dufferin's judgment had been right so far as it went; Mackenzie's ministers intended to pass the bill. But they could not move Blake, they could see no way to ignore him, and they could hardly imagine a government without that massive presence.

Yet it began to come to that. The search for an accommodation had been carrying on for months. In the Liberal caucus and cabinet the go-betweens were tiring. Holton, shuttling wearily between the Prime Minister and the recalcitrant, had almost had enough. A. G. Jones, the trusted friend of Mackenzie and the party's leader in the Maritimes, was equally the friend of Blake. He came to him and came again, was always courteously listened to, and invariably reported failure. Clear, intricately logical, pained, and faintly resentful, Blake's answers remained the same. There could be no entering the cabinet; the time had passed for that, though there might have been a time once if Mackenzie had made the request. Mackenzie had not made it, or not at the proper time, or not in acceptable form, and there was now the question of the railway. On that there could be no change; it would be a "public shame" for Blake.[40] As his ministers and confidants wearied Mackenzie himself gave up. In the cabinet and corridors of parliament there began to be other talk. The new Supreme Court would be requiring a

144

Chief Justice; perhaps the obstacle in parliament could be elevated out of the way.

It had not been done by the night of March 29, when the Nanaimo—Esquimalt railway bill came up for its second reading. Instead there had been shifts in the wind, vaguely promising. In his first reaction to the cooling mood about him Blake had been quite in character. "I have only to say, as I said in 1873," he wrote Jones, "that if the government thinks the step will lessen their difficulties I will cease attending parliament."[41] Yet in three days, not without help from Jones, the act of abnegation had been recalled. "You have so forcibly put before me the responsibility under which you think I labour," he wrote, "that I believe I must accede to your proposal . . . if all the world differs from me I must be wrong." Through the rare meekness, surrounded by intricate phrasing, the shape of an offer appeared. Without specifying terms or defining his prospective status, Blake seemed resigned to inducement into the cabinet. "I may be, and I confess I am, unable to announce myself," but he supplied Jones with a list of seventeen friends, all leaders in the party, who might be inclined to draft him.[42]

There had been no draft, however, as the crucial hour for the crucial bill arrived. Blake rose, following Mackenzie's argument, and was instantly tearing it down. He had returned with a new asperity to all his old positions. There was no need for a railway on Vancouver Island; it would be a waste and more than a waste of federal funds. It was meant to buy peace, it was part of a bargain offered to British Columbia, not by the Canadian parliament but "through the medium of the Colonial Secretary."[43] More than that, if the railway were once ratified, so would be the other terms. He could not approve the terms, he could not justify the railway, and he would not assent to the bill.

The view of the House was otherwise when the division bells rang. Blake stood, voting with Macdonald and Tupper among a minority of sixty-four. He was newly divided from Mackenzie and over-ruled by the party, the obstacle pushed aside. Yet there remained the other obstacle, more potent even than

Blake. The bill passed to the upper House and came to an abrupt stop. Richard W. Scott, the old friend and colleague, was not only a cabinet minister but Liberal leader in the Senate. He had dutifully proposed assent to the bill but duty was not enthusiasm and he had not persuaded his peers. "I observe," Blake wrote to Mackenzie on April 5, "that the Vancouver Railway Bill is lost in the Senate."[44]

స్

The game was again at stalemate, but Mackenzie was now prepared. Government had to go on, and he had hardened himself to govern. Even while the Senate deliberated he had made that plain to Blake. There was going to be a settlement made that would quiet British Columbia. It would be better with Blake's concurrence, but it would still be made without him. If politics were a dead end, the office of Chief Justice was at Blake's disposal. If not, the cabinet was open to him if they could agree on a railway plan. Mackenzie would discuss revisions and consider any arrangement; the object was peace with the westerners and it should be made with Blake's help. If that were not to be had, then he had done the best he could. "I will put off my coat and drive the machine myself."[45]

For nearly a month more there was a passing of letters and emissaries with ever-renewed frustration. "He no doubt believes the railway difficulty is the sole obstacle," Holton reported to Mackenzie after one of his talks with Blake, "because he is incapable of dissimulation or intrigue, but his idiosyncrasies are so peculiar that one cannot help going behind his avowed motives in search of the real springs of action."[46] They lay deep, amid the old broodings and the growing train of new regrets and resentments. Blake was not Prime Minister; he had offered to repair the mistake of his first decision and the offer had been declined. He could now be Chief Justice. William Hume Blake had left politics for the bench, and had hoped the same for his son. Yet he had feared the move too, for he had been savagely criticized himself and that might happen again. It was a change hardly to be thought of, at least at the present

time; there was the law firm and the income that would be far
too drastically reduced. Sam Blake was against it, the family
were all against it, and in any case it would have seemed a
defeat. Yet it would be worse still, unbearable now, to be out
of politics with nothing.

On April 30 the letter went off to Mackenzie, dilating for
eight pages on the subject of British Columbia. Blake was
prepared now "in no dogmatic or controversial spirit" to consider revised proposals.[47] He even offered suggestions. They
were vague, qualified and involved, but they were sign enough
for Mackenzie. "I come to the general conclusion," he replied
on May 5, "that we can find a ground of common agreement."[48]

On the same day the *Liberal*, which had been ailing for several months and was bound for an early demise, came out with
an important announcement. The Honourable Edward Blake
had been offered the Chief Justiceship of the Supreme Court.
That much being publicized, the editor hoped he would decline
"in order to sustain with his abilities the Liberal cause."[49] The
hint of what was coming meant dismay for Goldwin Smith, and
was equally disconcerting to the Governor-General. Blake
would be no asset, Dufferin warned Mackenzie. He would act
the traitor from within the cabinet as he had done on the outside.[50] On the 18th, however, Blake and Mackenzie met.

The result, Blake wrote that evening, "is that I agree to join
your government." He had held much of his ground; he had in
fact outlined the settlement that would ultimately have to be
made. "The government shall renegotiate with Columbia for
the payment of a cash subsidy in lieu of the agreement to con-
struct the Vancouver railway." There was to be no more interference on the part of Carnarvon or Dufferin, and no provision
in any agreement could be allowed to increase taxation. The
autonomy of the federal government, moreover, was once more
flatly affirmed. "It is understood that in case British Columbia
or England should raise any difficulty as to these provisions,
the government will notwithstanding proceed to carry them out
in good faith."[51]

On May 19 Blake took the oath of office as Minister of Justice. A day later, exhausted and grateful for release, Mackenzie left for England. He would return as he went, however, the Prime Minister of Canada, with Edward Blake confirmed in subordination. The decision of the November day, now receding eighteen months in the past, had a new air of finality.

MR. DAVENPORT BLAKE IS PUT INTO THE CABINET.

CHAPTER EIGHT

MACKENZIE'S MINISTER

O N JUNE 3 at Walkerton, during the by-election to confirm his cabinet appointment, a new Blake revealed himself to the electors. He still held to the views expressed at Aurora, but they were tempered now with a film of patience and discretion. Imperial federation was remitted to the long future, and he had only thought of it in any case as a strengthening of the imperial tie. For other domestic changes he had resigned himself to wait. Reformers must still reform, Liberals must still liberalize, but Blake would work with Mackenzie and presumably at Mackenzie's pace. He approved of the establishment of the new Supreme Court, and particularly of its independence in relation to imperial authority. There had been a meeting of minds on the question of the Pacific Railway and a new course was to be set, though it could not be announced now. Time, said the responsible minister, must be allowed to ripen policy, while the general principles of liberalism would govern his own conduct.

There was certainly nothing this time in the way of a disturbing speech, and the *Globe* was warm with its approval. Blake had shown, it commented, "how conscious he is of the personal limitations implied by the nature of constitutional government" and it congratulated him on his ability to "sink the doctrinaire in the public servant."[1] In other newspapers, however, the general tone ranged downward toward the flat verdict of the *Mail*. It could hardly believe, said that organ, that the "muzzled utterance" at Walkerton had come from the man of Aurora. "The Disturber" had descended from his pedestal to become "a joint in Mackenzie's tail, nothing more, nothing less."[2]

George Brown, privately, was more in agreement with the *Mail* than with his own newspaper. By July he was speaking complacently of the "Blake capture" which was having the effect hoped for. "His 'friends'," he wrote to Mackenzie who was still in England, "seem to have collapsed in surprising manner."[3] The *Liberal* was by then deceased, John Cameron, its editor, was reported to be in bankruptcy, and was trying to sell the type and presses to the *Globe*. Canada First was dying, Goldwin Smith was beginning to cool toward Blake, and even Holton was more enemy than friend. Still outside the ministry, he was not being pressed to join it, and he saw Blake's hand in that. The formidable "Blake faction" which had worried caucus and cabinet was now subsiding with its acquiescent leader. The Minister of Justice, settling into his office, seemed settling lower on the horizon as one of the party's problems.

He was also, at least for the moment, fulfilling its best hopes. With the political by-play ended, the abilities of the man came out and the difficulties fell away. Power and its responsibilities appeared to transform Blake, and his own powers transformed those around him. Clear, logical, direct, considerate, and incorruptible, he was a rock of assured strength in the shaky cabinet. For a few weeks, with his old total intensity, he bent himself to an immediate, specific problem. It was to comb the Canadian judiciary for its best available talent, secure the men he needed and reorganize for their replacement. When Mackenzie came back in August the work was largely done. Blake had selected his judges, secured the assent of most of them, and was ready for the inauguration of the Supreme Court of Canada.

Yet politics returned inevitably with the Prime Minister, and it was imperial politics first. The legal basis for the Court was still lacking, since the bill passed by parliament was in danger of disallowance. That Clause 47, evolved by colonials and touching the royal prerogative, had reared its ambiguous head. What was it supposed to mean? Did it mean anything at all? It raised hackles in the Colonial Office as an offensive gesture directed toward independence. To the law officers of the Crown it was redundant and ineffective. It purported to abolish appeals to a British court, yet the only court that could hear them was that of the Privy Council. The judicial committee of the Council, said Lord Cairns, the Lord Chancellor, was itself a prerogative court. Its rights were expressly retained — quite unnecessarily asserted — by the very clause in dispute. The Canadian parliament had limited appeals from the Supreme Court "saving any right which Her Majesty may be graciously pleased to exercise as her royal prerogative." In effect it had limited nothing and its words should be struck from the bill. They were mere "waste paper."

Blake was faced, after months of negotiation, with the collapse of his first achievement. Worse still, in the deep recesses of his mind, there was an embryonic suspicion that Lord Cairns' view was correct. Clause 47 had not been written by Blake but neither had Blake opposed it. He had to support it now for every reason. He was in full sympathy with its intent, if not convinced of its effect, and the Canadian government was committed. The bill could not be amended and neither could it be withdrawn; the imperial authorities had once more to be opposed. On that point he was soon firmer than Mackenzie, and the man in charge of the battle. He fought it throughout September with all his lawyer's skill, and with rather more than a hint of returning rancour. On the 23rd came his first threat to resign. It was followed a week later by suave withdrawal in London. The bill, Carnarvon cabled, was now considered acceptable except for Clause 47. This would be studied further and be subject to later amendment. The Court, however, in the meantime, might come into operation.

It was less a victory than a promise of future trouble, but the

Supreme Court was established. There were other problems now. By late September a new offer for the Columbians had been hammered out, and it was built on Blake's terms. There was to be no federal support for a Nanaimo–Esquimalt railway. Compensation to the province would be in the form of a cash bonus of $750,000 "for any delays which may take place in the construction of the Pacific Railway." "Any agreements as to yearly expenditure and as to completion by a fixed time must be subject to the conditions thrice recorded in the journals of Parliament, that no further increase of the rate of taxation be required in order to their fulfilment."[4] Not only the glaring reductions but the subtle changes in the offer would be certain to provoke an uproar. Compensation was no longer for past delays; it was for "any delays which *may* take place" in the building of the entire railway. Carnarvon's proposals of a time limit and of an annual rate of expenditure were in effect wiped out; they would not be met if it involved increased taxation.

Carnarvon and Dufferin were indignant and there was certain to be a fight in parliament. On both fronts Blake would be the principal target. He was detested by British Columbia, disliked by the Governor-General and already viewed with suspicion by the Colonial Secretary. He was drawn in as a cabinet minister on the seething troubles in Quebec. In that province, where Conservatism was in the ascendant and Ultramontane Catholics were the most conservative faction in the Church, there hardly seemed to be a Liberal party left. The *rouge* was equated by bishops, and firmly linked by the *bleus*, with the liberal Catholic heretics who were attacking the Church in Europe. Preached against from the pulpit and often damned in the confessional, Liberalism faced the threat of religious war. The spectre of a Catholic party was creating the spectre of a Protestant party, with English Liberals dominating it and Ontario soon drawn in. There were still men like Dorion seeking to avert disaster, but Dorion was now on the bench. The younger men who had followed him were as yet untried and raw, or worse than that they were old, corrupt, embittered.

There were French Canadians in the Liberal cabinet at Ottawa but they were almost rootless men, with their influence fading at home as they diminished under Mackenzie, the old Grit, the Upper Canadian Baptist.

Blake was as helpless in the face of it all as any of the English ministers. He was forced to accept as colleague the begrimed Joseph Cauchon, onetime *bleu* of Quebec, who was supposed to have influence with some of the milder bishops. He was compelled to agree with Mackenzie in postponing the entry to the cabinet of the promising young Laurier, because Laurier was marked as an anti-clerical *rouge*. He was often besought by Huntington and constantly beset by Holton, who were feuding as rival leaders of the distracted English in Quebec. All this could be endured as part of the trials of office, and much of it had been foreseen. There was one last drop of gall, however, distilled by the hands of journalists, that overfilled the cup. Blake as a cabinet minister with less time for his practice had reduced his share in the future profits of his law firm by more than the salary he received as Minister of Justice. Yet he was now being assailed in some of the hostile newspapers for appearing in court at all.

"I may say," he wrote Mackenzie in his first indignant surprise, "that if a lawyer who has spent the best part of his life in building up a valuable business and connexion is on taking office 'to step down and out' leaving his position to be filled by others, it is obvious that few such lawyers will take office, and it is equally obvious that those men who do are likely to become men dependent on their places for their living."[5] Yet the criticism cut to the bone because there was a shred of reason in it. When the Minister of Justice appeared before a judge the relationship became ambiguous. The pleader controlled the appointment of the man sitting on the bench and might potentially influence promotion. To Mackenzie it was no argument and he simply brushed it aside, for once openly impatient with his minister's scruples. Blake should take no notice of a ranting and malicious press. "I assure you it appears to me a most

THE POLITICAL SAMSON GRINDING FOR THE PHILISTINES.

extraordinary gratification of a morbidly sensitive disposition
. . . I would hold your personal and professional honour as
dear as my own."[6]

Yet he had not reassured Blake when the *Globe* came into the
controversy, and with that heavy hand the fat was spilled in the
fire. The country, proposed the *Globe*, should compensate the
Minister of Justice for his great professional sacrifice by paying him a larger salary. In effect, Blake wrote, he was to be

"bought off from practice",[7] and he had only one reply to such a proposal. He would not appear in court while Minister of Justice, and he had also decided "not to draw in future the salary assigned by law to my office."[8] It took four days of pleading by Mackenzie, Holton, Jones, and most of the cabinet to move him at last to a partially revised decision. He still refused to make any appearance at the bar, but he would continue to accept his stipend.

In the meantime Clause 47 was occupying the imperial mind, and Blake was much with Dufferin as the official channel to Carnarvon. As the talks went on and the cables and letters crossed and recrossed the Atlantic, the Minister grew wearily familiar with the man in Government House. That tall, flamboyant Irishman with the magnificent bearded profile and the ever-flowing eloquence was a high imperial adventurer who hoped for much from his Queen. There was India beyond Canada, and he would yet be Viceroy there. In the meantime he served, or preferred to say that he "reigned", alight with the work of empire building and determined to be its guide. He had all the qualities that froze Blake in his shell. He was Governor-General and a great peer of the realm; his position demanded respect. He had a quick, light grasp of the surface of any problem and was difficult to argue down. For all his social graces he had the imperial administrator's view of colonial statesmen, and was at too much pains to hide it. Blake could not be patronized and he saw through all pretence. He had not forgotten a word, nor given an inch of ground, in relation to their old disputes. He came to the presence disliked, he expected to remain disliked, and he presented his case for the most part with cold, punctilious reserve.

Yet there was Galway blood in his veins and he was not to be curbed forever, even by an imperial official waving an imperial despatch. There were times when he broke out, when they were two Irishmen together, and at such times Dufferin listened with some of his ebullience quelled. There was more than the Court involved in those discussions; there was the whole question of the relationship between Dominion and Home governments. Yet Blake's ideal of autonomy was embedded deep in his Britishness, and the two were at work together. The man might well be dangerous, he was obviously racked by his own obscure resentments, but he was not bent on breaking away from the empire.

Dufferin had many failings, but he was neither mean nor a fool. Without any sign of affection he grew to be impressed by Blake, and he impressed his views on Carnarvon. Carnarvon himself grew curious about "that very crooked-tempered Cerberus"[9] and intrigued by the hope of a conversion. On the subject of Clause 47 he had long memoranda from Blake, mounds of despatches from Dufferin, and still no ray of light. "I will not deny," came his letter early in November, "that it would personally give me much pleasure to confer with Mr. Blake not only on this but on many other questions in which we are all closely concerned."[10]

Dufferin was delighted with the suggestion and immediately conveyed it to Blake. "It is a most happy thought, your having Blake over," he replied to Carnarvon on November 19. "He is in very good humour and spirits."[11] If he was, they changed overnight. He had decided, Blake wrote to Mackenzie in the course of the next day, that a trip to England would be useless. "No reasonable expectation presents itself to me of changing by personal conference any opinions which high legal dignitaries may have formed and which they themselves have the power to enforce."[12]

The words were aggrieved and unpromising, and they hinted at doubts of his case. He was swamped with work in his ministry and there was a session of Parliament ahead. Yet Mackenzie pressed him to go, the affair of the Court was urgent, and Blake himself was oppressed by other urgencies. Imperial meddling in the imbroglio with British Columbia was only one of a train of interferences. To the Governor-General's older sins he was steadily adding new. He operated like all his predecessors under a set of formal instructions which were vague in defining his powers, and wherever a loophole opened Dufferin seemed to thrust out. In his own regal view he had the power of disallowance over Acts of the provincial legislatures. He claimed the prerogative of pardon, without the advice of his ministers, in the case of capital crimes. He had an itch now, in the case of the Supreme Court, to decide himself as to which appeals from its verdicts might be eligible to be heard in England. Dufferin had to be curbed and his limitations to be clarified; the Governor-General's instructions required revision. So did the procedures governing extradition, where slipshod treaties made by imperial authorities were hampering Canadian justice. On all this Blake and the Colonial Secretary had exchanged voluminous letters, but settlement called for discussion face-to-face. The great advocate must be heard at the seat of power, and Mackenzie at least had high hopes for the result. They were not shared by Blake in the depths of a December depression but at last, moodily, he agreed.

He would stay in Canada till the close of the present parliament, dispose of his most urgent work, and leave probably in May. Carnarvon would have to wait, but at least he would see his man. To Dufferin, who was now Blake's sponsor, the decision came in the way of a minor triumph. He was as optimistic as Mackenzie, though in a somewhat different vein. Blake, he confided hopefully to his friend in the Colonial Office, was "well worth being educated into a more generous and genial frame of mind," and the official meetings, accompanied as he knew they would be by appropriate hospitality, "will send him back to us in a better temper with England."[13]

෴

May came and passed, and there was still no hurrying Blake. He did not embark on "my unpleasant errand"[14] until June 3, 1876, and the prospect left behind him was as bleak as the one ahead. Parliament had begun its third session in February with a dreary Speech from the Throne directed to a depressed country. Neither politically nor economically had anything im-

157

proved since. *Rouges* and Ultramontanes were still at war in Quebec, Maritime free traders were dividing from Ontario Liberals on the question of a protective tariff, and British Columbia had refused the latest terms. While survey work went on, emptying the treasury by itself, the actual building of the railway seemed more remote than ever.

If there was a crumb of comfort when the session ended in April, it came from the chastened attitude of Macdonald's Tories. Only ten of them had dared vote against a resolution asserting for the fourth time that no expenditure on the railway could be allowed to increase taxation. The magniloquent bargain of the past was being all too gladly forgotten. Most Conservatives had swung round with the Liberals in the face of hard times, and were even muttering vaguely of the "extravagance" of the latest offers. The parties seemed tacitly united in an agreement to stand still.

Yet against this was Dufferin, alight with a new proposal. He had secured Carnarvon's support for a visit to British Columbia, which he intended to begin in August. "I think," he had written to Carnarvon in his first flush of enthusiasm, "if I were to appear upon the scene in the double capacity of your delegate, and also as the representative of the Dominion, I might manage to make an amicable arrangement about the Nanaimo Railway and perhaps all other matters."[15] From that spacious intention he had been steadily whittled down, not without acrid debate. The Prime Minister, once bitten by imperial intervention, was having none of it again. Cartwright joined the discussions as a worried Minister of Finance, to whom the thought of "amicable arrangements" was suggestive of new concessions. To Dufferin, however, it was Blake, the ominous and dominant figure, who summed up all hostilities and eventually imposed restrictions. The Governor-General's progress was to be something less than planned. He would not be empowered to decide for a Canadian government, still less to discuss or arrange for concessions to British Columbia. He would go if he went at all, and it was devoutly hoped he would not, merely as observer and reporter with an officially closed mouth.

He was still going, and he was still resentful, as Blake departed for England. He had had, he reported to Carnarvon, "a long and very disagreeable discussion"[16] on the subject of his own mission, and some of the purposes of Blake's mission he considered highly suspect. On the matter of the Supreme Court Dufferin was neutral; he did not, in fact, consider it very important. In the proposal, however, to restrict his own powers he detected "an irritable desire to limit and curtail Imperial authority and influence over the domestic affairs of the colony."[17] Carnarvon should not be misled by Blake's gentlemanly manners "for the pot boils over without giving any warning . . . In the first place he is a lawyer and in the next place he has the Celtic craving for logical symmetry, which is such a stumbling block in France."[18] Yet, Dufferin added, with his own touch of Celtic generosity, "I do not wish unduly to depreciate him . . . he is imperious and ambitious, but with his ambition there is mingled a genuine strain of pure, patriotic passion."[19]

Preceded by this analysis and accompanied by some of his family, Blake arrived in London and established himself at 19 North Audley Street. With Margaret came their daughter, Sophia, who was a personable fifteen, and Sam, the youngest son, who was now eight. There would not be the usual summer at Murray Bay and, except perhaps for the children, London was a poor exchange. Margaret Blake would at least see more of her husband for he would be all too much at home. But she would also be required to endure, accompany and sustain him through festivities and negotiations and periods of waiting and suspense to which his most frequently applied description was "intolerable."

He had arrived at his own convenience rather than that of his hosts, and the man sought in November was less desired in June. The session of the British House was dragging on through the summer, the government's program was far behind schedule, and it was much involved with imperial foreign affairs. "Everyone," wrote Carnarvon to Dufferin, "is far too hot and cross at being kept in London to find a good word for their neighbour."[20] Even Carnarvon's grammar was suffering from haste and distraction, and it was all too obvious to the visitor that he was one of a host of problems.

The memoranda and documents on the various subjects of his mission had all been sent ahead of him and had all presumably been studied. On June 16, when he presented himself at the Colonial Office, he was gracefully welcomed by Carnarvon and invited to dine that evening. But "we did not talk business."[21] He was passed on almost immediately to R. G. W. Herbert, the permanent under-secretary, and it was ten days before Carnarvon could find an hour for official discussion. The next day there was an allotment of forty-five minutes and a week later, for the crucial interview with Lord Cairns, the Lord Chancellor, he was granted an hour and a half. There were meetings arranged with other ministers and officials, but by that time the pattern of the visit was established.

Blake, the colonial supplicant, would talk, propose, and go home to await decision. For everything he could say with one eye on the clock there was a careful and friendly auditor. There were endless requests for supplementary drafts, for revisions of his memoranda and suggestions as to new bills. In the lodgings at North Audley Street there was a drift of invitations from imposing names. He was received by intelligent men absorbed in imperial affairs, but only as part of a long official parade. He was to be fittingly entertained, he would wait and write in the intervals, and he remained the outsider from Canada on the fringe of great concerns.

Everything pivoted on Henry Howard Molyneaux Herbert, fourth Earl of Carnarvon. The Colonial Secretary was neither a novice in office nor a stranger to Canadian affairs. He had been a powerful supporter in England of the plans for Confederation, and the presiding figure in London during the work of framing the Act. It was Carnarvon who had introduced the

British North America Bill in the House of Lords and piloted it with skill and firmness through a largely indifferent parliament. For all that he was not impressive to meet. In contrast to the lordly Dufferin he was small, clerk-like and diffident-seeming. Known as "Twitters" to Disraeli, his Prime Minister, he was overwhelmed with cabinet business and inclined, as it seemed to the visitor, to use the charming Herbert as a protective buffer. One saw too little of Carnarvon, too much of Herbert and the anteroom, and altogether too much of dinings-out.

The great houses were open enough, and the great names generously provided. The Harcourts, the Hollands, Trollope and Froude the historian were all at table with Blake. He dined at the Duke of Marlborough's and "struck up a friendship with their son, Lord Randolph Churchill . . . he is quite a young fellow."[22] He was anxious for the family to meet Churchill, who was planning to visit Canada. There was an invitation for the Blakes to the Queen's Ball, but the statesman developed a headache — "I could not stomach the dress."[23] Among many "swells" at another dinner he took down the daughter of Lord Adderley, "the Vice-President of the Board of Trade and a donkey. The latter appellation he will not lose even if he loses his office."[24] He was intrigued by Lady Elgin, "so shy that she always wanted to come into a room backwards",[25] and by stories of Lady Holland who was so terrified of thunderstorms that she hid from them in closets, and was said during the course of one storm to have dressed her maid in her own clothes "in order to deceive Mr. Thunderbolt."[26] He dined with Henry James, of whom he had nothing to say, and one midnight after hours of conversation with John Bright "I walked with him to his lodgings. He was the man I most wanted to meet in England."[27]

There were few such meetings, however, and neither the splendours of the great houses nor the eccentricities of their owners could rouse him to much enthusiasm. There was an ever-present tincture of colonial envy. "The more I see of life here, the more convinced I am that save for the very rich men

and bachelors it is no place ... I always feel that English-
men think themselves, though they do not say so, the superiors
of *Colonists*, and I don't like it."[28]

The explosions in letters home began early. "I might as well
have been sight-seeing and gadding about!"[29] he confided to
R. W. Scott on June 28. "My bulletin will show you how frightfully slow the progress is," he commented glumly to Mackenzie after an interval of two weeks. "I have kept myself
absolutely disengaged and indoors all the time so as to be
ready at any moment at which our Lords and Masters can find
that they have half an hour to consider the affairs of their
servants."[30] Brooding, writing, and resenting through the fretful days in his study, he had time to spare for dutiful reports
to his mother. They were for the most part of the socializing,
and Catherine Blake as usual was thrilled and moralistic.
"I advise you to answer *at once*, and in the affirmative, any
invitation which appears to be a duty ... I go step by step with
you in all your meetings with the great of the earth."[31] To the
son, however, worn down and irritable from most of his meetings with the great, the writing of his "Court Journal" was an
exercise in heavy irony. "For me, who you know have no small
talk at my disposal ... these affairs are *intolerable*."[32]

He was more than usual with Margaret and the two children
and more involved in their concerns, but there was irony even
in that. The Canadian statesman, in the intervals between writing drafts, supplementing memoranda and awaiting the next
summons, was often to be found with his womenfolk debating
in London shops. "We were yesterday on the look for Versy's
Turkey carpet, but have not finished our search . . . We have
devised a plan for utilizing the fancy stuffs . . . the extra velvet
and half the fur is to be made into a mantle or jacket for Margaret, and the remainder of the fur is to trim a silk one for
Sophia . . . I indulged myself in buying two bracelets for
Margaret . . . for myself I have to buy studs, plain gold, cheap
and neat and inconspicuous." His new clothes, he reported, "fit
very well, I think, at least for me, on whom you know nothing
fits like a glove."[33]

It was another of the Court Journals, compiled on July 26, "after a week or ten days absolute inaction".[34] He had met members of the government concerned with his various affairs, but everything was standing still. He had forced himself, against all of his inclinations, to an uninvited call at the Colonial Office, and had been turned away with promises. Herbert, the charming evasionist, was now "Herbert the Poke",[35] master of all delay. "I am fighting with one arm tied behind my back," Blake wrote to Mackenzie, "and I hope never again to go through this experience. Our whole relations to the Home Authorities are such as to render the negotiations intolerable to me. With every desire to oblige and to do what is right according to their lights, *they have no light!*"[36]

The comment reached Carnarvon by way of Dufferin, to whom Mackenzie rather informally had transmitted Blake's reports. It changed nothing in the bland, official manner, and wheels continued to turn at their own pace. Yet by mid-August, when Blake came down for a stay at Highclere Castle, the Carnarvon family home, there had been a series of other meetings and a considerable change in mood. He was charmed by the Carnarvon children, impressed by the great estate, and had even a reserved warmth for the Colonial Secretary. He had made such progress is his business, he wrote Catherine, that he would soon be able to leave. "I can't say that it is satisfactorily adjusted, for I have not been given the opportunity of talking over some things which want discussion; but on the surface it looks well and a good deal has unquestionably been done."[37]

With that Carnarvon agreed, and in the high ranks of officialdom there was a new opinion of Blake. It hardly approached liking, but it certainly involved respect. The colonial was less the trouble-maker than the exposer of potential trouble, which he obviously hoped to avoid. He was thin-skinned, subtle, elusive, and no man living could follow him in all his arguments; there simply was not time. But he had come to London with a batch of difficult problems, and for some at least he had brought acceptable solutions.

In the matter of the Supreme Court he had agreed largely

with Cairns on the emptiness of Clause 47. They had enjoyed the debate as lawyers, dissected each other's briefs, and Blake had opened the judicial mind to the larger political question. Empty or not, the clause was part of a bill, passed by a Canadian parliament which was not prepared to amend it. A dispute now might reopen deeper questions of Canadian autonomy, which Blake at least was prepared to reserve for the future. It would certainly embarrass the government and the Minister of Justice, and they hoped to be spared that. The bill, Blake ventured to suggest, should be allowed with the clause intact, and the limitation of all appeals be discussed in confidence later. That was now to be done. Privately, the imperial government would request a further study of the regulation of appeals. Publicly, it would allow the bill.

It would also alter the Governor-General's instructions, in accord with Blake's ideas. He had won on that, he had largely solved the question of extradition, and on a number of lesser matters he had opened the imperial mind. His voluminous memoranda, his always curtailed discussions, and his weeks of weary waiting had accomplished much. Yet it was perhaps on the greater question, still overhanging everything and totally unresolved, that his best work had been done.

He had been ushered into Carnarvon on June 30 for a short and wary discussion of the Pacific Railway. The talk had gone on longer and within a wider frame of reference than Carnarvon had first intended. On that day the young Dominion was completing its ninth year, and to the representative of a government with "no light" Blake had imparted the light as he saw it. Confederation, he said, was conceived by many of its critics to have been premature. He was not himself convinced of that but there were some grounds for the view, and the first was the lack of a real desire for unity. Ontario and Quebec, as Upper and Lower Canada, had already been bound together and fiercely quarrelling. Confederation for them had been a divorce rather than a union. New Brunswick had joined from fright, Nova Scotia through coercion, while not only the North-

West Territories but British Columbia and Prince Edward Island too had simply been bought. The demands for "better terms", the thirst for provincial grants from the federal treasury and the promise of the Pacific Railway had all risen from that. Money was to surmount geography, but it promised no real union.

What it promised instead was an already imminent revolt in the central provinces. It was Ontario and Quebec, the settled revenue-producers, who had contributed most of the taxes to fulfill Macdonald's arrangements. They had paid the shot for the acquisition of territory, while their own needs for development had been simply brushed aside. They were awake to that now, particularly in hard times, and the disproportion in expenditure was the greatest problem of the country.

Upon all this came the demand to build a railway through to the Pacific. It threatened to push imbalance to the verge of national disruption. Even for the work of survey, revenues needed in the east were being spent in the west, and they were being spent wastefully and recklessly because of the cry for haste. Survey work would be completed, probably by the end of the year, but it would only lead to another and greater problem. The government would be faced with the actual work of construction, and how was that to be done?

It would search for private builders and private capital, but the times were such that it would probably find neither. Nor would it dare use more than a dribble of public funds. The east had given too much and it would certainly give no more. It would not increase taxes at the risk of national solvency, nor would it longer forego its own development to placate British Columbia. For years yet, this promise to defy geography would be the greatest of the threats to unity, and there was no sane man in politics who would attempt to force it on. Macdonald's mad bargain had been forgotten; it would not be revived by any Conservative party. Later and lesser offers had been rejected by British Columbia and even the least was hardly possible now. All that remained was reasonable, rational progress, in the light of present conditions and in line with the country's needs. It would be slow, certainly, and much of it must be in the east, where the country's revenues were generated and the strength for future expansion could be built on a firm base. It would certainly not be enough to satisfy the Columbians, but that would have to be endured. They would complain, perhaps for years, but they would find that their own interests forbade their leaving the union. They would remain in the Confederation, they would grow along with Canada, and the government would set the pace.[38]

Carnarvon had listened to it all, impressed and thoughtful. He had had a part himself, after all, in the making of this nine-year-old Dominion. "We are laying the foundations of a great state," he had told the House of Lords, "perhaps one which at a future date may even overshadow this country. But come what may, we shall rejoice that we have shown neither indifference to their wishes nor jealousy of their aspirations, but that we honestly and sincerely, to the utmost of our power and knowledge, fostered their growth, recognizing in it the condition of our own greatness."[39] They were good words and he had meant them; he was a conscientious official. They imposed a responsibility; they involved listening to Blake, even remeasuring Blake. It seemed now, perhaps, that the trans-Atlantic analyses so carefully compiled by Dufferin had exhausted neither the railway question nor the potential of this man.

Toward the end Carnarvon had demurred a little on one or two of the points. Mad or not, the Pacific bargain had been made; Canadian honour was involved. He felt himself somewhat committed to his own earlier proposals, and there was the prospect of Dufferin's visit to British Columbia. Was there still not hope of a compromise? The hope, said Blake, must be founded on convincing Victoria that it could not be the western terminus of the Pacific Railway. It would involve convincing Victorians that there could be no gigantic profits on their own investments in land. He did not believe that either could be accomplished. Let Dufferin go and return and make his report; it would not change the westerners and it would certainly not change the facts. In Blake's eyes there would be one most helpful thing; he had one suave prescription. Let Carnarvon leave the affair to the Canadian government and announce himself as prepared to endorse their policy.[40]

It was a large suggestion. In the matter of the railway dispute the Colonial Secretary was invited to leave the arena, accompanied by the Governor-General. Blake could not know when he made it, nor did he know two months later, whether he had scored a point or touched an official nerve. He sailed for Canada on the 24th of August with his own nerves in ribbons and hardly in a mood to care. "I know not how I shall ever make up for the long three months these people have taken from me."[41]

CHAPTER NINE

"THE UGLY WORD"

B Y SEPTEMBER 5 he was in Ottawa, facing his heaped-up desk. On the 25th he abruptly resigned from the cabinet. On the 26th, after twenty-four hours of urging by baffled and dismayed colleagues, he was back at his desk again. It was sign enough, if Mackenzie had need of signs, of the mood of his returning minister.

Blake had been bombarded in England with letters from worried friends, bemoaning the state of the party. Its organization was weak, there was no cohesion or leadership, and it was losing ground as it approached the next election. All this he had known, and it was confirmed in his own case. There was a letter awaiting him in Ottawa from his organizer in South Bruce, who was eager to arrange a welcoming "Demonstration". Something had to be done, the letter clearly implied, because Blake along with the party was losing his hold on Bruce. Nevertheless he could not face the meeting. "I have not an hour at my disposal. It is possible that I may be able to run up for 24 hours to Toronto to see my mother, but that is the furtherest."[1]

Dufferin had left for his progress to British Columbia, and trouble was expected from that. The Dominion treasury was fast emptying itself and would have to be recouped by another loan from England. There were no signs of improving conditions in the country, and there was every sign of

168

revived Conservative strength. John A. Macdonald, miraculously renewed and restored, had crossed Ontario in a series of political picnics and he had been for a delighted countryside the one cheerful feature of a dismal summer. He was an image of buoyant confidence attacking stagnation and drift, while Mackenzie slaved at his desk pinching pennies. Nor for all the grim honesty of the devoted Prime Minister, was he wholly successful in that. Contracts had to be let, appointments had to be made, and somehow graft crept in. There were Liberal scandals and blunders now, to be defended by red-faced ministers.

There was no surcease from religious strife in Quebec, and there was no policy to assuage it. Holton and Huntington were helpless as English leaders, and were immersed in quarrels of their own. Cauchon, the friend of bishops in Mackenzie's cabinet, had little to show for his work on behalf of *rouges*. Despised and distrusted by most of his own party, he could not manoeuvre around a fixed idea. Political liberalism was Catholic liberalism, the detested heresy of Europe, and was to be attacked by a Catholic party. The party had now been formed, supported by embattled bishops, by most of the younger priesthood and by all too many of their flocks. It was opposed by the wiser clergy, it was causing concern in Rome, yet it would be a deadly force at election time, not least to Quebec herself. Pulpit, press, and confessional, at war with the Liberal party, would be at war as well with the English and with all the Protestants of the nation.

It was another part of the prospect confronting the returning minister, with the thoughts of England behind him and the railway overhanging. "I am very busy and far from well," he had written to Mills on September 23, "partly caused by worry. I am more and more determined to change my mode of life after we get through next session. I cannot continue."[2]

A day later there was a sudden advance in plans. To Blake, as Minister of Justice, came the sentences of execution in the case of capital convictions. He had commuted far too many of them, in the opinion of some of the press. He was given to poring endlessly over the evidence in every case, searching for the thread of doubt, the saving factor or circumstance that might make mercy possible. The cold equity lawyer, in the face of a sentence of death, was no longer the man of Riel's time, demanding blood for blood. He seemed rather to be compelled and capable of imagining himself into the shoes of the worst backwoods blackguard or the drabbest town slut, and of picturing the form in the cell waiting for the rope. Years later he was to confide to one of his grandchildren his deepest reason for not becoming a judge: he could never have brought himself to put on a black cap and sentence a fellow human being to be hanged by the neck until dead. Now, while he was still in the mood of England and unimproved by the homecoming, there was a new spate of criticism in some of the hostile press. Justice was being mocked — Blake was "the best friend the Canadian murderer ever had"[3] — even the *Globe* had published some hostile letters. The Minister of Justice, on the morning of the 24th, walked into a cabinet meeting to find that they were being read. There seemed to be a general impression, Mackenzie remarked irritably, that the government had been too free with commutations.

It was not much but it was enough; it came from the party leader, the wrong man in the place, the echo of Brown's *Globe*. It came after all that had been done and endured in London, and the thunderbolt fell next day. "I have carefully considered the circumstances mentioned in council," Blake wrote to Mackenzie on the morning of the 25th, "that public opinion is adverse to our course in reference to the exercise of the prerogative of mercy in capital cases . . . I cannot conscientiously alter my conduct or advise the adoption of a different line . . . it is then fit that a minister so circumstanced should retire . . . I have to beg you at once to lay my resignation before His Excellency."[4]

The appalled Mackenzie replied in a matter of hours. He could not accept the grounds, nor quite believe that they were actually the sole reason. There had been "newspaper conceit or malice" and it meant nothing. Blake's cabinet colleagues were all firm in support of him, and it would be a disastrous time to resign. There must be some other cause, some other dissatisfaction, and Mackenzie was eager to repair it. "Let me beg of you to consider your letter as not written."[5]

It was not to be so that day; in a second note there was only renewed farewell. Of the attitude of his cabinet colleagues Blake had no complaint, "but I cannot bear the existing condition of things . . . there is a danger that human life may be taken when it should be spared, and the consequences which may flow from a murderer's hurried death are too awful to contemplate."[6]

So perhaps they were, yet Blake supported in cabinet would have the more chance to avert them. The metaphysical argument was quickly shifted to the practical. "I think you quite overestimate the effect of my retirement. I have, as I expected I would, lost the greater part of what little strength I ever had in the country; I shall lose the rest by retirement. I shall make no effort to regain it and the ranks of the party will supply you with another and more fortunate minister. It is not a very happy ending; you will not suppose that it involves no sacrifice on my part; but I have made up my mind, and see no need for changing it."[7]

He was shown the need, through the night and the next morning, by several eloquent persuaders despatched from cabinet. A third note for Mackenzie arrived on the 26th. He had thought over, wrote Blake, what the Prime Minister and Cartwright and other ministers had said. "Though I continue of the opinion that I am placed in a false position . . . yet I yield in my own views and authorize you not to proceed any further in the matter of my resignation . . . I am truly sorry to have caused my colleagues trouble."[8] It was handsome, duly repentant, and could now be dismissed by the colleagues as merely a passing mood. Blake had returned from England faced by enormous problems, and he was still tired and unwell.

All that was true, but the damped-out fuse remained, ready for lighting again. "I continue of the opinion that I am placed in a false position." It always would be false to him, and it always would be dangerous, while he served as the second man.

✎

By October 9 Dufferin was back from the west, aglow with new enthusiasms which Mackenzie promptly squelched. The Scot, it seemed to Dufferin, in the matter of the Pacific Railway, had grown depressingly firm. There would be no London conference, as the Governor-General proposed, with Carnarvon sitting as arbitrator between British Columbia and Canada. There would be no increase in the subsidy nor offer of revised terms, and there was no desire for imperial intervention. The Canadian government, said Mackenzie, had the problem well in hand.

In Dufferin's opinion, however, the Canadian government pivoted on Edward Blake, and there was no Blake to be seen at the regal homecoming. He had been at Murray Bay for a week, and was to be there for three weeks more. "My headaches became so bad," he explained to Cartwright, "that I had to go for fresh air."[9] In the meantime, showering letters on Carnarvon and preparing the ground for battle, the Governor-General waited. It was difficult to describe, he reported from his own experience, the hatred and suspicion of Blake in British Columbia. "The first inscription which met my eyes on landing on Esquimalt was 'Welcome to our Sea of Mountains'."[10] Blake, he was informed in Ottawa, was "as cross and ill-tempered as ever in his domestic relations with his colleagues."[11] David Mills had just entered the cabinet as the new Minister of the Interior, and that was ominous to Dufferin. Mills was an echo of Blake, certainly an enemy of the railway, and the two had persuaded Cartwright to adopt most of their views. Blake, wrote Dufferin to Carnarvon, was head of a dangerous trio, a continual threat to Mackenzie, and in any potential decision-making "the most important man."[12]

All this coloured the background when Blake and Dufferin met on November 1. With that day began a new series of "long and painful discussions", the more exasperating for Dufferin because he was standing on solid ground. He had not returned in his own eyes as a partisan of British Columbia, but as a friend of the Canadian government who was anxious to redeem its honour. Canada had defaulted once on the commencement of the Pacific Railway. It was in default again on the Nanaimo-Esquimalt Railway, and it was liable for compensation. Had it evolved an acceptable settlement? It had done nothing of the kind; it had merely imposed an offer on British Columbia. Worse still, the offer had become a sham. It was twisted by new phrasing and restricted by new conditions that belied the original intent. Compensation for past delays had become compensation for any delays "which may take place" in future. To the Canadian government now, if building the railway meant increasing the taxes, there would be no railway built. "The real truth," said Dufferin in one of the heated moments, "is that Canada has first blundered into a horrid mess, and has ever since been seeking to extricate herself by every kind of shabby and disingenuous plea and manoeuvre."[13]

There could be no denial of that, and Blake writhed at the predicament. At one point, wrote Dufferin, "he gave a great groan and said, 'It is all too true.' "[14] The anguish of the man who had not made the bargains was clear enough as the lawyer sought to defend them. But he had come stonily prepared. From the very beginning of the Pacific Railway question there had been one firm condition established by the Liberal party. Whatever agreement was made, whatever building was done, it could not add to the burden of the nation's taxes. The inhibiting factor remained, and on this ground Blake stood. He would talk and listen to Dufferin but he had said everything to Carnarvon, and he was not to be moved from that. He had made a full report for Mackenzie of his talk with the Colonial

Secretary on June 30 and there was a copy now in the files of the Governor-General. It was Blake's final answer to proposals for the Pacific Railway, and it had become Mackenzie's too. Through twenty days of wrestling, and wherever discussion turned, it came back to the same reply.

By November 14, though the struggle with Blake and Mackenzie was still in mid-course, Dufferin had drafted the report on his findings in British Columbia. Through some hundred and eighty pages it dealt with the history of the railway question, the claims of the angry province and his own views and proposals. It was intended eventually for Carnarvon but it went first to Mackenzie, with a stiff request to be informed as to "the course you are disposed to take." From Mackenzie it went to Blake and came back again to Mackenzie with a crisp sardonic echo. "You are now afforded the opportunity of stating 'the course you are disposed to take', and the question is how you can avail yourself best of the chance."[15]

The question was answered on November 16, when Mackenzie was summoned alone to Rideau Hall. The course he was disposed to take was exactly Blake's course; he intended to do nothing. British Columbia had rejected reasonable proposals, and they were now no longer in force. Conditions in the country and the mood of the country had both swung against them. Railway building would proceed at the government's pace, as and when means permitted.

The question of compensation reared its head, and again received Blake's answer. On that point Mackenzie had been vague before, but he was wholly clear now, and the last straw snapped for Dufferin. The shouting match that followed became historic in Rideau Hall. It was apologized for next day but it was renewed on the 18th, and this time Blake himself was one of the shouters.

By the end of the afternoon he was racked by another of the headaches that had sent him to Murray Bay. His strained eyes were streaming and his voice shaking with exhaustion, but the points impressed on Carnarvon had been doubly driven home. Over the tired intricacies of the railway question the talk had raged and subsided, as usual settling nothing. There was nothing that could be settled in this time and place, or by the man in Rideau Hall. Dufferin had had no authority to negotiate with British Columbia, or to prepare or propose a plan. His official report, as drafted for the Colonial Secretary, was a constitutional outrage. It was almost wholly political and should never be sent at all. It was imperial interference, uninvited and undesired, and the Governor-General who suggested it was in need of further instruction. That he received in full, from each of his two ministers and it was summed up by Mackenzie in a last acidulous thrust. Carnarvon should be informed, he suggested grimly, that the Dominion was no crown colony and that four million Canadians would manage their own affairs.

It was to Blake's arguments, however, that Dufferin referred next day, in a subdued and placating letter. Though he would "not exactly put my 180 pages of laborious composition into the fire",[16] he would make very sure that they were kept from the public eye. There were three more days of writing for Carnarvon's private eye, and the Governor-General's altered views went off on their way to London. The horrid mess remained but it had become a Canadian mess, for Canadians to clean up. "P.S." Dufferin scrawled at the conclusion of one of his letters, "I am getting quite sick of this business."[17]

In that, at least, the Colonial Secretary concurred. Hardly changing a paragraph in the revised recommendations sent by Dufferin, he transposed them to the first person and despatched the official reply. The petitions of British Columbia and the replies of the Canadian government were consigned to ageless pigeon-holes where the dust would never be stirred. What reached Dufferin from Carnarvon in the closing days of December was a washing of the imperial hands. "I wish to inform your advisers and the Provincial Government that, while I do not feel myself in a position to decline to entertain the

representations pressed upon me by the province, I am nevertheless at the moment unable to pronounce an opinion as to
the course which should be taken, either with regard to the
Esquimalt and Nanaimo Railway or with regard to the delays
which have occurred, or may yet occur, in the construction of
the main line."[18]

In effect the controversy was over. If anyone could claim to
be winner of the grey victory, it would have to be Edward
Blake. He had fought Macdonald, he had controlled and
dominated Mackenzie, and he had withstood the imperial
pressures. He had redirected the country onto a sane and
possible course, the only course for that day. He had never
believed that the first of the railway bargains had been anything but a political promise, designed to win an election.
There would have been no more of railway if Macdonald had
remained in office than there was of railway now. Through
all the battles and confusion the essential work of survey had
been pushed forward. There was building in Manitoba and
there were plans for the North-West. The great project was
shaping itself in line with the country's means, and there was
not a man of the Conservatives who dared to ask for more.
Dufferin had learned that too, and it had brought his final
yielding; the country believed with the Liberals that they
were doing what could be done.

It was only that witless promise, that vision of the plunge
to the Pacific, that remained behind to haunt and distract
affairs. Mackenzie had not made it but he had not been able
to quiet it; under his hands it had become inflamed with a new
venom. Nor had Blake quieted it; he had not been in a position
to do so; he had accepted three years earlier the position of
second man. "It has sometimes struck me," Dufferin wrote to
Carnarvon while he was still in the midst of the quarrel,
"that Blake all this time wishes to drive matters to extremity
in the hopes of tripping up Mackenzie."[19] It was shrewd, but
it was off the point; the bitterness lay deeper still. The humiliated rescuer of blunderers had imposed the task on himself.

If he had chosen to be Prime Minister how much might have been redeemed?

It was not to be redeemed now, and the consequences lay ahead. Blake could see them foreshadowed in one figure, rising jaunty and incredible from the trampled mud of defeat. They had not escaped the eye of the Governor-General. He had talked, he wrote Carnarvon, with some of the British Columbians after the official verdict. They were prepared to watch and wait but they were not prepared to give up; and one of them had been much fortified by a talk with a faithful friend. It was John A. Macdonald, "who of course told him that the Conservatives were quite ready for office, and that if they were once back every man in British Columbia should have a branch railway to his own door."[20]

Against that, when the fourth session of parliament opened in February of 1877, there were only the dismal realities of the country's actual state. There were depression and rising taxes, and there was new tumult in Quebec. There was revived and truculent Torydom scenting the approach of an election, showering mud with one hand and raising hopes with the other. The spectre of a protective tariff and the fantasy of a National Policy were shaping in Macdonald's hands. Mackenzie, exhausted and failing and blind to the party's weakness, was newly in need of Blake, yet somehow newly distrustful. "I sometimes think he would not be sorry to see me worsted."[21] It was true and it was not true; the Minister of Justice had arrived at bleak indifference. He slaved grimly at the affairs of his own department and it had never been better run, more fruitful of useful bills, more intent on sound procedures. In questions of law and the improvement of law Blake was, as always, powerful, dominant, and admired even by official enemies. For the most part, however, the figure in the black slouch hat, hunched over his desk, had little to offer the House but moody silence. There was increasing alienation from an increasingly divided cabinet, and with the old torture of the headaches came a new fear in the nights.

"Blake is ill," wrote Dufferin on the day before the session ended, "thoroughly broken down with excitement and irritability of the brain. It is the affection which killed his father and to which it is known he is liable."[22] Parliament closed on the 28th of April, and two days later Mackenzie received Blake's note. "I can no longer remain a Minister. As the state of my health disables me from adequately discharging my official duties, I am spared the necessity of adding any other to this sufficient ground for retirement."[23]

✑

The resignation, as usual, could not possibly be accepted. It would be imputed to the troubles in Quebec, to differences within the cabinet, to every cause that might weaken the party's prospects. "I begin to feel," wrote Mackenzie, ailing and desperate himself, "that I can no longer sustain the struggle."[24] To the sick man from the sick man, with a list of the crowding urgencies, came the echoes of old friendship and the old pleadings for delay. They were answered by another yielding, but it was firmly restricted now. Blake would remain in the cabinet for perhaps a matter of weeks, but he could no longer act as an adviser on any but routine affairs.

By late May he had been won to a little more. As he escaped Ottawa the relentless headaches eased. He had more thought for the man who could not escape. There was a new link between them, forged by the Colonial Secretary and a forgiving Governor-General, as they were offered Knight Companionships in the Order of St. Michael and St. George. Each declined officially in graceful letters, and exchanged more private letters reflecting a common mood. "Lord Carnarvon is very kind," Blake wrote to Mackenzie, "but I am, as you may conceive, less disposed than ever toward these trappings."[25] He recoiled with the same weariness from increasing Mackenzie's woes. "My soul is sick of contention."[26] He must be free, he said, of the burden of the Ministry of Justice, but he would remain in a lighter post.

On June 8 the change was made, and three weeks later he left for Murray Bay. Installed in a cabinet sinecure as President of the Privy Council, he replaced Joseph Cauchon who had been a flat failure in Quebec. He was replaced as Minister of Justice by the *rouge* Rodolphe Laflamme, who could certainly not bring peace with the embattled clergy. That would be dependent now on the efforts of the young Laurier, who was about to enter the cabinet but was steering his own course. He was the one hope in the province if there was any hope at all, but he was feared by the Ultramontanes as a *rouge* protégé of Laflamme. Determined to confront the clergy in a direct and dangerous speech, he might destroy the last of Liberalism in a rash attempt to defend it. Whether he had or not one hardly knew, on the night of June 26 when the speech was made. Mackenzie had advised postponement, so had Blake and Laflamme, and there were as always good reasons for delay. Rome was intervening in the disputes of its Quebec clergy, and an Apostolic Delegate was actually in the province then. He was a bishop but not an Italian; he seemed to be a reasonable Irishman and it might be better to wait on his decisions. But Laurier had not waited.

At Quebec City he had stood up in the Salle de Musique before a crowded audience of the political and clerical élite, a pale, frail-looking man, rather too spectacularly handsome but tall and very firm. "I do not deceive myself," he had said, "with regard to the position of the Liberal party in the province of Quebec . . . I know that in the eyes of a portion of our people . . . liberalism is a new form of evil, a heresy carrying with it its own condemnation." He had hammered down that fallacy, and turned on the listening *bleus*. "In our adversaries' party it is the habit to accuse us, Liberals, of irreligion. I am not here to parade my religious sentiments, but I declare I have too much respect for the faith in which I was born ever to use it as the basis of a political organization. You wish to organize a Catholic party . . . have you not considered that if you have the misfortune to succeed you will draw down upon your coun-

179

try calamities of which it is impossible to foresee the consequences?" Then it was the turn of the bishops and of the clergy behind the *bleus*, preaching politics by right as the spiritual advisers of the people. "We have no absolute rights . . . the rights of each man end precisely at the point where they encroach upon the rights of others. The right of interference in politics finishes at the spot where it encroaches on the elector's independence . . . When by terror you force him to vote, the opinion you cause him to express is your opinion . . . if after each election the will expressed is not the real will of the country, you do violence to the constitution, responsible government is no longer anything but an empty name, and sooner or later, here as elsewhere, the pressure will culminate in explosion, violence, and ruin.²⁷

Explosion, violence, and ruin there were apparently not to be. Bishop Conroy, the Apostolic Delegate, departed Canada and the curbs came back from Rome. In every Catholic pulpit, throughout the course of that summer, the words of superior authority and the reminders of old injunctions were at least submissively read. It was forbidden a priest "to teach from the pulpit or anywhere else that it is a sin to vote for any particular candidate or party. You are never to give your personal opinion from the pulpit."²⁸ How much Laurier had done to affect the change in Quebec no man could say, but his words were already ringing across the nation. They had at least helped in the rescue of a political party, and they had made a public man.

Yet it was all remote from the broodings in Murray Bay. Rescued or not, the party remained what it was, politics remained what they were, the game went on. There were still the relentless headaches; not even the cool St. Lawrence seemed able to induce sleep; and Blake returned to Ottawa much as he had gone away. The general election was still a year off, but the background seethed with the prospect. He could neither face it nor make himself turn away from it; he parried, delayed, and fretted. At the little town of Teeswater, on Septem-

ber 24, he stood up strained and shaking before the electors of
South Bruce. If he were considered worthy, he said, "I shall
challenge a continuance of that confidence with which you
have so far honoured me; nor do I believe that I shall challenge it in vain." It was his one speech of the autumn, it was
an acceptance of nomination, and it purported to defend the
government. Yet its whole theme and burden was a defence of
the name of Blake and he returned with his peroration to a
eulogy of William Hume "whose bright example of active,
fervent devotion to the cause of freedom, truth and justice, of
indomitable perseverance in the thorny path of duty, it has
been my earnest aim to follow, with steps however unequal,
and at a distance however great."[29] It was the speech of a sick
man who was clawing at old scars, alienated from his party's
problems and wholly obsessed with his own. It foreshadowed
the letter to Mackenzie that arrived on November 6.

Yet not quite. There was a new dimension this time. Blake
could not stay in office as "a useless hulk",[30] and that was the
prospect now. He enclosed a note from his physicians dilating
on possible consequences if he remained through the next session. It was just short of explicit and it was, he commented
grimly, "milder than their talk. They did not wish, any more
than I do, to put down on paper the ugly word they used as to
probable results."[31]

For a moment politics yielded and old friendships warmed,
shocked by the unuttered word. "My fears are realized," Mackenzie wrote to Holton. "You can guess what the word is. I
cannot under such circumstances urge him further."[32] Holton's
resentments vanished, transformed into generous grief. He
found it "dreadful to think of the appalling possibility . . . in
the shadow of which he must walk until his nervous system re-
gains somewhat of its normal tone." That it must do so, wrote
Holton, was "the fond hope not only of friends who love him
but of a country that is proud of him."[33] It was a recalling of
old comradeships, it was all perfectly sincere, and it was all
eroded steadily as expediencies again prevailed.

ANXIOUS JOHNNY,

WAITING FOR A CERTAIN PARTY TO "RETIRE."

Laurier was a national figure now, and had been called to
Mackenzie's cabinet. Yet at Drummond-Arthabaska, in the by-
election for his constituency, he had suffered incredible defeat.
Newly become a key man for the Liberals, he had been faced by
embittered Torydom, undermined by bribery and corruption,
and he had been over-confident himself. He was to try again in
the constituency of Quebec East, and the fate of Laurier had
become a national issue. Every resource, not only of Quebec

bleus but of the entire Conservative party was being brought into play against him. Every resource of Liberalism was being strained in his behalf, and the first of these was unity in the federal cabinet. It would vanish with Blake's going, whatever the reason given, and Mackenzie for all his sympathy was determined to prevent that. He delayed, pleaded, evaded, and achieved partial success; Blake agreed to remain till after the election. The day came and went, bringing victory in Quebec East, but Mackenzie was still reluctant and still pleading. Could Blake not go away for an extended rest, yet still remain in the ministry?

"In the first place," came the reply on December 3, "neither my circumstances nor my temperament invite a lengthened absence from home and friends. In the next place I could not, if I were to go away, retain the responsibilities and emoluments of office . . . you say it is important at present to avoid further complications. But this is the point which has always been taken. The convenient moment never comes . . . I ask you without further delay to place my resignation before His Excellency."[34]

The request was sharper on the 7th and drew a short answer on the 8th. Once more the dialogue of friends was becoming acrid. It had not been possible, said Mackenzie, to arrange an immediate appointment with the Governor-General. "I suppose you can wait for two days."[35]

On the 11th the thing was done. Still under cloak of secrecy the resignation was accepted; Blake was out of the cabinet. Six days before, in pouring rain and a mud-splashed march of victory, Laurier had arrived in Ottawa. The new Minister had come. The old was free to go.

∽

On January 17, 1878, he composed a letter from a cabinet office for the last time in his life. "I have . . . cleared out my pigeon-holes and left my room empty and swept and garnished," he wrote Mackenzie. "I part from my colleagues

THE RETIRING MINISTER.

with pain so great that I find it impossible to speak and difficult to write . . . I must leave you to say goodbye to them for me."[36]

The pain, however real, must have been mixed with other feelings. Through the long last session of parliament that went on from February to May Blake as a private member was occasionally a sombre presence, once more ambiguous and discomforting even to his own party. "If you resign," David Mills had written him months before, "you will discover that your

184

quondam friends will be found pouncing upon you . . . I know
that you will be asked to withdraw from parliament. I believe
there are some more anxious to get you out of public life than
they are to get rid of Sir John A. Macdonald."[37] Mills had
always his cherished little suspicions, but there was a measure
of truth in these. Blake could sense the mood, sometimes even
in Mackenzie. But there was no request for withdrawal, and he
could not withdraw himself. On May 10, after a great concluding brawl, came prorogation and the end of the third parliament. The elections loomed in September and he felt defeat in
his bones. In any case, he would not be present for the battle.
Yet he turned aside with just short of a refusal the offer of a
nomination for West Durham, and he accepted in South Bruce.

Once more his relations with Mackenzie were on a too familiar course. He was the official friend, with his support or at
least his silence still essential. He was the detached adviser,
free of responsibility. Through the cool exchanges and wary
discussions of issues, there were often genuine flashes of the
old warmth and respect. Yet it was Cartwright now and Laurier
who were assisting with the election plans. "You ask my news,"
Blake wrote on July 3, "I have literally none. I never see anyone who knows anything of politics."[38] He sensed confidence
he said, in the mood of some of the party, but he did not indi-
cate that he shared it. On July 4 he sailed with Margaret for
England, to be gone at least three months.

In Europe too a pattern that had grown familiar began to
repeat itself. The grip of Ireland held firm, and there were
relatives to be visited there. There were the friends and relatives in England, the historic sites and the watering-places all
to be seen again. For three months, eager for escape from politics yet feverish for letters from Canada and devouring Canadian newspapers, he followed the trail established by William
Hume. He came home in early October, free indeed.

Mackenzie's hopes for the election had ended in complete
disaster. He was the beaten leader of a Liberal opposition,
wrecked and bewildered, facing a revived Macdonald. Those

old tarred hands would again be guiding the country; the standard of public virtue had been trampled and cast aside. Cartwright was one of the defeated, and so was Edward Blake.

"Thank God you are out of it," wrote his mother. "You have shown how a man not only ought but *can* be a pure, unselfish, self-sacrificing statesman."[39] Whatever the truth of that, there was no disputing the ballot-box. It only remained for the statesman to leave the scene with grace.

Yet there was to be little grace, and never a real departure. By December, as the dazed party sought to rebuild itself, Mackenzie struggled with necessities. He had to find places in parliament for some of his old advisers who were now outside in defeat. West Durham, which had, as usual, elected a Liberal, was considered a safe constituency and it was held by a dispensable man. He seemed prepared to resign, it would mean the offer of a vacancy, and the prospect spread on the wings of political gossip. So did word of Mackenzie's inclination. The man most needed now, for the one seat that was available and the seat that had once been Blake's, was the former Minister of Finance.

It was only one of a distracted leader's problems, shaken in his own position and beset by the squabbles of defeat. Yet he was soon aware of the effect of his proposed solution. "I am informed," he wrote to Cartwright, "that Mr. Blake is much offended at me because I named you in connection with West Durham. The truth is that . . . I said 'I must get seats for Blake and Cartwright if possible, *especially Cartwright*, as I must have him in the House at the opening to discuss financial matters.' "[40]

Especially Cartwright. In the event there was no change; the riding was not opened. H. V. Burke, the elected incumbent of Durham, decided to retain his seat, but the acid letters trickled in on Mackenzie. He did feel pained, wrote Blake, that Cartwright had been given the preference in his old constituency, but the matter was now forgotten. "I don't want to enter into any correspondence or invite any reply."[41] It had been a small affair, wrote Cartwright, since he had never intended to accept in West Durham; Blake was imagining trouble. "The only possible thing to be done in such a case is to let him severely alone."[42]

The obsessed leader was nourishing his own dark thoughts. Trouble was being fomented everywhere, directed against himself, always with Blake at the centre. It seemed to Mackenzie now that for all his generosity, all his years of work, he was being "paid back by an organized attempt to belittle myself and my services with a view to supplant me."[43] In the conspiracies, Cartwright thought, Blake was not involved, but he was hardly allied with the party and would certainly stand apart. It would be better, Holton wrote, if Blake were absent from parliament, at least for a session or two. "I have been told on what I consider undoubted authority that he will not act again in a secondary capacity either in opposition or in an administration."[44]

For Mackenzie the year closed with the painful draft of a letter that was much revised. It reached Blake in its final form on January 3, 1879. In regard to West Durham, said the leader of the opposition, "I was very much concerned to learn that you thought I had not acted fairly and openly in this matter." He enclosed papers to disprove the charge but would not discuss it further "as you express a desire to avoid correspondence." He had called on Blake in Toronto to offer him the season's greetings, but had not found him at home. "I now embrace this opportunity of wishing you and yours a very happy new year."[45]

The old tone had resumed. Stiff, suspicious and now in the abyss of defeat, the two went on. Neither in nor out, neither enemy nor quite friend, Blake overshadowed Mackenzie and the hopes of the Liberal party.

187

CHAPTER TEN

"WHO IS LEADER?"

LORD DUFFERIN had departed Canada in late November, to be replaced by the Marquess of Lorne. The arriving Governor-General had been met at Halifax by a Conservative Prime Minister who was recovering from a Homeric drinking bout and still showing the effects. On February 13, 1879, when the first session of the fourth parliament convened, Macdonald was again to the right of Mr. Speaker, with Tupper, Tilley, and other familiars beside him. The country buzzed with talk of the Pacific Railway and even more with talk of the National Policy, which was to build prosperity behind a wall of tariffs. Manufacturers and industrialists, most of them eager Tories, were filling Ottawa hotels, tramping official corridors, and pressing their claims on the receptive ear of government. "Tell us what you want," Macdonald was said to have said, "and we will give you what you need." For a Liberal out of office and out of parliament the bad old days had returned.

"Come at last!" said the Liberal *Stratford Beacon*, greeting the new era with its own sour salute. "We tremble at the thought of our readers invading our sanctum next week with their fists full of crisp new bank bills and shaking them in our face ... manufacturers will have a champagne supper every other night next week, and laborers will dine off boned turkey and garden 'sass' every day. Once for all we say, hurrah for the N.P. and high prices! Hurrah for Sir John, the great magician!"[1]

Mackenzie, who had sold his Ottawa home and moved his family to a cheaper house in Toronto, lived in a rented room throughout the session. It was bleak but adequate, for he was not much visited socially by the diminished band of his friends. Among these he did not count David Mills, always the friend of Blake. He liked Laurier and trusted him, but could summon no real warmth for the untried *Rouge*. George Brown was his prop and stay as always, Holton was renewed in loyalty and Huntington was still about. But the master of the *Globe* was drawing away from politics and was even leaving the newspaper to the care of his brother, Gordon. Holton was often absent on family cares of his own, Mills was difficult and abrasive, and Huntington was an able lightweight. The work devolved on Mackenzie, and there was more work than he could do.

If there was one crumb of comfort in the reduced and straitened circumstances of the leader of the opposition it was provided by the return of Cartwright, who had been found a new constituency. For Cartwright himself there was to be the additional comfort of a knighthood, which Mackenzie had recommended in the waning days of power and had later urged on Lorne. Sir Richard, already distinguished for his whiskers and his devotion to free trade, had none of his chief's objections to the acceptance of official honours and had suggested himself for the award. It did not come, however, until the Birthday List of the 24th of May, and for neither man in the meantime had there been any joy in parliament or any help from Blake.

"My dismissal from public life having set me free to pay some attention to my own affairs,"[2] the squire of Humewood was rebuilding his legal practice. He had joined with Mac-Kenzie and some of the other leaders in clearing off party debts and purchasing premises for a headquarters. If he saw irony in the fact that the new home of Liberalism was to be the defunct National Club established by Goldwin Smith, he made no comment for the record. He had few comments for any record as the weeks of the session drifted by without him. In the newspapers and in the talk of politicians there was the usual flow of questioning as to his future in the Liberal party. He neither stemmed it nor fed it by any public pronouncement. He saw little of Mackenzie and had no advice for his countrymen as they settled to Conservative rule. "As they made their bed so they must lie in it,"[3] Catherine Blake had written him, and it appeared to be his own view. Always faintly aggrieved, yet seeming at least to Holton to be enjoying excellent health, he was polite, formal, and reticent with his old political friends. He was a stonily detached observer of their hopeless battles in parliament. For three months, a passenger in the ship of state, he watched as the new pilots swung off on an altered course.

There was to be one sharp change, in the context of provincial rights, over the question of Ontario's boundary with Manitoba. The issue was ten years old, much aggravated by politics, and threatening to grow with the advance of western settlement. In 1869, when the Dominion government took over the territories of the Hudson's Bay Company, the western limits of Ontario had not been clearly defined. They had remained undefined when Manitoba was created, and between the two provinces there was a large region in dispute. Blake as provincial premier and Macdonald as Prime Minister had sparred for a while on the question and eventually let it drop. Mowat had carried on when he succeeded Blake in Ontario, and when Mackenzie succeeded Macdonald there were bright hopes for a solution. In 1874 the Liberal Prime Minister and the Liberal Premier of Ontario had agreed on the establishment of a commission that would recommend an award. This was done, and there was a four-year study of the question, protracted just too long.

It was August of 1878 when the commission announced its award. Since it was highly favourable to Ontario, Mowat promptly accepted. By that time, however, the Dominion parliament was dissolved, Mackenzie's government was facing a general election, and when the election came it fell. It was then Macdonald's government that would have to ratify the award, and Macdonald flatly refused. He would not accept the verdict of Mackenzie's commission. He would not aggrandize Mowat at the expense of Manitoba. He had a genuine fear that over-large, over-wealthy provinces might come in time to disrupt the balance of the union. What he intended now, it appeared, was to run a line due north from the American border and well east of Fort William. The rich western timber lands, the promise of wealth in minerals, the lakehead ports and much of the territory around them would be shorn away from Ontario and given to Manitoba.

All this, to federal and provincial Liberals, would be ammunition for the future. It had no effect, however, on the present course of affairs. On March 14 came budget day and the day of Leonard Tilley, the precise, diminutive New Brunswicker who was now Minister of Finance. He stood up, with his eyes red-rimmed from the study of tariff schedules to unveil the working frame of the National Policy. It was both less and more than expected, and promised no instant miracles. Prosperity remained a glimmer along the horizon and there would still be a budget deficit at the end of the current year. In general the tariffs established by the Liberals at 17½ per cent would rise to 20 per cent, an increase they had themselves projected as a necessity for raising revenue. What they had not projected, however, and the heart of the National Policy, lay in open and avowed protection for the factories, shops and refineries, the mines and infant industries that were under the American threat. To build them up, to encourage the growth of more, and to defend their products and workers against foreign competition, there would be new duties established to a maximum of 40 per cent.

The tariff had taken centre stage in politics, never to leave it again. For Mackenzie, devoted to free-trade Britain and speaking for rural Ontario, protection was worse than a fallacy, it was a displacement of the natural order. The flow of goods, as part of that natural order, was to be interrupted and distorted for the benefit of a chosen few. The price of the farmer's products would depend on open markets, but it was not so with the industrialist and manufacturer. Protected from competition by his wall of tariffs, he would charge whatever he liked and he would pay what wages he liked. He would grind the faces of his workers while he took his toll of the poor. Sugar, coal, clothes, flour, would inevitably cost more; every daily necessity would be burdened with a new tax. Protection, in Mackenzie's eyes, was "contrary to the beneficence of the Maker of the world," contrary to "all just law, human and divine."[4] To the maker of goods in Canada, however, it was a source of electric hope. Even farmers, inherently against tariffs, saw the prospect of rising prices in a widening domestic market. While Mackenzie preached and Cartwright flailed the measure with his bitter eloquence, a wave of acceptance rippled across the country. It was duly reflected in the House when the time for the vote came. Tilley's budget was safe; the National Policy was in being.

The railway policy that hovered over everything remained in doubt as the session came to a close. Land, people, money, and British Columbia; it was Tupper now, the new Minister of Railways, who must somehow link those factors of the enormous problem. He took up the work where Mackenzie had left it off, and in spite of politics and depression much work had been done. The Intercolonial had been completed and the Grand Trunk had grown; the provinces of Quebec and Ontario were moderately well served. From Halifax westward as far as Georgian Bay there was complete railway connection. Through the rocky wilderness to the north of Lake Superior one could not yet think of railways, but steamers carried traffic to the western lakehead. From there, commencing at Prince Arthur's Landing, Mackenzie had envisaged a combination of transport by rail, road, and water. While rail was building the Dawson route would serve, linking the east with Winnipeg by small steamers on the lakes and corduroy roads between.

The Dawson route had failed; immigrants would not face it. Its dreadful trails were settling in bush and muskeg and its steamers rusting at their docks for lack of passengers. Yet with that failure acknowledged, work had gone grimly on. West from the lakehead and east from Selkirk just to the north of Winnipeg there were now two sections of railway, building or under contract. They were each of a little more than a hundred miles, and there were tenders called for the section of line between them. The westerners' link with the east was being forged while the just-completed Pembina line, running south to the border, provided connection with Winnipeg by way of American railways. When Mackenzie left office Manitoba was no longer isolated. From the Atlantic ocean to the heart of western settlement one could go by rail and steamer.

Beyond that, on the way across the prairies and mountains to the Pacific, there were at least lines on the map now that would be intelligible to prospective builders. Forty-seven thousand miles of country had been "examined" and twelve thousand miles surveyed. The route west that was now considered most feasible would cross the prairies and climb through the foothills to Jasper, thread the Yellowhead Pass and descend the Fraser valley to Burrard Inlet. It would end there on the mainland; there would be no island terminus to please Victoria. There had been no construction as yet in British Columbia, and despite some tentative gestures there were no plans for construction. But the road was more than a promise now, it had become an actual project, with its frightening dimensions known.

Most of this Tupper freely conceded. While he questioned some of the routing and was still inclined to the terminus on Vancouver Island, he was unwontedly suave and conciliatory in admitting the central fact. Neither a Conservative government nor a Liberal government could have redeemed the promises of 1872. What could be done had been done. On this issue the six-year war of politics had been mainly fought for nothing, and Tupper proposed a truce. It remained now for both parties, proceeding from a *tabula rasa*, to face the completion of the task.

The olive branch was rejected by the party across the aisle, and Tupper was soon embroiled in familiar difficulties. While Liberals sniped, British Columbia ranted, and the core of his own dilemma was that he had no definite plan. He could not find private builders for the vital sections of the railroad, and there was as little of public money as there had been in Mackenzie's day. What there was, however, was a rising sense of optimism that had come with the National Policy, and a westward shift of peoples that was argument and inspiration.

Thousands of immigrants from Europe and hundreds of native Ontarians were already moving in the direction of Manitoba. Yet most of them never got there, Tupper argued; they were filling the American west. Why? Because they came to the lakehead faced by the Dawson trail, and turned south to go on by rail from Duluth. They settled in Minnesota or went south to Iowa or Nebraska or they took up land in the Dakotas, and were permanently lost to Canada. Neither to nor from Winnipeg, except for the stretch of the Pembina line which stopped short at the border, was it possible to move by any but American railways. There was always the southward pull of the mighty union, dragging settlement with traffic to people its own lands. And when those lands were filled it would be Americans who moved north, bringing their ways with them and perhaps bringing their flag. The National Policy would build the Canadian east, but the hope of a Canadian west depended on the Pacific Railway, and the two must work together. The immigrants would not wait, the Americans never waited, and the time to move was now.

By the close of the session Tupper had advanced a program, though it was hardly yet a plan. From Callander on Lake Nipissing, just above Georgian Bay, the government would complete the railway to the Pacific coast. One hundred million acres of public land would be appropriated to finance the work. Also, in case of shortfall, there would be a possibility of obtaining imperial help. The railway, after all, would be a great imperial work, an all-red land route linking two of the oceans. More than that, with the mother country still deep in depression, she had thousands of idle men. They could be shipped out to Canada and put to the work of building; she would be relieved of her unemployed. She in turn would provide what money was needed, by loan or guarantee. The arrangement had not been settled on or even much discussed, but Macdonald, Tupper, and Tilley were to go to England to conclude it. In the meantime, with an appropriation of $6,000,000 the government intended to go on with work where it could, notably in British Columbia.

The only thing that was definite in relation to British Columbia was that a section of line should be built "not exceeding 125 miles in length." This turned out, later on in the summer, to be exactly the distance from Yale on the Fraser Canyon to Savona's Ferry near Kamloops. It was at least as difficult as any section in the mountains, but it had political potentialities. Mackenzie had once eyed it, and had actually called for tenders. He had called for tenders on many sections, but here he had done more. Amid the election pressures of 1878 he had permitted some favourable comment on the line's prospects, shipped rails to the commencement site, and allowed the impression to be created that he actually intended building.

Nothing at all had come of it. When the tenders were in Mackenzie had recoiled from the figures. He was out of power and would certainly recoil now. But he would be embarrassed in opposing Tupper and explaining his old position, and the rusting rails at the building site would tend to weaken his case. Nor was that his only or even his greatest problem. He had never consulted Blake regarding the Yale-Kamloops section, and Blake was stirring again.

❧

For three months, as the shifts of politics opened up constituencies, there had been rumours of Blake's return. He was being spoken of for North York, Holton had reported to Mackenzie in early February, but nothing had developed from that. There had been other talk of one of the Huron ridings, but again it had died away. Blake had allowed it to die, and with good reason, since he was being left to fend for himself. He was not encouraged by Mackenzie, he was no longer Holton's friend, and though he had his own friends among the newspapers they did not include the *Globe*.

There had been a change for the worse in that respect as the younger brother took over the *Globe*'s direction. With George Brown Blake had been cool enough, but with Gordon Brown he verged on open contempt. As a result he was being ignored in the *Globe*'s columns. Neither the great organ of the party nor any of the party leaders seemed inclined to force the opening of a seat for Blake. It would have to be a safe seat, it would mean the displacement of an already-elected Liberal, and in any case there were few such seats to be had. Even in West Durham, the obvious and desired constituency, Mr. Burke declined to make way. In that course, moreover, he had now the tacit approval of the Liberal party leader. After the calamity of the general election, wrote Mackenzie, "such was the state of feeling . . . that it would not be safe to open up the county even for Mr. Blake."[5]

By the end of June, however, there had been a rather dramatic change. Oliver Mowat had provided it with a solid Liberal victory in the Ontario provincial election. He had been faced with the new euphoria induced by the National Policy and with determined federal Conservatives who were bent on cutting him down. In spite of it all he had been returned once more as premier and with newly enhanced prestige. He was the defender of provincial rights, the old enemy of Macdonald, and the man whom Blake had chosen to replace himself. To many he was Blake's deputy, to Macdonald he was Blake's "jackal", and certainly on the suspended boundary question the two were a united team. The projected "rape" of Ontario's western territory was becoming a useful issue. It seemed that in the greatest province, so crucial to either party, the fortunes of Blake and Liberalism might be once more on the rise.

By late May, though he had declined to take much part in Mowat's campaign, Blake had begun to appear on public platforms. By July, with his intentions obvious, his words were being studied by nervous leaders. "Blake's speeches are not very clear," Cartwright wrote to Mackenzie, "but I suspect he is holding back by design. He may be afraid of committing himself on questions of trade and policy just yet."[6] Cautious he certainly was, yet time was ripening. There were wheels turning in the constituency of West Durham and pressures and pleadings mounted around the reluctant H. V. Burke. He announced his resignation in early November, induced by suitable promises according to hostile gossip. The seat was vacant, the by-election was called, and there was much talk by Conservatives of making a bitter fight. Then that talk died; there was to be no Conservative candidate, and of the identity of the Liberal aspirant there had never been any doubt.

On November 18, 1879, Blake came down to Bowmanville for the performance of the official rites. They were as brief and bleak as they could be made by a disgruntled Tory returning officer who was a good friend of Macdonald. "The election is over," he wrote that night to his chief, "and Blake returned by acclamation. I took the liberty of holding the election in my law office which is a capacious building capable of containing at best fifteen people with seats for nine, as I hate to hear the jeers and cheers of Grits." For the same reason he had not appeared at the drill shed when Blake spoke in the evening, "but I am told by his friends that they were terribly disappointed in him . . . George Brown told me that he (Blake) was utterly unfit for public life, and I believe that instead of blocking you in any way he will be setting up straw men for you to knock down when you feel inclined to play."[7]

It was a wishful thought, and quite belied by the scene

"HIS CUSTOMARY AT-TI-TUDE!"

"I ALTOGETHER DECLINE TO ACCEPT, ON MY RE-ENTRANCE INTO PUBLIC LIFE, ANY MORE *STRAIGHTENED* CONDITIONS THAN HERETOFORE."—HON. E. BLAKE, IN WEST DURHAM.

earlier that evening. Blake stood up in the flagged and gar-landed drill hall, once more the elected member for West Durham. "It was not, as you know, my desire to have returned to public life." The words came familiarly, delivered from old habit, but they were not borne out by anything in the speaker's manner. He was vigorous, restored, jovial and al-most effusively grateful; to any impartial observer a man delighted to be back.

He was reunited with the friends of his first constituency, "never, I trust, to be dissociated as long as I keep to the stormy sea of politics." He almost seemed to be repentant of his straying to South Bruce. It had been imposed on him by duty but it had kept him away from his own. He had genially barbed thanks even for the Conservatives of Durham, since whether from grace or prudence they had decided not to oppose him. To all, everywhere as always, he announced his terms of service. "Although I have been condemned during the course of my public life for having on some points differed from the bulk of my party, I altogether decline to accept on my re-entrance into public life any more straitened conditions."

From that point, through the next two hours and a half, he unfolded the ripened views that would now guide him. Cartwright's questions seemed to receive their answer; he was merciless with the cant surrounding the National Policy. The tariff which had provided revenue was now to be used as an instrument to provide protection, and the whole theory was wrong. It involved government in the distortion of the channels of trade, and in the development of "hot-house industries" that required unnatural shelter. Manufacturers would fatten and great monopolies grow up, while the tax concealed in the tariff would be a burden on the common man. There were barriers raised against the purchase of American goods. For whose benefit? Certainly not for his farmer friends in Bowmanville. What did John Jones care whether he bought his goods in Oshawa or crossed the lake to buy in Rochester, New York? "Your patriotism, about which these people talk so much, does not induce you to buy in this country if you can make a better bargain elsewhere. You buy, if you are a sensible man, and I think you are, where you can buy cheapest."

What was this talk of unity, supposed to be induced by the tariffs of the National Policy? The people of the Maritime provinces would pay more for their flour, because they were barred from the American market and must haul it down from Ontario. Would they love Ontario for that? Would Ontario love the Maritimes because it was forced to buy their coal, at a higher price than it would pay in Pennsylvania? Nor would either region benefit from the increase paid by the other; it was freight that raised the prices and that would go to the railways. It was not unity that would be fostered by this bland ignoring of geography and this wrenching-around of trade; it was new and dangerous friction that might tear the country apart.

It had been a year of good crops, and because of the increased tariffs the national revenues were rising. "Providence has at length smiled upon our harvests, and frowned on the harvests of Europe." Was that the government's work? Did the increased revenue from the tariff mean any real prosperity? It did not; Government was overtaxing to support its overspending; it was merely aggravating and enlarging the country's oldest malaise.

He lingered on that malaise, tracing it back to its source. From Confederation onward "it was obvious, it was plain as day, that we were not increasing in population, in realized wealth, in power of paying taxes and making importations to the extent that we were actually importing and paying taxes for. What necessarily followed, to the eye of the most limited observer? Why, that a day of reckoning must come."

It was in the midst of these conditions that the Pacific Scandal had broken and the Macdonald government gone down. Blake had foreseen the consequences and had not welcomed them. "Nor was I anxious that the Liberal Party should at that time accede to power, believing that . . . the reaction would very soon set in." It had set in — depression had duly come — and for five years the Liberal government had coped with it while "the opposition who had produced this state of affairs sat on their benches complaining."

Now there was another change. The opposition had become the Government again, but it was no wiser than before. At a time when the country's condition was still critical, when frugality, economy, and retrenchment were the only watchwords, it had revived Conservative railway policy in a new, more reckless form. It admitted now that its first scheme had been impossible. It was asking for imperial help in the promotion of a second scheme because it knew the work was beyond its own resources. Yet it had pledged itself, without any promise or agreement, to the Yale-Kamloops project in the interior of British Columbia. He read out from hair-raising accounts in newspapers a description of the country through which the line must run, of the mountain walls to be tunnelled and the rivers to be tamed and bridged at a cost no man could reckon. Nor was that all. "They are embarking upon what I consider to be a fatal policy, that of making a trifling section of the work independent of the main policy . . . you cannot pause in this work when you have once engaged in it without utterly losing all you have spent. We are committed practically to the construction of the whole railway through British Columbia. I, for my part, protest against it, though I know it is useless to do so."

The echoes of Aurora sounded as he turned to other questions. The matter of an elective rather than an appointed Senate was "a question which ought to attract our attention at a tolerably early day." Proportional representation and compulsory voting were still much in his mind. "Tell me that it is necessary to reform the tariff; I tell you if you had a representative machine which properly recorded the balance of public opinion you would have no tariff to reform." He had intricate calculations made through his months of retirement which proved that point to himself. In the last general election Ontario's vote had shifted by a mere 5 per cent, yet it had doubled Conservative strength in the House of Commons. There was even more distortion because voting was not compulsory. The 55,000 truants who had stayed away from the polls had made the election meaningless. "Actually it remains unsettled whether Ontario was in favour of protection."

For these evils at the moment Blake had no remedy, "but they should be considered by thoughtful men." As he prepared for his return to parliament "I do not find the sky so clear or the immediate future so brilliant as some sanguine men, and perhaps of better judgment, expect. I know perhaps as well as most men the difficulties of organizing the Canadian Liberal Party and apprehend some difficulties."

To former and prospective colleagues they might have been chilling words, though there was warmth enough when he came to his peroration. "I believe, sir . . . that after nearly nineteen hundred years since the message came to earth of peace and good will to men, that the cause which is the greatest element productive of peace and mutual good will, the cause of freedom of commercial intercourse, the cause of freedom of transactions between man and man, between people and people . . . is one which we may vindicate on these higher grounds. I believe that the laws of morality, the real interest of the world in its highest sense, are and will be served by the cause of Free Trade."

There was more of it and it rose higher. He sat down to great applause. But it was not echoed in the private councils of the party. Mackenzie's name had hardly been heard in the speech. There had been no softening reference in his diatribe on Yale-Kamloops. For Senator George Brown, who had once appeared to consider support of the project, there had been an old additional irritant in his talk of Senate reform. There was no grist for politics in his musings on other reform. He had soared beyond even Cartwright in his eulogy of free trade, yet he had remained curiously ambivalent on the question of the tariff as it stood. Wrong in principle, certainly, it required to be judged in practice, and by every man for himself. There had been that odd injunction, tucked in the middle of the speech: "You will agree with me that every one of you is vitally interested in looking into the matter and in seeing how this tariff does operate . . . while you see the brick structure of a manufactory go up, while you see the workmen, etc., and while you are told that this is the consequence of a restrictive tariff, you have to decide whether this is mere coincidence or whether it is a consequence of the tariff."⁸ It was the balanced utterance of a responsible public man, yet it diluted much that he had said. To crude political gymnasts it was a careful balancing on the fence.

Whatever the friends felt, and whatever George Brown had said, the *Globe* refrained from comment. It reported the speech, as the *Mail* observed, "in almost painful fullness . . . because it dares not do otherwise; but having conceded thus much, it invariably lets him severely alone in the editorial columns."⁹ Even to that the *Globe* did not reply, and the Liberal party settled to watchful waiting. There was cause enough for discretion, and more than enough for tension, in the fact that Blake was back. He had returned through his own efforts, he had returned with his own objects, and he had returned his old self.

〰

"Who is Leader?"¹⁰ Within a day of the speech at Bowmanville it had become the question of the hour. Launched first by the editor of the Hamilton *Spectator*, it was kept alive for months by the Conservative press. According to these authorities Mackenzie had outlived his usefulness, Blake intended to replace him, and had accepted the Durham riding as a first step to that end. Conservatives by mid-December were indignant at Liberal apathy, not only to the speech itself, but to the matter of Blake's return. "The election of Mr. Blake was announced all over the Dominion as one of the events of the hour, and yet he remains an unhonoured and unnoticed member of the Grit party, who think they can freeze him into insignificance by ignoring his presence among them, and even his very existence."¹¹

It was useful Tory mischief-making, designed to create an atmosphere for the opening of the next session. When that came, on February 12, 1880, the assistance was hardly needed. "I will see Blake in person,"¹² Mackenzie had promised Laurier, and it was ominous enough that the promise had to be extracted. The two first men of the party no longer wrote to each other, they certainly did not confide, and whatever passed at the meeting it was not a meeting of minds. For sixteen months, as Mackenzie was to write later, he had felt around him "a process of sapping and mining . . . zealously carried on in and out of parliament by Blake and his partisans . . . all were as fair as sunshine to me and as cordial as possible, but I knew from various incidents that a conspiracy was on foot, and I knew the conspirators."[13] He was charging more than he could prove; there was no conspiracy. There was the mere force and thrust of the returning presence, thrusting Mackenzie aside. As Blake entered the Commons and settled with massive humility in a back bench one could feel the party shift and crack with the weight.

Early in March the debate on the budget came, and Mackenzie led the attack on the National Policy. Cartwright joined him, loyal as ever in that. Prosperity was still a fiction, protection was still iniquitous; neither of the two had given an inch of ground. Yet around them in Quebec and Ontario there were brick factories rising and workers streaming to jobs. Coincidence it may have been, but fact it certainly was; the country was coming alive with the change in tariffs. Some protection was good, some protection was essential; in spite of Liberals the heresy was gaining ground. It was rippling through the ranks of the party, eroding Mackenzie's footing, and it ran unchecked by Blake. He asked, and was granted by Macdonald, the elimination of duties on books in braille for the blind. Beyond that, through the whole debate on the tariffs, he had not one word to say.

Ahead on the order paper was the question of the Pacific Railway, and the core of that for the session was the Yale-Kamloops project. In their larger schemes Tupper and Macdonald had failed. Free-trade England was resentful and disapproving of the new Canadian tariffs. It was not lured by the promise of work on the railway for its thousands of idle men. There was to be no imperial money nor an imperial guarantee, and the only remaining prospect lay in the sale of public lands. In this respect there were new plans in the making, but not even Tupper could present them as other than dubious and vague. In mid-Canada, still with the impetus provided by a Liberal ministry, there was railroad crawling painfully toward a linking with the North-West. It was not enough for a new Conservative government or for British Columbia or for Tupper. The great project was stalled but it could not appear to be stalled; there would have to be some work begun. Tupper had let contracts for the line from Yale to Kamloops and he intended to have them ratified.

As the time neared for the debate Blake had moved forward from his desk among the back-benchers. On the night of April 15, with the session two months old, he sat between Cartwright and Laurier among the leaders facing the aisle. Mackenzie was beyond Cartwright, and to the right of the greying leader there was no Luther Holton sitting in his usual place. Holton had died suddenly, exactly a month before. George Brown was dying, shot by a drunken printer in his own office. With his great supporters gone and the party drawing away from him, Mackenzie was already grim in isolation. Living in his rented room, refusing to call a caucus, he had studied his own position on the matter of Yale-Kamloops. Certainly he would have to oppose the work, yet he had once seemed to consider it, and he had been supported in that by the *Globe*. There had been good reasons but they were mainly political reasons, and the change of front would require a careful defence. He had worked it out painfully in an elaborate resolution and had shown the result to the friends he still trusted. They had all given it their approval, but there remained the former friend. "One day I showed it to Blake. *That same evening* he gave a formal notice on the minutes that he would move the question."[14] Brusquely and without comment the leader was shoved to the sidelines; Blake was to speak first.

He rose about nine o'clock on the evening of the 15th, with the galleries packed and the corridors seething with latecomers. By midnight the House was wilting and some of the benches emptying under the vast three-hour barrage of his facts and figures. Cartwright noted the signs and asked for adjournment, much to Macdonald's umbrage, who had noted the signs too. The relief was granted, however, and the speech resumed next day to a restored and refreshed audience. Two hours from its resumption and five hours from its commencement it swept up to a conclusion that reserved the sting for the tail.

He had started with the "antiquities" of the railway question and marched forward to the present, combing the ground as he came. Nothing was left unmarked, nothing forgotten. When he came to the latest plans conceived by Tupper he was in full ironic sweep. The Honourable the Minister of Railways, "not content with taking charge of the suffering thousands of Canadians . . . took charge of the unemployed poor of England . . . this great scheme of outdoor relief — so far outdoors as the North-West — was to be carried out for the relief of the suffering poor in Great Britain." What had become of that plan? Nothing was heard of it now and nothing would be. England, with its trade shut out by Canadian protective tariffs, was in no mood to help with a Canadian railway.

Neither were private builders. Whatever was done must be done with public money, from the sale of the public lands. There was a new policy now, though to Blake it was barely discernible through the fog of Tupper's figures. For an hour he dwelt on them, lovingly, exhaustively, disastrously, and emerged with his own conclusion. The calculations were dreams, the projections beyond belief. There would be no such flood of immigrants as Tupper professed to foresee, and there would be no such sales of land. The land would have to be free to induce immigrants to take it, and new men settling on homesteads would require additional help. For years the revenues generated would be a fraction of what Tupper claimed. "Every dollar we are paying and are to pay for interest on the con-

struction of the Pacific Railway has come and must come out
of increased taxation or from further additions to our
burdens."

It was the east that would bear this burden, and he surveyed
the condition of the east. It was losing people to the west, and
that was likely to continue. What was the effect on old Canada
of such western emigration as there had been to date? Blake
was not opposed to it, the emigration was essential, he welcomed reasonable development with all his heart. But the shifting of population took its toll. The young farmer from Ontario
was no longer buying in Ontario as he worked his western
homestead. Nor would he, for years to come. "He will live as
hard as he can, smuggle as much as he can, and smuggle a good
deal too under the present tariff." Meanwhile Ontario had lost
him, as it had lost thousands of others. With her own farms
deserted in favour of newer lands, provincial revenues were
declining, real estate values falling and the demand for goods
reduced.

These were the real conditions underlying the false inflation
of the National Policy. They were everywhere, they were en-
demic, and they would only be vastly aggravated by the government's present course. "I am not now discussing the general
question of Free-trade and Protection," but there were these
facts to consider: in ten years the population of the country,
the tax-paying powers of the country, had increased at the most
hopeful estimate by 16 per cent. Its expenditures on current
needs and on the cost of capital construction had increased in
the same period by over 50 per cent. And yet in the face of
this — in the face of these "appalling figures" — the government was plunging on. "All that we can raise by taxes or loans,
all that we can beg or borrow, is to be sunk in the gorges of the
Fraser."

He had reached the gorges as his principal destination. The
whole course of his speech had been directed and intended
to culminate with the Yale-Kamloops railroad. The project had
once been thought of by a Liberal Ministry; he did not deny

it and made no attempt to explain it. "I had then long since ceased to be a member of the government, was not even in the country and knew nothing about the matter." What he did know was contained in a grim addendum, addressed directly to Tupper and without a glance at Mackenzie. Had there been any proposal made to commence the work, "the Honourable the Minister of Railways would have found me, as he complains I sometimes was, restive again."

He made as short work of a claim advanced for the project. "Well, Sir, we have this road for 125 miles lying in this ditch ... the Honourable the Minister of Railways talks of placing there within four or five years a population of 100,000."

It was the *Globe* that said it first, Tupper retorted.

"And does the Honourable gentleman agree with that?"

"Yes."

"I tell the Honourable gentleman he could not do it. If such a population went there within the time he names they would stay there as bones, not as living men."

He had ignored Mackenzie and brushed aside the *Globe*. Now he came to his point. The House was considering a vote of nine million dollars for this line which "begins nowhere, ends nowhere and will serve no earthly purpose" if it were not extended westward to the Pacific coast. And with that done, what then? There would have to be eastward building as far as Edmonton, which was now proposed as the terminus of the prairie section. There was no prairie section; there would have to be money for that, and the money was not yet found. There was no policy to find it that any man could believe in. Yet once the work was begun in the Fraser Canyon all this would be called for, all this would be inevitable. The nine millions would become thirty millions, the thirty would vault to fifty and would rise to a hundred millions to prevent the loss of the whole. Was the country ready for that? Did the government dare to ask for it?

"If in all else you be rash, in this at any rate be discreet. Learn that our position is grave and serious and that our future is dependent on present prudence. Complete the rail-

way to the Red River; go on with the prairie section as fast
as settlement demands. For that risk something, since the die
is cast . . . Postpone meanwhile the western work and do not
by your present action based on airy dreams and vain imagin-
ings risk the ruin of your country."

He was ready to move his amendment, a matter of twenty
words. It owed nothing to the draft prepared by his leader. The
contrast was sharp and clear, insulting by its very starkness.
"The public interests," he asked the House to resolve, "require
that the work of constructing the Pacific Railway in British
Columbia be postponed."[15]

When he sat down he had shaken the party across from
him and shaken Macdonald himself. "We were obliged to sit
for the best part of *two days* in caucus," Macdonald reported,
"in order to get them to vote down Blake's motion."[16] He had
done more than that, however, to the man a seat away. "I about
this time," Mackenzie was to write later, "determined to pre-
cipitate a crisis."[17]

৶

The crisis came within a matter of ten days, and it was not
brought on by the leader. On Monday, April 26, for the first
time in the session of 1880, the members of the Liberal party
met in caucus. They had not been summoned by Mackenzie,
and Mackenzie was not present. He was informed next morning
of the result of the deliberations. A resolution had been passed
asking him to "consider the question of the leadership."

Among the delegation of five which came to his office Blake
was conspicuously absent. Cartwright and Laurier were there,
however, the onetime trusted friends. As they fumbled with
explanations Mackenzie cut them off. He had heard about the
meeting yesterday; it was another of the Blake conspiracies.

No, Laurier urged gently, it was no conspiracy. But there
was a general feeling . . .

"Very well. If that is so I shall very soon cease to lead the
Liberal party."[18]

It was two o'clock next morning, at the close of a long sitting, when he made his curt announcement to a silent House. Among the late-lingering members Blake sprawled at his desk, his black hat over his eyes. "Mr. Speaker," said Mackenzie, "I yesterday determined to withdraw from my position as leader of the opposition, and from this time forth I will speak and act for no person but myself."[19]

A day later, in another Liberal caucus, Blake stood up to accept Mackenzie's place. Around him in the crowded room

A BIT OF FATHERLY ADVICE.

SIR JOHN. "NOW, EDWARD, BE STEADY, SOBER, STRAIGHTFORWARD, AND KEEP YOUR HANDS CLEAN, AND YOU MAY BECOME AS GREAT A SUCCESS AS I AM."

there were many of the familiar faces, many of the old reminders, much of the persuasive eloquence of 1873. He was more easily persuaded this time, since he had come here to be persuaded, that he was the inevitable man. Yet he was not and he could not be empowered to lead the nation; he was seven years too late for that.

CHAPTER ELEVEN

"WE ARE GOING TO WIN IN 1883"

H E WAS forty-six now, generally recognized as the greatest lawyer in Canada, and a comparatively wealthy man. He had built well on those first investments and properties over which his father had agonized, and he had also followed his father in other fields. For the past seven years he had been Chancellor of the University of Toronto. His brother sat on the bench as Vice-Chancellor of Ontario. His law firm, with the choice of the best business had also the choice of the best legal talent, and merely to be a partner in "Blakes" was the sign of a marked man. Few distinguished visitors came to Toronto without the hope of meeting Blake, and he was able to entertain them in a style he considered fitting. Humewood, mellowing more graciously with each passing year, was only another symbol of professional and social success.

Marriage was a serene companionship, and there was pride in his four children. Margaret was the restful confidant, the perfect wife, concerned only with him. Sophia, the one daughter, was a handsome twenty-two, with a gift for music which her tone-deaf father admired, "though I know nothing at all of music and am rather partial toward her."[1] Edward Hume, the eldest son, was now approaching twenty, Edward Francis was fourteen, and Samuel Verschoyle twelve. Their development hinted, as their names hinted, at a burden of family legendry that might prove difficult to bear. Their father himself had experience of the same burden. He had tried too hard to be worthy of William Hume, to rise to the beloved ideal. The boys tried now to be worthy of Edward Blake, and of Blakes and Cronyns and Humes who had gone before them. They were sometimes strained and shaken when they fell short of their goals, and it occasionally made the father a little fearful. He was gentle, concerned, tolerant to the last limit, but still the goals were there. He could not change himself nor the boys' ideal of himself, and life in any case was a continuing struggle. He must press on, driven by his own compulsions, and the boys press on behind him.

The family circle was close, and enclosed in the wider circle of the knitted kinships. There was brother Sam and his family, always near and devoted. There was Kerr, the favourite partner who had married the dearest sister, and there was the Cronyn family in London, bound by so many ties. It was among these and a few others that life was most richly lived, that one felt truly at home. It was here that the sense of roots, strong and secure, reached back to the Irish past. It was here that the conviction of worth, nourished on older worth, provided a sterner strength for the paths of duty. They were hard paths, set in a raw new land, but God did nothing in vain.

He was no longer so sure as he had once been of his nearness to that God, but he was near to Catherine Blake. Now in her late seventies his mother was still unchanged, the daughter of Irish Protestants, the daughter of Irish gentry, and the essence of mid-Victorianism translated to Upper Canada. In her eyes and in his she had forged the chains of his rectitude. She was the thread of steel and gold that ran through his life, drawing him away from the herd, binding him in with the elect. She still advised on his diet, she still commented on his speeches, and he sometimes squirmed a little or dismissed it, tolerant and amused. But he could not escape the image she had built of him, transmuted to his very blood-stream and made his guide and master. He was a man born for the summits, reserved for the toils and duties of the highest place. Elsewhere, for the diminished exile, there could be only the common grind of common men.

In his thirteen years of politics he had been offered the highest places and had turned away from them. He might have been Chief Justice, he might have been Prime Minister, and he was now neither. Politics itself, that daily, grubby business of wheedling, bargaining, and persuasion, he had found to be unendurable. Yet he must endure it; the sense of exile was worse. He had been driven back, whipped by the lash of duty; what other reason could there be? What other had there been for William Hume Blake? That brisk, able, opinionated, driving lawyer, always so firmly fixed on his own ambitions, had attained the status of sainthood in his son's eyes, cherished, challenging, often and passionately defended. Even his gout, even his diabetes, even his money worries had been transformed. They had become an "affection of the brain", incurred in the line of duty, breaking a devoted man. It would break the son too; he fully expected that. As he pressed on in those footsteps he had already given way; time and again he had felt those intimations. Yet somehow he had fought back, somehow he had been called back; duty was not yet done.

They were conceptions somewhat foreign to the House of Commons, and in spite of his familiarity he was foreign to the place himself. That crowded, restless chamber stinking of drains and sweat, redolent of the bars below, had little of Victorian rectitude or charm for the Victorian man. On the nights when members reeled and swore in the aisles, when the books flew and the wrestlers locked in combat, Macdonald could watch amused. Blake could not; he was witnessing degradation. Yet it was here that the forces met, that the muscles of the nation flexed, that the guiding mind was needed. He came in his rumpled tweeds and his broad black hat, self-summoned to give that guidance.

Since it was not always welcomed, he rose justifying himself, true to himself alone. Tariffs, railways, taxes, the public business — whatever the issue dealt with, it must be seen in its grand totality as conceived of by Edward Blake. There could be no flaws, there could be no gaps, there could be nothing skimmed or omitted in the course of the mighty argument. He came to each of the occasions prepared by weeks of study, steeled to the great effort, conscious of error and enmity to be battered down by facts. He had them, he had them all; the masses of books and documents, the marshalled ranks of statistics, the examples, precedents and warnings that history could bring to bear. He moved on, sweeping the ground before him to the limit of every horizon, too often clearing the House of numbed listeners. It did not matter; it was their own loss and peril; he had come to establish truth.

The work as it absorbed his energy had involved his emotions too; the reasoner had become the prophet and the argument had become the vision. It had been clear, precise, beautiful in the lamplit quiet of the study, in the last small hours of the night. It had been duty done, duty to God and country, duty to father and mother. The thought had driven him on, lifted him to crests of eloquence, and occasionally swept him over. The cold, sardonic clarity, the relentless waves of conviction, had sometimes washed to their conclusion in a swelling tide of bilge. It was the last effect of the effort, the invariable warning of strain, the release of the exhausted phrase-maker surrendering himself to words.

They cost him dear, those words, wasted or not. The spectacles with the steel frames and the thick lenses had been part of his life since childhood. He read painfully and he read endlessly, and with every recurring crisis there was still more to be read. The strain increased with the effort and the effort magnified crisis, yet the widening ramifications must be pursued to the last end. When he stood up in the House, his notes prepared at last, it was always with a throbbing head, always with taut-drawn nerves, and with those faces across the aisle a hostile blur.

Nor was that all that he owed to those tired eyes, "to my blindness which is notorious."[2] He had "cut" Lady Dufferin in

215

the corridors of the House of Commons. He was forever cutting other important friends, and being told of the fact later. Always the apology went forth, often profuse and agitated, but he could never be reassured that he was quite forgiven.

He must live with that, however, once he had made amends. There could be no outreaching beyond the due and proper; it would be a cheapening of Edward Blake. If he must walk deprived of friends, or uneasily among half-friends, that was another cross to be accepted. He loved the ideal of friendship and yearned often for its warmth, but of how it was made and perpetuated he had almost no conception. He was removed from that by the walls of his own upbringing, as he was removed from the common man. He could not court, he could not stoop, certainly he could not flatter and there were few with whom he could share. The first and the last loyalty was to his own conception of himself.

He had broken Mackenzie in friendship, loyal to that conception. He would break others and make others, loyal as ever still. He was servant of "the public interest" and the phrase was destiny and burden, to be interpreted by Edward Blake and to be shouldered in his own way. He could not retreat from duty, he could not be bound by friendship, he must obey the joyless call.

It made for a joyless man, and that he was, at least to the public view. When the tall, thickening figure rose in the House of Commons the face was pasty and set, the spectacles glinted icily. There was no warmth in the corridors when he passed among party friends; corridors were a way for Blake to reach his office. "His paw, chilly as the fin of a dead fish"[3] was a proverb with lesser members, and there was truth in an acid paraphrase of the general trend of his discussion: "If you believe me, what need is there for explanations? . . . if you do not believe me you stand condemned."[4] Hardly more warming, apart from the set speeches, were his appearances at party occasions and the great formal banquets. "I looked at his shirtfront and then at his face," a guest reported to Macdonald, "and concluded that it didn't matter which I looked at as they were both starched and ironed. He will never be a real leader of men."[5]

Time and again he had confessed failure himself, failure in the common terms of political warfare. He had not been able to mould and manoeuvre men, to set a party on the twisting course to power. If anything he had disrupted party; if anything, he had cost it power; and his insistent harping on virtue made him all the more fiercely blamed. The rich lawyer from Toronto could afford to despise corruption; the man borne up by the cloud of his own self-righteousness could refrain from common work. Yet some work had been done in the course of those thirteen years, and much of it by Edward Blake.

Always the Ontarian first, he had fought the battles of his province in the name of federalism, and federalism was stronger than before. He had lost on those Better Terms for Nova Scotia, he had lost a battle in the creation of Manitoba, he was steadily losing his war with British Columbia, yet he had forced Macdonald to terms. The deep-set, never relinquished urge to centralize was being checked on many fronts. The two older provinces, the heart of the Confederation, had been held to their original purposes and recalled to their earlier fears. Ontario was now alive to the danger of a little Ontario, powerless in the grip of an over-mastering Dominion. Quebec was alive to the danger of a French people, swallowed in an English nation.

He had stood for "purity" in politics, and it was still a distant hope. But the game was a little cleaner now than it had been before he came. It was more dangerous to buy votes, more difficult to steal elections; and he had nagged in every parliament for the laws that made it so. It was Blake together with Mackenzie who had reduced corruption and patronage, and it was Blake rather than Mackenzie who had forced a Liberal government to adopt the secret ballot. Respectful of his own money, he regarded the public monies as a sacred trust, and saw to it that they were so regarded by the public servant. Little as he knew or wished to know of the average common man, he had a high view of the rights and duties of the voter. Above all in his own person, and even in his own faults, so rigid, privileged, and ludicrous in his pious self-esteem, dreaming of his vast reforms, his perfect electoral system, he stood for a new ideal. Few politicians liked it, no one fully attained it, yet still the ideal was there. It was the conception of a responsible citizenry to be served by responsive leaders and to be served with clean hands.

Almost from the first he had stood out in Canadian politics as the one comparable alternative to John A. Macdonald. He was the younger by twenty years, but he had entered the field as George Brown was leaving, and Mackenzie had only replaced Brown because Blake refused to do so. Nor, in refusing leadership, had he ever relinquished the influence that potentially meant power; it was Blake in the eyes of Macdonald who was the one real rival, the man to be watched and feared. They repelled each other, fascinated each other, and regarded their contrasting faults with real regret. If Macdonald smelt of corruption, Blake smelt of the vestry, and it made on either hand for a waste of talent. There was much that they might have done, much they might have improved if they had been able to work together. They had been almost eye-to-eye in the making of the Supreme Court, there were only shadings of difference in their stand on the autonomy of the Dominion, and in the development of the imperial relationship they drifted alike in mist.

Yet there were fundamental differences, and they imposed basic choices. Macdonald had grown up in Kingston, with the War of 1812 a recent memory. Blake had grown up in busy, bustling Toronto, with its Yankee lust for trade and much of that trade with Yankees. It had seemed safe enough, and certainly British enough. He did not share the earlier memories of Macdonald, nor Macdonald's fear of the Americans. They were forty millions to four millions but they were busy with their own concerns. Let Canada be the same, neighbour and trading partner when her interests so directed. Blake did not see the flag as inevitably following trade, nor the paths of trade as the determinants of political boundaries. He was not for the building of walls in North America, he was for the opening of roads to commerce. John Smith of Bowmanville, in Blake's opinion, would remain as British as ever, as British as he ought or wished to be, though he bought in Rochester, New York.

It was Blake's answer to the National Policy and it impelled his answer to the question of the Pacific Railway. Each had been conceived in haste, each dictated by fear. Roads must be built, certainly, but only as interest served, tangible, actual present national interest. It was one thing to talk of that westward leap, that bridging of the continent with steel, that filling of its empty spaces. It was another thing to attempt it in a generation. He foresaw the strain on the east, the problems of the opening of the west, the threat of national disruption in a wastage of lives and wealth. He foresaw the other problems that would be left to fester, shelved for the railway, aggravated by the railway. What of Ontario and Quebec, the compact, vital heartland of a nation that was still dual? Would the railway help in the welding of French and English? Macdonald hoped that it might; Blake was sure it would not. Macdonald stood for the mighty westward gamble; Blake for order and proportion with the east as the heart of growth. The issue was near to decision now, and both men were leaders. It would be the way of one or the other.

As Blake stalked at last to the head of the Liberal party there was a cooler welcome than there might have been before. He was the obvious man, the only man, yet he was the prisoner of his own record. "We are like a ship at sea without you," his closest followers conceded; but he had wrecked the ship too often, steering by his own star. There were many now who saw that star as set in its own cold heaven, hopelessly remote from earth.

Among these Laurier was not included, that rising man of Quebec. There was a companionship building here that would be one of the best of their lives, one of the most enduring, and fruitful for the nation itself. Laurier beside Blake was growing in the House and caucus, and more and more there were quiet hours together. Laurier was familiar now with the cluttered study at Humewood and the heaped masses of papers. He was sensing the causes of some of the moods and attitudes and he had come to know the charm of the other Blake. He had seen those spectacles come off, those thick, white lawyer's hands rubbing the tired eyes, myopic but still haunted by their glimpses of far-off goals. There was that shock of chestnut hair, always so carefully brushed, always so stiffly in place when Blake rose in public. Here, when he talked to a friend, when he thrust his truth at a friend, it tumbled over his forehead to be impatiently swept back, in a curiously boyish, suddenly revealing gesture. There were passion and purpose here, fretting and trapped; there were tremendous, priceless abilities struggling for release and use. Blake, said Laurier, "was the most powerful intellectual force in Canadian political history . . . he would have proved Canada's most constructive statesman had he held office . . . he cast a spell over every man in parliament. We felt in the presence of genius."[6] But he spoke the words long afterward, when they could change nothing. The unhappy warrior had not prevailed in his time.

∽

Through the last few days of April and the first few days of May 1800, Blake found himself turned relentlessly on the spit of the public press, the latest meat for the fire. The blaze kindled with his railway speech had become centred on himself. He was, however he had got there, the leader of a national party, to be toasted, roasted, and dissected as he had not yet been before. Under the hand of his friend John Cameron, the columns of the London *Advertiser* glowed with welcome. To the London *Evening Herald*, "The selection of Mr. Blake has created no enthusiasm in the party . . . they recall how he deserted them twice on the eve of a general election."[7] To the

Argenteuil *Advertiser*, a friendly voice from Quebec, "Mr. Blake is without doubt the premier intellect of Canada."[8] To *Le Canada*, however, *bleu* and also of Quebec, he was and always had been "L'élément de discord."[9] What was seen in Argenteuil as "the beginning of a new era" was "Mackenzie's Decapitation" to the Moncton *Daily Times*: "However the party may view it, common sense people will doubt that Mackenzie with all his failings would be more likely to achieve success than the impractical, poetical, unbalanced Blake . . . he develops idiosyncrasies in his day-dreaming and carries them with him into his wide-awake hours."[10]

"This change," said the Montreal *Gazette*, "was brought about in a very scurvy way,"[11] and the same view was held by the *Morning Herald*: "The Grit party may find an abler and better man to lead them, but they can never recover from the odium attaching to their heartless and relentless treatment in adversity of the man whom in prosperity they followed and fawned on." [12] Through the *Evening Chronicle* of Halifax, the organ of A. G. Jones, came suitable salutations: "It is no disparagement to the many other able men in the Canadian parliament to say that Mr. Blake stands head and shoulders above them all . . . with such a leader the Liberal party of Canada must draw to its ranks the best elements of the Canadian people."[13] It was seen otherwise by the people of Berlin, Ontario, according to the *Daily News*: "He moves about like an animated iceberg, giving everybody a chill."[14] To the *Daily Telegraph* of Saint John he was "the idol of young Ontario . . . the centre of many hopes,"[15] while in Brantford nearer home he was something less to the editor of the *Daily Courier* in Brantford, nearer home: "He is not a courageous man. He waves his arms on the bank and makes every preparation for a plunge into the stream; then he shuffles down the slope and wades carefully in."[16]

Whatever was to be made of it all there was one thing clear from the *Globe*: he was not welcomed by the party's senior organ. "There is little reason to doubt," was the best it could find to say, "that the new leader will fulfill all reasonable expectations, but he must be given time . . . we earnestly wish for Mr. Blake success in his new position, and hope that the new leader may have no more ground of complaint against the party than the party expects to have of him."[17] The *Globe*'s protagonist, the *Mail*, joyfully pouncing on that, found "sinister ambiguity" in the final sentence. "The *Globe* plainly states that it has such complaints to make, or plain English has lost its meaning." The English used by the *Mail* was certainly plain enough: "The bitterest enemy of the Reform party could desire nothing better than the selection of Mr. Blake. It means vacillation both in act and policy, and the ultimate disintegration of the party."[18]

He read everything as always and clipped everything as always, filing it away in his scrapbooks. He could ignore nothing and forget nothing, and much of it would fester later. Yet it was swept aside for the moment in the face of a greater change, altering all perspectives. The *Mail* spoke as expected, the *Globe* had sunk to a mumble, but it hardly mattered now. On May 12, 1880, Blake was one of the pall-bearers at the funeral of George Brown. He walked with the deposed Mackenzie and the group of the party leaders, but he was newly enlarged and alone. Whatever he had felt for Brown, whatever he felt at the passing, the Liberal party had become the party of Blake. It seemed to harden and steel him, to release some spring of confidence. "I will let you into a secret," he told a reporter only a few weeks later, "we are going to win in 1883."[19]

✍

He was aware by late June of the work that lay before him. On the 29th, at one of his party picnics, Macdonald had dropped a deliberate and portentous hint. Conditions had changed in the country and in the matter of the Pacific Railway. The opposition had said that it should not be built, and certainly that it should not be attempted with public money.

Well, he had met them half way. The railway was going to be built, but not with the people's taxes. "There are capitalists at this moment who, knowing that there is a certain fortune to be made out of the construction of the railway, are asking that the work be handed over to them."[20] Even as he spoke, he said, offers were being considered. They would be considered further in England, where he intended to go with Tupper, and he and the Minister of Railways would be back with a new plan. What Liberals could not do, Conservatives had now done; they had interested private builders.

There were alerting rumours through the summer and early autumn, and a sense of events in motion. All were well founded. Macdonald returned in September to announce that an agreement had been reached, and on the 21st of October it was made legal. On December 10, before a House that had been summoned two months earlier than usual, Tupper presented the terms for ratification.

Inevitably they recalled old scandal. Once more the Canadian government was contracting with a syndicate of capitalists which included American names. Once more there were names omitted, and perhaps significantly omitted. James J. Hill, the railway magnate of St. Paul, was one of the prominent figures. Where was the name of Donald A. Smith, that entrepreneur of the west, who was almost certainly involved? George Stephen, President of the Bank of Montreal, was official head of the syndicate, but he was Smith's cousin. He had only entered on railway business because of the urgings of Smith, and Smith was an old and bitter enemy of Macdonald. Had he become a friend now, and if so why? What had the inducements been? Everything was veiled in secrecy, everything hinted to Liberals of the return of the days of Allan.

Yet beneath the unanswered questions lay a hard and convincing fact. Hill, Smith, and Stephen had a record of success behind them and knew what they were about. As recently as a year ago they had completed the great coup that had given them possession of the St. Paul, Minneapolis and Manitoba

Railway embracing the Pembina branch in the North-West, and one of the most profitable lines on the continent. They had each made fortunes from the deal and were in a position to make more. Stephen was no Allan, this syndicate was not the old syndicate, and whatever the bargain offered it would have to be taken seriously.

It was the more monstrous because of that, in Blake's eyes. Here was the fruit of Macdonald's old obsession, that railway to be built in haste begot of fear, all on Canadian soil. It was to be hacked through mountain country where hardly a white man lived, to keep the Americans out of British Columbia. It was to go round by that empty wilderness to the north of the Great Lakes, rather than link with the Americans on their easy route to the west. Anything to prevent the Yankees, anything to shut them out; it was still Macdonald's goal.

At what cost? One looked at the terms and gasped. There were the familiar figures, battered from old debates. Twenty-five million dollars and twenty-five million acres, the syndicate was to have that. It was to have a choice of the best land, whether along its route or not, "fairly fit for settlement" in its own opinion. It was to acquire its roadbed free, with wide allotments for its stations, shops and round-houses. Its construction materials were to be imported duty-free. Nor was that more than the beginning. It was to receive as a free gift the sections of the line already built by government, and most of what was now building. It was the government, not the syndicate, that would have to complete the line to Yale from Kamloops, and push that line on westward to reach the Pacific coast. And the government, equally with the syndicate, would be bound to finish its work in ten years.

Actually, what the syndicate was contracting for was the building of two sections, the one from Kamloops to Winnipeg, and the other from Port Arthur to Callander around the hump of the Great Lakes. They were major sections, certainly, but they were still unnecessary sections, and what was the reward to be? The company now to be incorporated under the terms of this contract would be exempt in perpetuity from all forms of taxation. The unsold portion of its land grant would be exempt for twenty years. During the same twenty years, in that region of North-West settlement that was the crux of the whole scheme, it would be free of the fear of rivals. Clause 15 in the agreement, soon to become famous, would forbid competing railroads south of its main line if they ran within fifteen miles of the American border. The vast space of the land grants, the monopoly of western traffic and ten years of railway building at the cost of the Canadian people would all be totally surrendered. "The Canadian Pacific Railway shall become and be thereafter the absolute property of the Company."[21]

The debate began with some tentative ranting and foot-dragging while Liberals caught their breath. So great an issue should be decided by a general election. The contract made in secrecy should not be rushed through the House. There was information withheld, there was lack of time for proper study of the terms, there was a threat to the Christmas holidays. Mackenzie, grey and diminished now, with his voice beginning to fail, demanded the production of every scrap of paper, of every offer or tentative offer that had affected the negotiations. Macdonald flatly refused. He was equally flat with the complaints of the new leader; the debate would go on as planned. There was a rumour about, said Blake, "that if we are good boys and say our lessons well, according to the instructions of our masters opposite, we may get home on the 23rd, but if we are not good boys we shall be kept here at school."[22] Tupper demurred to the irony with more irony of his own; good boys ought to be pleased. Mackenzie's government, quite as much as Macdonald's, had hoped to find a private builder for the railway. Now that had been done. "The House will readily understand the gratification I expected to see spread over the honourable gentleman's countenance on learning that all that he had been unable to accomplish . . . his successors were in a position to present for the consideration of Parliament."[23]

From that beginning there were to be six weeks of debate,

broken by a Christmas interval that was no holiday at all. During the ten days between December 23, 1880 and January 4, 1881, the battle went out to cities across the country and the speeches were spoken over in jammed and tumultuous halls. Then, with the resumption of parliament, the flanking movement came.

"I am in a position to announce," wrote the Ottawa correspondent of the *Globe* on January 7, "that a syndicate of well-known capitalists, railroad contractors and business men has been formed for the construction of the Canadian Pacific Railway on terms eminently more favourable to Canada than those terms now waiting the ratification of parliament and which Sir John Macdonald is forcing upon the country." As to the terms themselves "I am not in a position to speak so authoritatively,"[24] but he was able to name the gentlemen who composed the syndicate and prepared to guess at their intentions. They would require in the first place less land and money. They would accept taxation and pay duties on their building materials like any private company. Nor would they be found inflexible if the scope of the plan were reduced. They would obligingly desist from the building of any section if the government so decreed.

The offer reached the Cabinet smelling to heaven of Toronto machinations. It had been framed in haste, subscribed to in haste and subscriptions were still being sought. Most of the principals named were flagrant Liberals, and all the terms were adjustable to Blake's ideas. Blake denied paternity and Macdonald was inclined to believe him; the gesture was too inept. Yet it drew Macdonald to his feet, sick and furious, pushing Tupper to the sidelines for the first time in the debate. Through most of what had gone before Macdonald had sat silent, enduring the month-long deluge, exhausting himself and his arguments in steeling his own supporters. But everything had been heard "*ad nauseam*", it had all gone on too long, and for the old man in a hurry this was the final straw.

The offer was a farce, he said, his voice rasping with strain.

226

It was a mere political plot hatched in Ottawa and he defied Blake to support it. "It won't catch the blindest — it won't catch the most credulous." Who were the men who made it? — generally a clutch of nobodies — defeated Liberal candidates from the last election. What was their one object? — it was merely to discredit a contract that was part of government policy. They could offer anything they liked — terms as low as they liked — because they were not responsible now and would never have to fulfill them. Well, they had said, "the Government are pledged to a contract. They cannot get out of it, and we are quite safe . . . the Government cannot in honour and decency, if their policy is defeated, remain in office, and therefore we will get in and we will take care of our friends . . . we will make things easy for them and so arrange it that, even if their offer was accepted by us when we go into office, we can let them out of it." The old familiar of politics, so knowledgeable of bygone schemes, dissected this one with savage and angry relish. "We must be blind as bats, and the country must be blind as owls in the day, if they do not see that there is a net, and they will avoid the net. They will not be caught."[25]

Hardly able to stand, he turned to excoriate Blake. Blake's hopes were well known. "Not a train would ever run through British Columbia if he could help it." What Blake wished was "to run off the trade into the United States, to strengthen, to renew, to extend and develop our commerce with the United States, to the utter destruction of the great plan, basis and policy of the Dominion which is to connect the great counties composing the Dominion from sea to sea by one vast iron chain which cannot and will never be broken."[26]

He was at the very core of the question, but Blake had arrived before him. In thousands of words, answered by thousands of words, the new leader of the Liberals had established his own position. Why were they now considering a private contract? It was because the work of a Liberal government had made it possible. Liberals had completed the surveys and advanced the building of railway lines toward the heart of the North-West; they had all but completed the connection. "Does anybody suppose that the circumstance that the road from Thunder Bay to Selkirk will be finished in a year or two is not an important factor in the building of the Pacific Railway?"[27] The Conservatives had also built since they returned to office, and more than Blake approved of, but that was beside the matter. The point was that it had been done with public money, and that the work the country needed now could be completed with public money. Why then, in view of all these circumstances, this vast gift to a syndicate?

Even if there were still an argument for private building it was negated by the contract's terms. Who would be paying for the Yale-Kamloops section, and for the section to the Pacific coast? The Government of Canada would be paying for it and completing it in ten years. Then, with the rest of the railway and the fruits of the public purse, with all that imperial, never-to-be-taxed domain, it would become the property of the syndicate. "Gentlemen, we will give you as much and half as much again as is necessary to build this railway, and we will let you own it afterwards." That was the effect of the agreement. "It is not the work of private capital at all. These men will, for a little while, until they make some land sales, invest four or five millions which will be recouped to them within a very short space of time, and they will then have their enterprise without having sunk a dollar of their own money in it, and will have millions of acres besides . . . Sir, these people will become landlords of the North-West."[28]

The North-West. It was the opening of the North-West that was the present goal of railway building, its imperative and justification. How did Blake propose to achieve the goal? There was that line to Thunder Bay, begun by Liberals and driving east from Winnipeg, to be a link for Manitoba with a lakehead port. "To what end did we sink millions more than was necessary to produce the extraordinary grades and splendid provisions with respect to curvature . . . to whose advantage

is this magnificent railway, constructed so that it can be run
and worked very cheaply, and enormous trains twice the length
of those on other roads be brought down?"[29] It was to the advantage of the western settler, because it would cheapen costs
to the lakehead and reduce by half the freight rates paid on his
grain. "That is the means, that is the inducement you have to
offer the people of Manitoba and the North-West within a year
or two."[30]

Would it be an inducement only to those north of the
boundary? Why should it be? In the American northwest there
was a railway monopoly now, exacting whatever it wished in
the way of freights. Would it last long if there were a cheaper
route to the east, half-Canadian or not? On either side of the
boundary the people were much the same, barely rooted as yet.
They were Germans, Swedes and Icelanders, Scots, English-
men and Irishmen, a newly-arriving Babel of the world's ambitious and hungry. Their hopes were centred on land, land to
produce grain, and on getting that grain to market. Would they
accept no way for its passage but a way on American soil? By
what distortion of patriotism, by what mysterious affinity,
would they insist on paying the freight rates of American
buccaneers? They would not insist; there would be branch
lines built to the north. Canada would tap that mounting flood
of grain.

But the grain was destined for the east, for Montreal and the
sea, and it would draw a westward tide of returning goods. The
problem of transport entered another phase. There would be
water movement and movement by rail on land, both as links
with the eastern and western lakeheads. Rail was the more difficult question, and what was Macdonald's plan? It was to em-
ploy the syndicate here, for a work no government would
consider. It was to build that endless Callander-Port Arthur
section through seven hundred miles of rock and bush and
muskeg that had hardly a white inhabitant and only the one
attraction: it was to the north of the Great Lakes, it was all on
Canadian soil.

That section, with the rest of the line, was to be completed in ten years. Ten years of wandering in this northern wilderness, while the easier, obvious alternative lay neglected. What was it? Blake pointed to Sault Ste. Marie. It was a scant two hundred miles from the region of Callander and it was a port at the very throat of Lake Superior. A line to Sault Ste. Marie could be built through easy country and could be completed in three years, perhaps even in two. What would be the position then? There would be passage from Port Arthur to the Sault by lake steamers, and there would be passage south of the lakes by connections with American railways, already built or building. Was there anything horrifying in the thought? Would Americans control the traffic? Exactly the reverse was true. They would be providing merely a nexus on the roadway across a continent, mainly on Canadian soil. From the North-West to Port Arthur and from the Sault east to the Atlantic, Canadian transport offered the better route. Over the whole long haul, as compared to anything the Americans could offer now, there would be a saving of hundreds of miles, thousands of dollars in freights on every trainload. From both sides of the border, and from as far west as the Pacific, Canada would draw the major portion of the traffic. "By this line . . . you get the shortest route from San Francisco to Europe.[11]

"Anybody who looks at the map, or who knows what is doing on the other side, must know that that road is the key of the position; that the future of Canada, and particularly of Montreal, is bound up in our having the shortest line by way of Sault Ste. Marie by which the traffic of the American North-West as well as of the Canadian North-West shall go to the ocean steamships . . . Sir, that line will give us the trade of about 400 miles in depth, as I estimate, from our boundary all across the continent. It will give us, at present, the trade to a point 60 or 70 miles south of St. Paul . . . it will give us trade not in the future. We are told to rejoice because in ten years we will get a road through to the North-West . . . I propose that you adopt a scheme which in three years will give you a short route to the North-West, and within three years and for all time thereafter the traffic of . . . the population of the United States which would be tributary to that route and which would be constantly increasing.

"I maintain that we will be able to control the traffic of the North-West legitimately, and I do not want to control it any other way . . . All we have to do to accomplish that result is to utilize the American lines." Why not? What did the Americans do? "Why, Sir, the western peninsula of Ontario is streaked with lines loaded with American traffic. Why do they send it through our country? Because it suits them; because it supplies the best route for them. They do not feel that it is anti-national to go through Canadian territory. They do not feel that there is anything humiliating in it, anything wrong in it . . . commerce knows no boundary line in this matter. Commerce seeks to make use of our neighbour's roads . . . in order to make the best, the nearest, the cheapest commercial connections between the two parts of our own country. If, Sir, we can annex commercially a part of Minnesota . . . why not do it? But I want to go further — I want to annex not only Minnesota, but Wisconsin, Michigan, Dakota, Montana, Idaho and Washington Territory."[32]

Here was the "timid" Blake, the "hesitant", "vacillating", "always negative" Blake, advancing his own alternative to the course set by Macdonald. It would have accepted geography and adapted it to common needs. It would have made of trade what it should be, an agent of natural growth. It would have overlapped boundaries and ignored boundaries, it might one day even have dissolved them, but it would have followed the course of settlement and the developed will of peoples. It would not have strained, and over-strained, the resources of a dual nation. It would not have forgotten Frenchness to bind Britishness in. Nor would it have abandoned so much of the shaping of North America to a handful of commercial tycoons.

In answering Macdonald on the offer of the second syndicate, Blake was comparatively brief. He was even a little evasive. He had not known what the terms were until they had

231

come before the House. He did not say that he had not known they were coming. He would himself have rejected some parts of the offer, yet there was much in it that was preferable to the present contract. Could there not then be a revision, an adjustment between the parties that would prove acceptable to both? "Are governments infallible? Do they never make mistakes? Are they bound to ruin their country to preserve their reputation for infallibility? Should they not retreat from a false step?"[33]

It was of no use. There was to be no retreat. Blake moved his enormous amendment and it was voted down. By the late days of January, as the bill crawled through committee, he was quibbling about "wills" and "shalls" in the financial terms, about the gulfs of difference between interest "accrued" or "accruing". "I cannot really comprehend," exclaimed the mild-mannered Tilley at last, "what the honourable gentleman is driving at." The question rose of the Indians who would be displaced in the North-West. "We can form no estimate of what the extinguishment of these titles will cost us," said an honourable member, "it might cost us an Indian war."[34] The remark passed without comment, from Blake or anyone else. On Tuesday, February 1, 1881, the act incorporating the Canadian Pacific Railway received its formal assent. False or not, ruinous or not, the great step had been taken.

Blake was forty-seven now and the Dominion of Canada was into its fourteenth year. There was time enough and youth enough for the correction of great mistakes. That great mistakes had been made Blake would always believe, and he was a man of enormous influence at the head of a national party. He might aspire to Macdonald's place; he might hope for the grip on power; he might alter wrong directions before they were firmly set. What still remained to be measured was the depth of his wish for the work, and no less than that the depths of the man himself.

A NOTE ON SOURCES

The Blake Papers in the Ontario Provincial Archives have been a principal source of material for this work. So have other collections in the Public Archives of Canada, such as the Laurier Papers, the Alexander Mackenzie Papers, and others. A large selection of Blake letters and other documents made by the late Professor Frank H. Underhill and deposited with the Public Archives of Canada was made available to me through the kindness of Mrs. Underhill and Professor H. Blair Neatby. Members of the Blake family have supplied me with a history in manuscript, largely concerned with the life of William Hume Blake, and with a number of private letters and other papers. Archivists in charge of various other collections have been consulted, and have been kind and cooperative.

For the work of research in the larger collections I have had extensive help, made possible by a grant from The Canada Council. Mr. Peter Yurkiw of the Public Archives of Canada and Mrs. Marion Beyea of the Public Archives of Ontario have been unwearying and invaluable assistants. M. Marcel Caya gave much help in investigating Blake's correspondence where it was concerned with Quebec politics, Mr. Daniel Livermore supplied me with material on Alexander Mackenzie, and Mr. Alan Bowker provided a special study of Blake's relations with the University of Toronto. Through the kindness of Mr. Arthur Pattillo and Mr. W. O. Chris Miller of Blake, Cassels and

Graydon, I was given access to considerable material on Blake held by the firm.

I should like here to acknowledge the assistance of Mr. Edward Phelps, Regional History Librarian of the University of Western Ontario; M. Jacques Prémont, Directeur de la Bibliothèque de la Législature, Québec; Mr. D. W. Rudkin, University Archivist, Department of Rare Books, University of Toronto Library; Dr. C. Bruce Ferguson, Provincial Archivist, Public Archives, Nova Scotia; Mr. K. R. MacPherson, Supervisor of Private Manuscripts, Public Archives of Ontario; Miss Edith Firth of the Baldwin Room of the Toronto Public Library; and Professor Henry C. Klassen of the University of Calgary. My thanks go to the numerous members of the Blake family who have patiently endured questioning, and to the equally patient business officers of the Department of History, University of Toronto — Miss Eileen Utterson, Mrs. Geraldine Rerup and Mrs. Erene Stanley.

Manuscript sources consulted are given below:

BP   Blake Papers, in Ontario Public Archives and University of Toronto. (All references in the notes are to the Public Archives of Ontario.)

BFP   Blake Family Papers, presently retained in the possession of the family.

BFH   Refers to the manuscript history of the Blake family, a copy of which is among the Blake papers in the Ontario Archives.

PAC   Public Archives of Canada
George Brown Papers
William Buckingham Papers
Carnarvon Papers
Charles Clarke
Dufferin Papers
Hayes Family Papers
Laurier Papers
John A. Macdonald Papers

John Sandfield Macdonald
Alexander Mackenzie Papers
R. W. Scott Papers
Goldwin Smith Papers
Sir John Thompson Papers
F. H. Underhill Papers
J. S. Willison Papers
Record Group 13 (Department of Justice), 1867-1906

OA   Public Archives of Ontario
Sir Alexander Campbell Papers, 1855-1908
Cartwright Family Papers, 1779-1913
J. D. Edgar Papers
Sir E. W. Grier Papers
T. C. Patteson Papers
Goldwin Smith Papers

David Mills Papers — University of Western Ontario
A. G. Jones Papers — Public Archives of Nova Scotia
W. S. Fielding Papers — Public Archives of Nova Scotia
Lande Collection, McLennan Library, McGill University
(various pamphlet reprints of Blake speeches)
Newspaper sources consulted are generally indicated by the
notes.

Of the published materials, those continually at hand for much of the work were such books as *Alexander Mackenzie: Clear Grit* by Dale C. Thomson; *Brown of The Globe* by J. M. S. Careless; *John A. Macdonald* by Donald Creighton; *Canada, 1874-1896: Arduous Destiny* by Peter B. Waite; and, particularly in relation to tariff questions, *Canada's National Policy, 1883-90* by Robert Craig Brown. *Edward Blake, Irish Nationalist* by Margaret A. Banks, was indispensable in dealing with Blake's years as a member of the British parliament and must still be consulted as a study of his actual involvement with the Home Rule movement. Also much consulted were the many writings on Blake by the late Frank H. Underhill.

A list of the principal secondary sources follows:

ADAMS, C. MERCER. *Canada's Patriot Statesman: Sir John A. Macdonald.* Toronto: Parrish, 1891.

ARMSTRONG, CHRISTOPHER. "The Mowat Heritage in Federal-Provincial Relations." In *Oliver Mowat's Ontario,* edited by Donald Swainson. Toronto: Macmillan, 1972.

BANKS, MARGARET A. *Edward Blake, Irish Nationalist: A Canadian Statesman in Irish Politics, 1892-1907.* Toronto: University of Toronto Press, 1957.

————. "The Change in Liberal Party Leadership: 1887." *Canadian Historical Review,* June 1957.

————. "Edward Blake's Relations with Canada During His Irish Career, 1892-1907." *Canadian Historical Review,* March 1954.

BARTHE, ULRIC. *Wilfrid Laurier on the Platform.* Quebec: Turcotte & Ménard, 1890.

BERTON, PIERRE. *The National Dream.* 2 vols. Toronto: McClelland & Stewart, 1970, 1971.

BIGGAR, C. R. W. *Sir Oliver Mowat,* 2 vols. Toronto, 1905.

BORDEN, ROBERT LAIRD. *Memoirs.* 2 vols. Toronto: Macmillan, 1938.

BOWKER, ALAN FRANKLIN. "Edward Blake and the University of Toronto, 1863-1900." Thesis in preparation.

BOYD, JOHN. *Sir George Etienne Cartier, Bart.* Toronto: Macmillan, 1917.

BROWN, ROBERT CRAIG. *Canada's National Policy, 1883-1900: A Study in Canadian-American Relations.* Princeton, N.J.: Princeton University Press, 1964.

BUCKINGHAM, WILLIAM, and ROSS, HON. GEORGE W. *The Honourable Alexander Mackenzie: His Life and Times.* Toronto, 1892.

BURKE, SISTER TERESA AVILA. "Mackenzie and His Cabinet, 1873-8." *Canadian Historical Review,* June 1960.

CARELESS, J. M. S. *Brown of The Globe.* 2 vols. Toronto: Macmillan, 1959, 1963.

————. "Frontierism, Metropolitanism and Canadian History." *Canadian Historical Review,* March 1954.

————. *The Union of the Canadas, 1841-1857.* Toronto: McClelland & Stewart, 1967.

————, ed. *Colonists and Canadians, 1760-1867.* Toronto: Macmillan, 1971.

236

————, and BROWN, ROBERT CRAIG, eds. *The Canadians, 1867-1967.* Toronto: Macmillan, 1967.

CARRINGTON, PHILIP. *The Anglican Church in Canada.* Toronto: Collins, 1963.

CARTWRIGHT, SIR RICHARD. *Reminiscences.* Toronto: Briggs, 1912.

COLLINS, J. E. *Canada Under the Administration of Lord Lorne.* Toronto: Rose, 1884.

CREIGHTON, DONALD. *Canada's First Century.* Toronto: Macmillan, 1970.

————. *John A. Macdonald.* 2 vols. Toronto: Macmillan, 1952, 1955.

————. "The Victorians and the Empire." *Canadian Historical Review,* June 1938. Reprinted in Donald Creighton, *Towards the Discovery of Canada.* Toronto: Macmillan, 1972.

CROWFOOT, A. H. *Benjamin Cronyn, First Bishop of Huron.* Incorporated Synod of the Diocese of Huron, 1957.

CURNOE, LORNE J. "John Charlton and Canadian-American Relations." M.A. thesis, University of Toronto, 1938.

DAFOE, JOHN W. *Laurier: A Study in Canadian Politics.* Toronto: Thomas Allen, 1922.

DALES, J. H. *The Protective Tariff in Canada's Development.* Toronto: University of Toronto Press, 1966.

DAVIN, N. F. *The Irishman in Canada.* Toronto: MacLean, 1877.

DAWSON, R. M. "The Gerrymander of 1882." *Canadian Journal of Economics and Political Science,* May 1935.

DENISON, G. T. *Soldiering in Canada.* Toronto, 1900.

————. *The Struggle for Imperial Unity.* London, 1909.

DENT, JOHN CHARLES. *Canadian Portrait Gallery.* Toronto: Magurn, 1880.

DURAND, CHARLES. *Reminiscences of Charles Durand of Toronto, Barrister.* Toronto: Hunter-Rose, 1897.

FOSTER, W. A. *Canada First, or Our New Nationality.* Pamphlet. Toronto: Adam, Stevenson, 1871.

FIRESTONE, O. J. *Canada's Economic Development, 1867-1953.* London: Bowes, 1953.

FRASER, BARBARA. "The Political Career of Sir Hector-Louis Langevin." *Canadian Historical Review,* June 1961.

GLAZEBROOK, G. P. de T. *Life in Ontario: A Social History.* Toronto: University of Toronto Press, 1968.

GRAHAM, W. R. "Liberal Nationalism in the 1870's." Canadian Historical Association *Report*, 1946, pp. 101-19.

———. "Sir Richard Cartwright." PH D. thesis, University of Toronto, 1950.

———. "Sir Richard Cartwright, Wilfrid Laurier and Liberal Party Trade Policy, 1887." *Canadian Historical Review*, March 1952.

GRAYDON, ALAN. *Some Reminiscences of Blake's*. Privately printed, 1970.

HAM, GEORGE H. *Reminiscences of a Raconteur*. Toronto: Musson, 1921.

HEISLER, J. P. "Sir John Thompson." PH D. thesis, University of Toronto, 1955.

HODGINS, BRUCE W. *John Sandfield Macdonald*. Toronto: University of Toronto Press, 1971.

HOPKINS, J. CASTELL. *The Life and Work of Sir John Thompson*. Toronto: United Publishing Houses, 1895.

HOUGHAM, G. M. "Canada First: A Minor Party in Microcosm." *Canadian Journal of Economics and Political Science*, May 1953.

de KIEWIET, C., and UNDERHILL, F. H. *The Dufferin-Carnarvon Correspondence*. Toronto: Champlain Society, 1955.

KLASSEN, HENRY CORNELIUS. "L. H. Holton, Montreal Businessman and Politician, 1817-67." PH D. thesis, University of Toronto, 1970.

LANDON, FRED. "The Canadian Scene, 1880-90." Canadian Historical Association *Report*, 1942, pp. 5-18.

LANGTON, W. A., ed. *Early Days in Upper Canada: Letters of John Langton from the Backwoods of Upper Canada*. Toronto: Macmillan, 1926.

LEDERLE, J. W. "The Liberal Convention of 1893." *Canadian Journal of Economics and Political Science*, February 1950.

LONGLEY, J. W. "Reminiscences." *Canadian Magazine*, October 1920-February 1921.

LOUDON, J. W. "Edward Blake." *University of Toronto Monthly*, May 1912.

———. Manuscript of unpublished autobiography in the University of Toronto Archives.

LOWER, ARTHUR. *Canadians in the Making*. Toronto: Longmans Green, 1958.

———. *Colony to Nation*. Toronto: Longmans Green, 1946.

MAC DONALD, NORMAN. *Canada: Immigration and Colonization, 1841-1903.* Toronto: Macmillan, 1966.

MAC INTOSH, A. W. "The Career of Sir Charles Tupper in Canada, 1864-1900." PH D. thesis, University of Toronto, 1960.

MAC KIRDY, K. A. "The Loyalty Issue in the 1891 Federal Election Campaign and an Ironic Footnote." *Ontario History*, September 1963.

MAC NUTT, W. S. *Days of Lorne.* Fredericton: Brunswick, 1955.

———. "The 1880's." In *The Canadians, 1867-1967*, edited by J. M. S. Careless and R. Craig Brown. Toronto: Macmillan, 1967.

MAXWELL, J. A. "Lord Dufferin and the Difficulties with British Columbia." *Canadian Historical Review*, December 1931.

MORRISON, J. C. "Oliver Mowat and the Development of Provincial Rights in Ontario." M.A. thesis, University of Toronto, 1947.

MORTON, W. L. *The Critical Years: The Union of British North America, 1857-1873.* Toronto: McClelland & Stewart, 1964.

———. *Manitoba: A History.* Toronto: University of Toronto Press, 1967.

NEATBY, H. BLAIR. "Laurier and a Liberal Quebec." M.A. thesis, University of Toronto, 1956.

———, and SAYWELL, JOHN T. "Chapleau and the Conservative Party in Quebec." *Canadian Historical Review*, March 1956.

Ontario Historical Society. *Profile of a Province: Stability and Progress in Ontario*, 1967.

ORMSBY, MARGARET. "Prime Minister Mackenzie, the Liberal Party and the Bargain with British Columbia." *Canadian Historical Review*, June 1945.

OSTRY, BERNARD. "Conservatives, Liberals and Labour in the 1870's." *Canadian Historical Review*, June 1960.

POPE, JOSEPH. *The Correspondence of Sir John A. Macdonald.* Toronto: Oxford, 1921.

———. *Memoirs of the Right Honourable Sir John Alexander Macdonald.* 2 vols. Ottawa: J. Durre & Sons, 1894.

POPE, MAURICE, ed. *Public Servant: The Memoirs of Sir Joseph Pope.* Toronto: Oxford, 1960.

PRESTON, W. T. R. *My Generation of Politics and Politicians.* London: Eveleigh Nash, 1915.

READ, D. B. *Lives of the Judges.* Toronto: Rowsell & Hutchison, 1888.

ROSS, G. W. *Getting into Parliament and After.* Toronto: Briggs, 1913.

ROSS, P. D. *Retrospects of a Newspaper Person.* Toronto: Oxford, 1931.

SAGE, W. N. "Federal Parties and Provincial Groups in British Columbia, 1871-1903." *British Columbia Historical Quarterly*, April 1948.

SAYWELL, JOHN T. "The Crown and the Politicians: The Canadian Succession Question, 1891-6." *Canadian Historical Review*, December 1956.

————. "The 1890's." In *The Canadians, 1867-1967*, edited by J. M. S. Careless and R. Craig Brown. Toronto: Macmillan, 1967.

————, ed. *The Canadian Journal of Lady Aberdeen.* Toronto: Champlain Society, 1960.

SHRIVE, NORMAN. *Charles Mair, Literary Nationalist.* Toronto: University of Toronto Press, 1965.

SKELTON, O. D. *The Day of Sir Wilfrid Laurier.* Chronicles of Canada Series. Toronto: Glasgow Brook, 1916.

————. *Life and Letters of Sir Wilfrid Laurier.* 2 vols. Toronto: Oxford, 1921.

SMITH, GOLDWIN. *Reminiscences.* Edited by Arnold Haultain. Toronto: Macmillan, 1910.

STAMP, ROBERT. "The Public Career of Sir James David Edgar." M.A. thesis, University of Toronto, 1962.

STANLEY, GEORGE F. G. *Louis Riel.* Toronto: Ryerson, 1964.

SWAINSON, DONALD, ed. *Oliver Mowat's Ontario.* Toronto: Macmillan, 1972.

THOMSON, DALE C. *Alexander Mackenzie: Clear Grit.* Toronto: Macmillan, 1960.

TUPPER, SIR CHARLES. *Reminiscences of Sixty Years.* London: Cassells, 1914.

TYLER, J. E. *The Struggle for Imperial Unity, 1868-1895.* London, 1938.

UNDERHILL, FRANK H. "Edward Blake." In *Our Living Tradition*, edited by Claude T. Bissell. Toronto: Carleton University and University of Toronto Press, 1957.

————. "Edward Blake and Canadian Liberal Nationalism." In *Essays in Canadian History*, edited by R. Flenley. Toronto: Macmillan, 1939, pp. 3-38.

————. "Edward Blake, the Liberal Party, and Unrestricted Reciprocity." Canadian Historical Association *Report*, 1939, pp. 133-41.

————. "Edward Blake, the Supreme Court Act and the Appeal to the Privy Council." *Canadian Historical Review*, September 1938.

————. *The Image of Confederation*. Reprint by Canadian Broadcasting Corporation of the Massey Lectures, 1963.

————. "Laurier and Blake, 1882-1891." *Canadian Historical Review*, December 1939.

————. "Laurier and Blake, 1891-2." *Canadian Historical Review*, June 1943.

————. "Political Ideas of the Upper Canadian Reformers, 1867-78." Canadian Historical Association *Report*, 1942, pp. 104-15.

————. *In Search of Canadian Liberalism*. Toronto: Macmillan, 1960.

WADE, MASON. *The French Canadians*. Toronto: Macmillan, 1955.

WAITE, PETER B. *Canada, 1874-1896: Arduous Destiny*. Toronto: McClelland & Stewart, 1971.

————. "The 1860's." In *Colonists and Canadians, 1760-1867*, edited by J. M. S. Careless. Toronto: Macmillan, 1971.

————. "Reflections on an Un-Victorian Society." In *Oliver Mowat's Ontario*, edited by Donald Swainson. Toronto: Macmillan, 1972.

WALLACE, ELISABETH. *Goldwin Smith, Victorian Liberal*. Toronto: University of Toronto Press, 1957.

WALLACE, W. STEWART. *The Memoirs of the Rt. Hon. Sir George Foster*. Toronto: Macmillan, 1933.

————. "The Mystery of Edward Blake." *Canadian Magazine*, September 1912.

WARD, NORMAN. "The Formative Years of the House of Commons." *Canadian Journal of Economics and Political Science*, November 1952.

WATT, JAMES T. "Anti-Catholic Nativism in Canada: The Protestant Protective Association." *Canadian Historical Review*, March 1967.

WESTERN, MAURICE. "Edward Blake as Leader of the Opposition, 1880-87." M.A. thesis, University of Toronto, 1939.

WILLISON, SIR JOHN. *Reminiscences Personal and Political*. Toronto: McClelland & Stewart, 1919.

————. *Sir Wilfrid Laurier and the Liberal Party*. Makers of Canada Series, 2 vols. Toronto: Oxford, 1927.

WILSON, BECKLES. *The Life of Lord Strathcona*. London: Cassels, 1915.

YOUNG, JAMES. *Public Life and Public Men in Canada*. 2 vols. Toronto: Briggs, 1912.

NOTES

CHAPTER ONE

1 Some material in this and other chapters is from an unpublished life of William Hume Blake, written by his great-grandson, Edward Hume Blake. There is a copy of the manuscript among the Blake Papers in the Ontario Archives and other copies are held by the Blake family. The life also includes material on Edward Blake. This manuscript will be referred to in subsequent notes as *Blake Family History* (BFH).

Additional material for the present chapter and others is from papers in possession of the Blake family, and is referred to as *Blake Family Papers* (BFP).

2 *Globe* (Toronto), Feb. 11, 1876.

3 From a letterbook of Edward Blake in the possession of Blake, Cassels & Graydon, Toronto, (referred to hereafter as "Letterbook BCG"), October 6, 1858.

4 Note from diary of Mrs. Amelia Harris, January 6, 1858. Extract is reprinted in *London Free Press*, but clipping in BFP bears no date.

5 Story told of Margaret Blake by Mrs. Nora Wright, her granddaughter.

6 Same source as above.

CHAPTER TWO

1 Letterbook 2, BCG, 1858.

2 Letterbook 3, BCG, 1859.

3 Letterbook 2, BCG, 1858.

4 *Globe*, Oct. 16, 1858.

5 *Ibid.*, Nov. 20, 1858.

6 BFH, IX, p. 4.

7 *Ibid.*

8 *Ibid.*, IX, p. 13.

9 *Ibid.*, VIII, p. 11.

10 *Ibid.*, VIII, pp. 5, 11.
11 *Globe*, Mar. 6, 1863.
12 *Ibid.*, May 11, 1863.
13 PAC, Macdonald Papers, PP91635-46, Hon. M. H. Foley to Macdonald, December 5, 1863.
14 In possession of Blake family.
15 BP, Blake Scrapbook, 1865. Quotation is from Mackenzie's speech in *Confederation Debates*, February 23, 1865.
16 PAC, Alexander Mackenzie Papers, P116-17, Brown to Mackenzie, March 12, 1867.

CHAPTER THREE

1 *Leader* (Toronto), Aug. 1, 1867.
2 *Leader*, quoted by W. S. Wallace, *Canadian Magazine*, September, 1912.
3 Account quoted in BFP, from John Squair, *The History of the Townships of Darlington and Clarke* (Toronto: University of Toronto Press, 1927), p. 156.
4 *Ibid.*
5 *Globe*, Sept. 5, 1867.
6 Squair, *Townships of Darlington and Clarke*, p. 158.
7 *Leader*, Aug. 20, 1867.
8 BP, Section II, no. 5, Edward Blake to John Bruce, September 24, 1867.
9 BP, Section II, no. 1, Wm. Hume Blake to Edward Blake, December 7, 1867.
10 PAC, Mackenzie Papers, M 197, 1-919, Geo. Brown to A. Mackenzie, August 18, 1867.
11 BP, Section II, no. 14, Scrapbook 5, 1864-71. (Scrapbooks contain clippings from various papers, often identified.)
12 Dale C. Thomson, *Alexander Mackenzie: Clear Grit* (Toronto: Macmillan, 1960), p. 93.
13 *House of Commons Debates*, November 8, 1867, pp. 10-20.
14 *Ibid.*, November 11, 1867, pp. 23-26.

CHAPTER FOUR

1 BFP. Pencilled note in papers dated July 7, 1831, and signed "K.C.B." from 661 Talbot St., London, Ont.
2 *Leader*, Sept. 18, 1867.
3 BP, Section II, no. 13. Scrapbook.
4 *Globe*, Mar. 4, 1868.
5 PAC, Brown Papers, Cartier to Brown, February 27, 1868.
6 PAC, Brown Papers, MG 24-B40, V.8, 1707-9, Mackenzie to Brown, March 19, 1868.
7 PAC, Macdonald Papers, 78455, Blake to Macdonald, December 28, 1868.

8 *Ontario Legislature Debates* quoted in the *Globe*, Nov. 24, 1869.
9 *Ibid.*
10 *Ibid.*
11 *Ibid.*
12 *House of Commons Debates*, quoted in the *Globe*, June 12, 1869.
13 *Leader*, Apr. 4, 1870.
14 BP, Section II, no. 1, Wm. Hume Blake to Edward Blake, May 9, 1868.
15 *Ibid.*, Section II, no. 1, Catherine Blake to Edward Blake, May 1868.
16 BFH, XI, p. 9.
17 BP, Section II, no. 1, Wm. Hume Blake to Edward Blake, August 22, 1868.
18 PAC, Macdonald Papers, 65068-71, Blake to Macdonald, November 7, 1868.
19 PAC, Underhill Papers, Macdonald offer quoted in Blake to Morrison, December 18, 1869.
20 Quoted in the *Globe*, Dec. 28, 1869.
21 *Telegraph* (Toronto), Dec. 10, 1869. (The *Telegraph*'s dates were wrong. William Hume Blake was appointed Chancellor in 1849.)
22 PAC, Underhill Papers, Blake to Morrison, December 18, 1869.
23 BP, Section II, no. 14, Blake Scrapbooks. Clippings from various unidentified newspapers.
24 *Leader*, Feb. 14, 1870.
25 PAC, Mackenzie Papers, Brown to G. Buckingham, February 4, 1870.
26 BP, Section II, no. 14. Clipping February 24, 1870 in Blake Scrapbook.
27 *Globe*, quoting *Stratford Beacon*, Feb. 14, 1870.
28 *New Era* (Clinton), Feb. 17, 1870.
29 *Globe*, Oct. 26, 1870. Report of speech at London, Ont.
30 Bruce W. Hodgins, *John Sandfield Macdonald* (Toronto: University of Toronto Press, 1971), p. 5.
31 *Journals of the Ontario Legislature*, February 2, 1871.
32 *Ibid.*, December 7, 1871.
33 *Ibid.*, December 11, 1871.
34 Sir John Willison, *Reminiscences* (Toronto: McClelland & Stewart, 1919), p. 18. See also Blake's explanation in *House of Commons Debates*, June 11, 1872.
35 *Journals of the Ontario Legislature*, December 15, 1871.
36 PAC, Mackenzie Papers, Blake to Mackenzie, December 12, 1871.
37 BP, Section II, no. 14, *Blake Scrapbook.* BFH, XII, p. 2.
38 Essay "Matthew Arnold" in *The College Survey of English Literature*, ed. B. J. Whiting (New York: Harcourt, Brace, 1945), pp. 1008-9.

CHAPTER FIVE

1 BP, D. A. Macdonald to Blake, December 19, 1871.
2 *Ibid.*, Blake to D. A. Macdonald, December 20, 1871.
3 *Ibid.*, Blake to Scott, December 24, 1871.

4 *Ibid.*, Scrapbook 10, *Daily News*, Dec. 28, 1871.

5 *Ibid.*, *Daily Telegraph*, Dec. 25, 1871.

6 PAC, Macdonald Papers, Letterbook Vol. 17, p. 16, Macdonald to M. C. Cameron, January 3, 1872.

7 C. B. Sissons — Ryerson's letters to Sophia, December 15, 1872.

8 *Ibid.*, January 29, 1875.

9 *Globe*, Dec. 23, 1871.

10 *Journals of the Ontario Legislature*, January 23, 1872.

11 *Globe*, Jan. 24, 1872.

12 *Ibid.*, Feb. 5, 1872.

13 George F. G. Stanley, *Louis Riel* (Toronto: Ryerson, 1964), p. 180.

14 PAC, Macdonald Papers, MG 26 A1(a), Vol. 188, Blake to Macdonald, March 4, 1872.

15 *Ibid.*

16 *House of Commons Debates*, May 8, 1872.

17 *Globe*, Jan. 9, 1873.

18 *House of Commons Debates*, May 29, 1872.

19 *Mail* (Toronto), July 8, 1872.

20 John Boyd, *Sir George Etienne Cartier, Bart.* (Toronto: Macmillan, 1917), p. 307.

21 *House of Commons Debates*, March 28, 1871.

22 *Ibid.*

23 *Globe*, June 27, 1872.

24 BP, Blake to J. G. Brown, June 15, 1872.

25 *Globe*, June 27, 1872.

26 *Ibid.*

27 BP, Section II, no. 5, Can. Gen. Political Correspondence, Proudfoot to Blake, June 19, 1872.

28 *Mail*, July 8, 1872.

29 PAC, Mackenzie Papers, MG 26B, Reel M 197, Blake to Mackenzie, August 8, 1872.

CHAPTER SIX

1 PAC, Mackenzie Papers, MG 26B, Reel M 197, Blake to Mackenzie, September 12, 1872.

2 Sir Joseph Pope, *Correspondence of Sir John A. Macdonald* (Toronto: Oxford, 1921). Macdonald to Mowat, October 25, 1872.

3 BP, Section II, no. 4, Blake to Mackenzie, December 7, 1872.

4 PAC, Mackenzie Papers, MG 24 B40, Vol. 9, Mackenzie to Brown, March 5, 1873.

5 Geo. Stewart, Jr., *Canada Under the Administration of the Earl of Dufferin* (Toronto: Rose-Belford Publishing Co., 1878), p. 130.

6 Donald Creighton, *John A. Macdonald, The Old Chieftain* (Toronto: Macmillan, 1955), p. 141.

7 OA, Cartwright Papers, Mackenzie to Cartwright, February 21, 1873.

8　PAC, Macdonald Papers, MG 26 A1(a), Vol. 124, Blake to Macdonald, July 3, 1873.

9　BP, General Political Correspondence, Dorion to Blake, June 26, 1873.

10　BFP, Section II, no. 15, Pamphlet, *Three Speeches by the Hon. Edward Blake on the Pacific Scandal.*

11　*Ibid.*

12　*Ibid.*

13　*Globe,* Sept. 16, 1873.

14　BFP, Section II, no. 15. Pamphlet, *Three Speeches by the Hon. Edward Blake on the Pacific Scandal.*

15　PAC, Brown Papers, MG 24, B 40, Vol. 9.

16　Ottawa *Times,* Nov. 1, 1873.

CHAPTER SEVEN

1　PAC, Kimberley Papers, PC/A/25b, Dufferin to Kimberley, November 13, 1873.

2　*Ibid.*

3　Thomson, *Alexander Mackenzie,* p. 182. Original in Public Archives of Nova Scotia, published in 1952 *Report,* PANS, Mackenzie to A. G. Jones, December 27, 1875.

4　PAC, Mackenzie Papers, January 3, 1874, pp. 294-5.

5　BP, Section II, no. 4-k, Mackenzie to Blake, January 4, 1874.

6　PAC, Mackenzie Papers, Blake to Mackenzie, January 29, 1874.

7　*Mail,* Feb. 16, 1874.

8　*Ibid.*

9　W. A. Foster, *Canada First or Our New Nationality.* Pamphlet. (Toronto: Adam Stevenson & Co., 1871).

10　*Ibid.*

11　Goldwin Smith, *Reminiscences* (Toronto: Macmillan, 1910), p. 439.

12　[Goldwin Smith], "Bystander," *Canadian Monthly & National Review,* April 1872, p. 321.

13　BP, Section II, no. 4, Box 20, Goldwin Smith to Blake, November 6, 1873.

14　*Ibid.*

15　PAC, Carnarvon Papers, Private 129-139, Dufferin to Carnarvon, April 23, 1874.

16　BP, Section II, no. 13D, L-O David, *Le Courier de Montréal,* December 2, 1874.

17　BP, Section II, no. 4-k, Mackenzie to Blake, May 28, 1874.

18　BP, Holton to Blake, June 14, 1874.

19　BP, Section II, no. 4-k, Blake to Mackenzie, September 6, 1874.

20　*Ibid.,* Blake to Mackenzie, September 17, 1874.

21　*Ibid.,* Mackenzie to Blake, September 18, 1874.

22　BP, Section II, no. 4-k, Blake to Mackenzie, September 24, 1874.

23　G. M. Hougham, "Canada First: A Minor Party in Microcosm," *Canadian Journal of Economics & Political Science,* May 1953, p. 183.

24 Edward Blake, "A National Sentiment." Speech at Aurora, October 3, 1874. Pamphlet (Ottawa: E. A. Perry, 1874).

25 Goldwin Smith, *Reminiscences*, p. 443.

26 *Bobcaygeon Independent*, Oct. 10, 1874.

27 PAC, Mackenzie Papers, Brown to Mackenzie, October 6, 1874.

28 *Globe*, Oct. 7 & 8, 1874.

29 *Mail*, Oct. 8, 1874.

30 BP, Scrapbook 18; *Mail*, May 6, 1875.

31 BP, Section II, no. 4-k, Mackenzie to Blake, October 12, 1874.

32 BP, Section II, no. 4-k, Blake to Mackenzie, October 14, 1874.

33 BP, Section II, no. 4-k, Mackenzie to Blake, October 15, 1874.

34 BP, Section II, no. 4-k, Blake to Mackenzie, October 16, 1874.

35 PAC, Mackenzie Papers, 651-2, Mackenzie to Brown, October 19, 1874.

36 PAC, Geo. Brown Papers, 2174-5, Mackenzie to Brown, November 5, 1873.

37 PAC, Carnarvon Papers, 185-8, Dufferin to Carnarvon, November 12, 1874.

38 *House of Commons Debates*, March 16, 1875.

39 *House of Commons Debates*, March 30, 1875.

40 PAC, Mackenzie Papers, Blake to Mackenzie, April 30, 1875.

41 BP, Blake to A. G. Jones, March, 19, 1875.

42 BP, Blake to A. G. Jones, March 22, 1875.

43 *House of Commons Debates*, March 29, 1875, p. 954.

44 PAC, Mackenzie Papers, Blake to Mackenzie, April 5, 1875, p. 752.

45 PAC, Mackenzie Letterbooks, Mackenzie to A. G. Jones, April 8, 1875.

46 PAC, Mackenzie Papers, Holton to Mackenzie, April 19, 1875.

47 BP, Box 92, Blake to Mackenzie, April 30, 1875.

48 PAC, Mackenzie Letterbooks, Mackenzie to Blake, May 5, 1875.

49 *Liberal* (Toronto), May 5, 1875.

50 PAC, Mackenzie Papers, Mackenzie to Brown, May 13, 1875.

51 PAC, Mackenzie Letterbooks, 314-5, Blake to Mackenzie (copy), May 18, 1875.

CHAPTER EIGHT

1 *Globe*, June 4, 1875.

2 *Mail*, June 4, 1875.

3 PAC, Mackenzie Papers, Geo. Brown to Mackenzie, July 15, 1875.

4 Order in Council, September 20, 1875, quoted by J. A. Maxwell in "Lord Dufferin and the Difficulties with British Columbia," *Canadian Historical Review* 12, December 1931.

5 BP, Letterbook 3, Blake to Mackenzie, November 26, 1875.

6 BP, Political Correspondence II, Mackenzie to Blake, November 27, 1875.

7 *Ibid.*, Blake to Mackenzie, November 26, 1875.

8 *Ibid.*

9 PAC, Dufferin Papers, Carnarvon to Dufferin, March 31, 1875.

10 PAC, Dufferin Papers, Carnarvon to Dufferin, November 4, 1875.
11 *Ibid.*, Dufferin to Carnarvon, November 19, 1875.
12 BP, Letterbook 3, Blake to Mackenzie, November 20, 1875.
13 PAC, Dufferin to Carnarvon, November 19, 1875.
14 BP, Blake to James Young, May 17, 1876.
15 C. W. de Kieweit and F. H. Underhill, eds., *Dufferin-Carnarvon Correspondence, 1874-1878*. (Toronto: Champlain Society, 1955). Dufferin to Carnarvon, March 31, 1876.
16 PAC, Carnarvon Papers, Dufferin to Carnarvon, May 26, 1876.
17 *Ibid.*, February 2, 1876.
18 *Ibid.*, June 1, 1876.
19 *Ibid.*
20 PAC, Dufferin Papers, Carnarvon to Dufferin, July 16, 1876.
21 BP, Letterbook 6, Blake to Mackenzie, June 17, 1876.
22 BP, Edward Blake to Catherine Blake, July 6, 1876.
23 *Ibid.*
24 BP, Edward Blake to Catherine Blake, July 13, 1876.
25 BP, Edward Blake to Catherine Blake, July 19, 1876.
26 *Ibid.*
27 BP, Edward Blake to Catherine Blake, July 26, 1876.
28 BP, Edward Blake to Catherine Blake, July 19 and August 3, 1876.
29 BP, Blake to R. W. Scott, June 28, 1876.
30 BP, Blake to Mackenzie, July 13, 1876.
31 BFP, Catherine Blake to Edward Blake, July 13 and July 25, 1876.
32 BFP, Edward Blake to Catherine Blake, July 13, 1876.
33 BFP, Edward Blake to Catherine Blake, July 26, 1876.
34 *Ibid.*
35 PAC, Mackenzie Papers, Blake to Mackenzie, August 2, 1876.
36 PAC, Carnarvon Papers. Enclosure, Dufferin to Carnarvon, July 27 and July 31, 1876.
37 BFP, Edward Blake to Catherine Blake, August 14, 1876.
38 PAC, Dufferin Papers, Blake to Mackenzie (reporting interview), July 1, 1876.
39 Quoted in D. G. Creighton, *John A. Macdonald: The Young Politician* (Toronto: Macmillan, 1952), p. 461.
40 PAC, Dufferin Papers, Blake to Mackenzie (reporting interview), July 1, 1876.
41 BP, Letterbook 6, Blake to Mackenzie, August 9, 1876.

CHAPTER NINE

1 BP, Letterbook 8, Blake to O'Connor, September 5, 1876.
2 *Ibid.*, Blake to David Mills, September 23, 1876.
3 *Free Press* (London), Mar. 5, 1877.
4 PAC, Mackenzie Papers, Blake to Mackenzie, September 25, 1876.
5 *Ibid.*, Mackenzie to Blake, September 25, 1876.

6 *Ibid.*, Blake to Mackenzie, September 25, 1876.
7 *Ibid.*
8 *Ibid.*, Blake to Mackenzie, September 26, 1876.
9 BP, Blake to Cartwright, October 13, 1876.
10 PAC, Carnarvon Papers, Dufferin to Carnarvon, October 8, 1876.
11 *Ibid.*, October 9, 1876.
12 *Ibid.*, October 26, 1876.
13 *Ibid.*, November 6, 1876.
14 *Ibid.*, November 4, 1876.
15 PAC, Mackenzie Papers, Blake to Mackenzie, November 14, 1876.
16 PAC, Dufferin Papers, Dufferin to Mackenzie, November 19, 1876.
17 *Dufferin-Carnarvon Correspondence*, p. 309. Dufferin to Carnarvon, November 20, 1876.
18 Quoted in Margaret A. Ormsby, "Prime Minister Mackenzie, the Liberal Party, and the Bargain with British Columbia," *Canadian Historical Review*, June 1945, p. 171; B.C. Sessional Papers 1877, Carnarvon to Dufferin, p. 581.
19 *Dufferin-Carnarvon Correspondence*, Dufferin to Carnarvon, November 23, 1876, p. 312.
20 *Ibid.*, p. 314.
21 PAC, Mackenzie Papers, 1548-51, A. Mackenzie to Charles Mackenzie, March 4, 1877.
22 PAC, Carnarvon Papers, Dufferin to Carnarvon, April 27, 1877.
23 PAC, Mackenzie Papers, Blake to Mackenzie, April 30, 1877.
24 BP, Mackenzie to Blake, April 30, 1877.
25 PAC, Mackenzie Papers, Blake to Mackenzie, May 21, 1877.
26 *Ibid.*
27 Ulric Barthe, *Wilfrid Laurier on the Platform* (Quebec: Turcotte & Menard, 1890), PSIF.
28 Mason Wade, *The French Canadians* (Toronto: Macmillan, 1955), p. 369.
29 BFP, *Reform Government in the Dominion.* Pamphlet. Speech by Blake at Teeswater, Ontario, September 24, 1877.
30 PAC, Mackenzie Papers, Blake to Mackenzie, November 5, 1877.
31 *Ibid.*
32 *Ibid.*, Mackenzie to Holton, November 9, 1877.
33 *Ibid.*, Holton to Mackenzie, November 11, 1877.
34 *Ibid.*, Blake to Mackenzie, December 3, 1877.
35 BP, Mackenzie to Blake, December 8, 1877.
36 PAC, Mackenzie Papers, Blake to Mackenzie, January 17, 1878.
37 BP, Mills to Blake, May 24, 1877.
38 PAC, Mackenzie Papers, Blake to Mackenzie, July 3, 1878.
39 BFP, Catherine Blake to Edward Blake, October 1878.
40 PAC, Mackenzie Papers, Mackenzie to Cartwright, December 20, 1878.
41 *Ibid.*, Blake to Mackenzie, December 21, 1878.
42 *Ibid.*, Cartwright to Mackenzie, December 27, 1878.

43 *Ibid.*, Mackenzie to Cartwright, December 20, 1878.
44 *Ibid.*, Holton to Mackenzie, December 22, 1878.
45 *Ibid.*, Mackenzie to Blake, January 2, 1879. (Draft dated December 31, 1878.)

CHAPTER TEN

1   *Stratford Beacon*, Feb. 14, 1879.
2   PAC, Currie Family Papers, v2, Blake to Currie, April 28, 1879.
3   BFP, 271, Catherine to E. Blake, October 8, 1878.
4   Thomson, *Alexander Mackenzie*, p. 351.
5   PAC, Mackenzie Papers, Mackenzie to John Simpson, January 25, 1879, p. 609.
6   *Ibid.*, 2292-3, Cartwright to Mackenzie, July 28, 1879.
7   PAC, Macdonald Papers, 167732-3, Robt. Armour to Macdonald, November 18, 1879.
8   *Advertiser* (London), Nov. 20 and 22, 1879. Report of a speech.
9   *Mail*, Nov. 21, 1879.
10 *Spectator* (Hamilton), Nov. 18, 1879.
11 *Free Press* (London), Dec. 18, 1879.
12 PAC, Laurier Papers, 207829-32, Mackenzie to Laurier, January 7, 1880.
13 PAC, Mackenzie Papers, 673-8, Mackenzie to L. H. Davies, May 20, 1880; 2356-7, Mackenzie to Charles Black, May 20, 1880.
14 *Ibid.*, Mackenzie to Black, May 20, 1880.
15 *House of Commons Debates*, April 15-16, 1880, pp. 1425-69.
16 PAC, Macdonald Papers, Vol. 279 (draft), Macdonald to Trutch, May 17, 1880.
17 PAC, Mackenzie Papers, 673-8, Mackenzie to L. H. Davies, May 20, 1880.
18 O. D. Skelton, *Life and Letters of Sir Wilfrid Laurier*, Vol. 1 (Toronto: Oxford University Press, 1921), p. 221.
19 *House of Commons Debates*, April 27, 1880.

CHAPTER ELEVEN

1   BFP, 229, Edward Blake to Catherine Blake, August 3, 1876.
2   BP, Blake to Geoffrion (draft), February 13, 1880.
3   PAC, Macdonald Papers, 170487-94, J. Maclean to Macdonald, May 1880.
4   *Mail*, Apr. 2, 1881.
5   PAC, Macdonald Papers, 174787-90, A. I. Bray to Macdonald, April 13, 1881.
6   O. D. Skelton, *Life and Letters of Sir Wilfrid Laurier*, Vol. 1, (Toronto: Oxford University Press, 1921), pp. 223-4.
7   *Evening Herald* (London), May 1, 1880.
8   *Advertiser* (Argenteuil), May 5, 1880.

9   *Le Canada* (Quebec), May 20, ,1880.

10   *Daily Times* (Moncton), Apr. 30, 1880.

11   *Gazette* (Montreal), May 8, 1880.

12   *Morning Herald* (Montreal), Apr. 29, 1880.

13   *Evening Chronicle* (Halifax), Apr. 29, 1880.

14   *Daily News* (Berlin, Ontario), May 5, 1880.

15   *Daily Telegraph* (Saint John), Apr. 27, 1880.

16   *Daily Courier* (Brantford), May 5, 1880.

17   *Globe*, Apr. 30, 1880.

18   *Mail*, May 1, 1880.

19   BP, Scrapbook, *World*, 1880.

20   *House of Commons Debates*, December 13, 1880, p. 42.

21   *Ibid.*, December 10, 1880, p. 29.

22   *Ibid.*, December 10, 1880, p. 12.

23   *Ibid.*, December 14, 1880, p. 55.

24   *Globe*, January 8, 1881.

25   *House of Commons Debates*, January 17, 1881, pp. 485-90.

26   *Ibid.*

27   *Ibid.*, December 14, 1880, p. 76.

28   *Ibid.*, December 15, 1880, pp. 99, 100.

29   *Ibid.*, December 15, 1880, p. 101.

30   *Ibid.*, December 15, 1880, p. 102.

31   *Ibid.*, December 15, 1880, p. 103.

32   *Ibid.*, December 15, 1880, pp. 103-6.

33   *Ibid.*, January 18, 1881, p. 515.

34   *Ibid.*, January 31, 1881, pp. 771-86.

INDEX